语法隐喻中的语义变化

聚焦"性状"转"事物"类概念隐喻

董 娟 著

中国海洋大学出版社

·青岛·

图书在版编目（CIP）数据

语法隐喻中的语义变化：聚焦"性状"转"事物"
类概念隐喻 / 董娟著 . -- 青岛：中国海洋大学出版社，
2020.11

ISBN 978-7-5670-2500-4

Ⅰ. ①语… Ⅱ. ①董… Ⅲ. ①隐喻—研究 Ⅳ.
① H05

中国版本图书馆 CIP 数据核字（2020）第 079338 号

出版发行	中国海洋大学出版社			
社　　址	青岛市香港东路 23 号		**邮政编码**	266071
出 版 人	杨立敏			
网　　址	http://pub.ouc.edu.cn			
订购电话	0532 - 82032573（传真）			
电子信箱	1922305382@qq.com			
责任编辑	邵成军		**电　　话**	0532 - 85902533
印　　制	日照日报印务中心			
版　　次	2020 年 11 月第 1 版			
印　　次	2020 年 11 月第 1 次印刷			
成品尺寸	170 mm ×230 mm			
印　　张	16.5			
字　　数	314 千			
印　　数	1—1000			
定　　价	55.00 元			

总序（一）

　　中国海洋大学出版社将国内外国语言学及应用语言学博士生的优秀论文集中出版建立文库，对学界来说是件极好的事。目前已经出版了第一辑总计15本专著，引起了学界很大的反响和广泛的关注。现在，第二辑论文专著正在筹划与编辑中，希望挑选出来的优秀博士论文能够丰富该文库的学术内容，促进该领域的学术争鸣。

　　作为一门学科，外国语言学及应用语言学涉及的面极为广泛，几乎"包罗万象"。因此，要规划好第二辑出版主题，先要对该学科有个明确的范围界定，以期有的放矢地挑选相关的优秀论文。

　　外国语言学及应用语言学，顾名思义，是指与外国语言紧密相关的语言研究学说，且应用相关理论解释语言问题。这样界定似乎较为完整，但仔细分析，其中却存在着概念界定模糊、内容划分不明等问题。

　　首先，学科名称"外国语言学及应用语言学"就值得商榷。外国语言学是大概念，其他的语言学分支包含其中，如心理语言学、社会语言学、应用语言学，而不应把语言学和其分支并列作为学科名称。因此，外国语言学及应用语言学似有概念混淆之嫌。其次，语言学有国内、国外之分虽也说得过去，但时常造成共性语言现象研究的归类困难。而且应用语言学因涉及领域过于广泛而很难界定其确切的研究范围。当然，现在外国语言学及应用语言学作为学科名称已约定俗成，在人们心目中也已经有了一个大概的范畴，但鉴于中国海洋大学出版社要出版此学科的第二辑博士论文专著，理应对这一学科有一个理性的解读。

　　语言学的研究（无论国内还是国外），大致分为理论层面的研究和应用层面的研究。理论层面的研究主要集中于对语言的描述以及人类语言的普遍规律或语言与某一领域的结合,如语音研究有音位学,词汇研究有词汇学,句子研究有句法学,还有语法学等;与某一领域结合起来的研究有心理语言学、社会语言学、神经语言学、计算语言学、系统功能语言学等。应用层面的研究又可以分为宏观、中观和微观三个研究视角。宏观研究视角主要与语言政策及语言教育政策的研究有关,如语言的地位规划、语言的本体规划、语言的习得规划以及教育上使用何种语言等问题。中观研究视角大多关注语言在社会生活中的使用,如语言的翻译、语言的社会交际、语言的态度、专门领域中的语言使用以及方言、民族语言和外国语言的和谐共存和发展。而微观研究视角与外语教育教学有关,包括语言课程、教学方法、教学大纲、课堂教学、信息技术与外语教学、教育技术与外语教学等。综上所述,外国语言学及应用语言学与语言的理论研究和应用研究息息相关,并涉及上述的方方面面。

可见,学科研究范围的解读界定了博士文库所包含的内容。第一辑的15本博士论文专著主要涵盖两个方面:语言本体研究与语言教学研究,符合学科的理论研究和应用研究的两个层面。即将出版的第二辑博士论文专著,除了涵盖第一辑的研究内容外,其研究焦点应集中在以下几个方面:语言和认知的结合、语言的普遍规律、语言的变化与发展(理论层面);语言政策与语言规划、课程开发与课堂教学、信息技术与语言教学、互联网＋语言教学解决方案(应用层面)等。

博士文库的建立主要是为了把相关领域的最新研究成果集中展示,供人参考、研究和借鉴,因此,必须体现文库的开放性、内容的完整性、论述的创新性以及研究的科学性。这样才能充分发挥博士文库应有的学术价值!

中国海洋大学出版社以先进的出版理念和敏锐的学术意识策划并设计了外国语言学及应用语言学博士文库,为广大的优秀博士人才提供了展示自己学术研究成果的交流平台。相信该博士文库的不断丰富和完善,必将极大地促进该领域的研究和发展。

陈坚林

上海外国语大学教授,博士生导师

《外语电化教学》主编

总序（二）

    在我国外语研究中，语言学自 20 世纪 80 年代后期开始蓬勃发展，先是作为英语语言文学、日语语言文学、俄语语言文学等二级学科的一个研究方向，稍后外国语言学及应用语言学被列为外国语言文学一级学科下面的二级学科。当前，在外语语言学方面具有较强实力的院校一般具有数个一级学科或二级学科。语言学蓬勃发展的另一个表现是研究生培养规模的扩大。90 年代初，语言学硕士研究生还不多，博士研究生更是凤毛麟角。当时招博士研究生的只有北大、北外、上外、广外等院校，招生人数也是屈指可数。后来，随着增设外语博士点的院校稳步增加，现在招收外语语言学博士研究生的院校已经超过 40 所，招生人数在 200 人左右，学制一般为 3～4 年，最长不超过 8 年。随着高校对外语教师水平和学历要求的不断提高，广大教师考博的热情高涨，20 余人竞争 1 个名额已属常见。报考语言学方面的博士研究生一般需要对语言学有一定的兴趣和热情，硕士研究生阶段已打下较好的基础，其后能经常研读相关学刊，最好有一篇或数篇较高质量的论文在外语类核心期刊上发表。被录取后，通常要刻苦钻研，潜心修炼，短则 3～4 年，长则 5～6 年。其博士论文要经过开题、预答辩、盲审、答辩等严格的环节，所以往往具有较高水平，甚至能达到国内外的领先水平。对个人来说，博士论文也代表了学术生涯的一个高峰，其后要超越并非易事。正是因为博士论文的质量较高，将其出版能有效促进学术发展，国内外出版界也时常为之。这些以博士论文为基础的专著经常能为出版社赢得美誉。

    在过去十多年间，国内几家出版社，如河南大学出版社、上海交通大学出版社、科学出版社、陕西师范大学出版社、中国海洋大学（简称海大）出版社等出版了一系列外语方面的博士论文，其中有很大一部分属语言学，产生了良好影响。其中,海大出版社自 2008 年开始,重视外语语言学研究,出版了外国语言学及应用语言学博士文库,共计 15 本,并通过多种方式进行推广,产生了良好的社会效益。

近几年来,因工作关系与海大出版社邵成军老师交往较多。2015 年下半年,邵老师打电话与我商量,想对外语语言学博士论文进行新的策划,后商定为"外国语言学及应用语言学博士文库(第二辑)",以国内高质量的相关博士论文为对象,为专业性开放式学术系列,旨在为广大外语教师和研究生呈上丰盛的学术大餐。这套文库具有以下特点:(1)加强策划:表现在限定选题范围、请知名学者做序,统一开本、封面,加强后期宣传等方面;(2)严把质量:对申请出版的博士论文呈送两位相关领域的专家进行指导,以进一步提高其学术水平;(3)精心编辑:由专业编辑对书稿进行高质量的编辑,确保其文字无差错,体例与规范等符合国家的出版要求;(4)立体推广:该文库的专著出版后会通过传统与网络形式进行书目推送、网络营销、会议赠送、撰写书评等多种方式向广大读者推介。

对广大外语教师和研究生来说,仔细阅读这套文库,将会在以下方面收获匪浅。

第一,能快速了解某一专题的国内外研究现状。博士论文要求有创新,前提是对国内外相关研究了如指掌。因此,通过答辩的博士论文的文献综述部分通常会对国内外相关论著进行梳理,并有的放矢地进行批判性评论。阅读这部分可以使读者快速掌握某一专题的最新情况,为自己今后开展相关研究打下初步基础。

第二,了解所读专著的创新之处及创新思路。细读作者在对前人研究评论后所提出的研究内容、思路以及具体研究方法,可以窥见作者为什么选定某一专题的某个侧面,用什么理论框架及原因,研究方法有何创新等。了解这些内容并思考背后的原因能帮助读者提升在研究选题方面的功力,而好的选题对高质量研究而言是第一步。

第三,独立思考,发现其不足。阅读专著仅仅停留在吸收知识层面是不够的,还要对所读内容进行批判性思考,英语叫 critical thinking。孔子也说过"学而不思则罔,思而不学则殆",强调思考的重要性。我们阅读专著时,只怀着学习的态度是不够的,还要有质疑和批判精神。可以思考:选题是否有意义?理论框架是否能为研究内容服务?受试是否有代表性?数据收集方法是否可靠?统计分析方法是否恰当?是否对结果进行了深入讨论,能否较好地解释所得出的发现?只有通过思考,发现所读专著存在的不足,我们才能在今后研究中予以克服,加以超越,学术才能发展。就阅读方法而言,读者适当关注博士论文的最后一章往往有事半功倍之效，因为作者通常会在该部分指出其研究的不足，并对今后研究进行展望。

第四，写书评与综述，并进行原创研究。读了一本专著及相关论文，有些收获，对某个专题产生了兴趣，这是非常难得的，此时宜趁热打铁，有所行动。比较容易入手的是对所读专著撰写书评，写好后既可以向期刊投稿，也可以在网络和微信上发布。其后，应进一步阅读相关文献，特别是最新论文，对该专题撰写综述性论文。综述性论文要写好并不容易，其选题首先要有意义，其次要具备全面性、逻辑性、批判性，如能适当采用一些新方法，如元分析、CiteSpace 软件，往往显得不落俗套。前两步只是做学问的"练手"步骤，更重要的是做原创研究，这最能体现一个学者的水平和贡献。原创性研究一般具备以下特点：选题新、方法新、结论新，但如何实现要靠自己的琢磨与钻研，"纸上得来终觉浅，绝知此事要躬行"。

在海大出版社推出"外国语言学及应用语言学博士文库（第二辑）"之际，我应约作序，一方面很是惶恐，同时也为这份信任所感动，遂不揣浅陋，与大家分享一点治学的体会。

蔡金亭

上海财经大学教授，博士生导师

《第二语言学习研究》主编

序　言 //////////

　　欣悉董娟的《语法隐喻中的语义变化:聚焦"性状"转"事物"类概念隐喻》一书即将付梓,十分高兴,特表示热烈祝贺。该书是在她博士论文的基础上经过修改完善而完成的,重点探讨系统功能语言学创始人 M. A. K. Halliday 的系统功能语法中"语法隐喻"的一个重要方面。该书的出版不仅标志着系统功能语言学理论中语法隐喻研究又增加了一部新著,也标志着董娟博士经过多年的不懈努力,已经开始出道,进入中国学术研究队伍的行列,可喜可贺。

　　董娟博士为人正直坦诚,工作兢兢业业,做事认真仔细。她本科毕业于我的母校聊城大学,虽然学校的层次不如其他"211 工程""985 工程"学校高,但外语学院却为山东省以及国内的许多大学培养了很多学术带头人、学术骨干、学术带头人培养对象等,董娟也属于其中之一。她做博士由我指导,学习系统功能语言学,并且从事这个领域的研究工作。尽管她是在职学习,又有繁重的家务工作,压力大、时间紧,但还是以优良的学习成绩和科学研究成果完成了博士论文。在读博士期间,她还获得了教育部人文社科青年基金项目(14YJC740017),毕业后仍在上海理工大学外语学院从事教学与科研工作。

　　语法隐喻是 Halliday 在其概念语法研究中提出来的一个重要概念,而且逐步成为功能语法研究的重要课题之一,至今已经历了 30 余年的发展。隐喻概念是传统修辞学中修辞格一个主要类别,经历了几千年的研究和发展。最近,隐喻概念得到了扩展,成为人们日常一种普遍的思维方式。无论传统的修辞格,还是认知语言学的隐喻概念,都是建立在意义层次上的,表示一种特定的意义转换现

1

象。但功能语法中的语法隐喻,顾名思义,首先是语法转换,即语法范畴的转换:由一种语法结构形式转换为另一种语法结构形式,如由一种过程的及物性结构转换为另一种类型的及物性结构,或者由一种词类转换为另一种词类,如由动词或形容词转换为名词。

如果语法隐喻主要是一种语法转换现象,那么它是否也涉及意义的转换或变化呢?这是一个需要认真研究的问题。问这个问题是因为,语法隐喻的假设是:语法隐喻是对同一客观现实和概念的不同的表达方式。它的存在基础是它的一致式表达方式和隐喻式表达方式是对同一客观现实和概念的体现方式。这样,再谈意义变化或转换是否是背离了语法隐喻提出的初衷呢?这可能是困扰许多研究者的一个问题。但这里需要说明的是:客观现实和客观概念和语言的意义并不是一一对应的。在这里,认知语言学和系统功能语言学都可以对这种现象做出解释。认知语言学区分客观主义语义学和认知语义学。根据客观主义语义学的观点,意义是要受到真值条件的检验的,不符合真值条件的命题是假命题。而认知语义学则认为,人类不对客观现实范畴化就无法认识世界。语言中表现的客观现实及其结构是人类大脑和心灵活动的结果,所以,客观现实和语言体现的意义是不一一对应的。也就是说,同一客观现实,可以根据人类在他们的大脑中的概念化的不同而不同。从这个意义上讲,语法隐喻的一致式和隐喻式虽然基于相同的客观现实,但其意义可以是不同的。系统功能语言学虽然不区分客观主义语义学和认知语义学,而且其概念意义是表现客观现实的意义,但这并不是说,对于同一客观现实,只能有一种意义。从这个角度讲,系统功能语言学和认知语言学虽然理论框架不同,但它们背后的假设是一致的:对于同一客观现实的不同表达方式其意义是不同的。这种不同可以表现为概念意义的不同,由语境引起的对同一客观现实的不同释解方式,如:"They arrived at the summit on the fifth day." 和 "The fifth day saw them at the summit." 并不是简单的同义句,而是涉及不同的过程。前者的重点是"他们"到达山顶的行为和时间,而后者的重点则是感知这个行为的结果:"到达了山顶"。与此同时,两种结构的人际意义和语篇意义也有区别。从人际意义上讲,虽然两个句子都是陈述句,是提供信息的,但它们的主语不同,即对命题的负责者不同。前者是人:"他们","他们"的行动是信息的重点;后者是时间:"第五天",重点是第五天的行动结果。从语篇意义上讲,前者的主位是人:"他们",这条信息是关于他们的;后者是时间:"第五天",这条信息是关于到达山顶的时间的。明确了这一点就解除了一致式和隐喻式同义的限制,可以大张旗鼓地探讨两者在意义上的差别。

迄今为止,虽然国内外学者在这一领域做了大量研究,明确了语法隐喻的分类、发生机制以及该理论的发展模式,还进行了与不同语域或学科相结合的应用研究,但对于一致式和隐喻式意义上的差别还没有进行深入研究。笔者认为,这并不是因为此研究不重要,或者大家忽视了它们的区别,而是对于两者的同义性不知如何处理。

该书作者认识到此研究的必要性,致力于探讨一致性和隐喻式在意义上的差异,聚焦于"性状—事物"概念语法隐喻的意义变化研究。此研究的基本思路是:根据情景语境,从词汇语法层面寻找意义变化的依据。通过聚焦"性状—事物"类概念语法隐喻,探讨在语法隐喻形成过程中在意义(主要是经验意义)上发生了哪些类型的变化,同时提出探讨人际和语篇意义变化的可行视角。

该书主要采用实证研究,定性与定量分析相结合,选取了 10 种著名科学期刊的 35 篇研究性论文(约 164 300 词)作为语料,析出 900 个含有"性状—事物"类概念语法隐喻的小句,对它们的一致式和隐喻式进行比较分析。该书运用 UAM Corpus Tool 3.3h 分析统计了 900 个小句的及物性结构,包括这些小句的过程类型以及含有隐喻性事物的名词词组在小句中所承担的功能角色,并分析统计了所有小句中含有该类隐喻的名词词组的经验结构。

通过研究,该书发现:(1)"性状—事物"类概念隐喻从一致式到隐喻式的转变过程中,主要产生四种类型的概念意义变化,即语义抽象、语义概括、语义特化和语义模糊。(2)不同类型的经验意义变化在语料中呈现出有规律的分布模式。语义抽象是普遍性的变化,其他类型为具体变化。(3)语义抽象源于语义交联,经验意义的各种变化都有具体的词汇语法体现形式。该书还提出了"过程+性状+事物"三种语义范畴融合的"三重交联"。(4)语法隐喻中的人际和语篇意义的变化可分别从评价意义和指称系统的视角进行探讨。总体上讲,该书对语法隐喻在意义上的变化做了较为系统的分析阐释,在一定程度上进一步完善了语法隐喻理论。

虽然作者已经获得了博士学位,在学术上取得了一定成就,但在学术界还是一个新兵,还需要进一步发展和提高,书中可能还有个别不尽如人意的地方,还请读者提出宝贵意见。

张德禄

同济大学教授,博士生导师

2020 年 8 月 22 日

前　言 ////////////

　　语法隐喻(grammatical metaphor)这一概念是由系统功能语言学创始人 M. A. K. Halliday 提出的,历经 30 余年的发展,已经成为系统功能语言学的重要组成部分和理论创新。不同于传统修辞学的词汇隐喻和认知语言学的概念隐喻,语法隐喻产生于语义范畴与词汇语法范畴的交叉耦合。它不仅是一种特殊的表达方式,也是生成意义的方式,是语言系统意义潜势扩展的重要资源。国内外学者在这一领域做了大量研究,明确了语法隐喻的分类、发生机制以及该理论的发展模式,还进行了与不同语域或学科相结合的应用研究。但语法隐喻理论的核心问题一致式与隐喻式在意义上的差异性却没有引起足够重视。语法隐喻涉及同一意义的不同表达,但一致式和隐喻式又不完全同义。尽管语法隐喻过程中新的语义特征的增加以及信息丢失等问题多次被提及,但缺乏基于实际语料分析的、系统的、全面的研究,语法隐喻中的意义问题始终没有得到充分的解决。因此,本研究将充分探讨语法隐喻过程中的语义变化问题。

　　本研究以系统功能语言学理论为指导,基于语言的五大维度,通过实际语料分析,结合语境,从词汇语法层面寻找意义变化的依据。通过聚焦"性状—事物"类概念语法隐喻,考察语法隐喻过程中在意义(主要是经验意义)上发生了哪些类型的变化,并初步提出探讨人际和语篇意义变化的可行视角。本书遵循实例与系统的互补关系,选取 10 种著名科学期刊的 35 篇研究性论文(约 164 300 词)作为语料,共获得 900 个含有"性状—事物"类概念语法隐喻的小句,对它们的一致式和隐喻式进行比较。本研究运用 UAM Corpus Tool 3.3h 分析统计了 900 个小句的及物性结构,包括这些小句的过程类型以及含有隐喻性事物的名词词组

1

在小句中所承担的功能角色,并分析统计了所有小句中含有该类隐喻的名词词组(共 996 个)的经验结构,结果在 Excel 中呈现。词汇语法层面的分析与语境参数的考量为语义层面的讨论提供了依据。

本研究的主体部分由八章组成。

第一章是绪论,介绍研究背景、理论依据、研究目标和研究问题。

第二章是文献综述,包括三个方面的相关研究:语法隐喻理论的发展模式、语法隐喻中的意义变化、不同语言学视角下的名物化。第二章分析已有研究的意义和不足,在此基础上说明本研究的特点和价值。

第三章是理论基础,首先介绍系统功能语言学提出的语言的五大维度(结构、系统、层次化、实例化、元功能),随后探讨语法隐喻理论的基底性概念——"一致性"的发展脉络,明确形式、功能与意义的关系,界定"性状—事物"类概念语法隐喻的主要概念,并基于以上讨论构建本研究的综合理论框架。"性状—事物"类概念语法隐喻的语义变化是指三大元功能即元意义上的变化;变化具有系统性,每种意义模式的变化都有其变化系统。语义变化是由词汇语法层的变化来体现的,同时由语境层控制,因此两个层面都要考虑。本研究将从词、词组、小句等不同级阶进行语法分析,通过一致式与隐喻式的对比,寻找经验意义变化的依据。本研究是基于语料分析的实证研究,通过语境中的大量实例,找出变化规律,从实例到系统。

第四章是研究方法,介绍语料的选取、处理、标注、分析工具及其操作方法。本研究基于语料分析,采用定性和定量相结合的方法。语料中所有包含"性状—事物"类概念隐喻的名词词组统一拆解为一致式:构型为"载体+过程+属性"的关系小句,性状在小句中被识解为属性。在性状转为事物的过程中,一致式小句的过程消失,同时其他成分的功能也发生变化,产生综合反应链。本研究对语料在词、词组和小句三个级阶上进行分析、标注和统计。在词这一级阶上,本研究统计"性状—事物"类隐喻的词汇实现形式及其出现次数,通过分类比较,发现共有特征。在词组级阶上,本研究分析所有含有该类语法隐喻的名词词组的经验结构,考察名词词组的语义生成力,结果在 Excel 中呈现。在小句级阶上,本研究分析小句的及物性构型:(1)包含该类语法隐喻的小句的过程类型;(2)包含该类语法隐喻的名词词组在小句过程构型中充当什么功能成分。本研究利用标注统计软件 UAM Corpus Tool 3.3h,采用自建标注体系,手动标注。过程类型的标注体系按照功能语法对小句过程及其内部分类的描述来建构;功能成分的标注体系包括级阶、地位和类型三个方面。

第五章是语料的及物性语法分析,统计分析名物化名词词组所进入的小句过程类型以及这些名物化词组在隐喻式过程中担当怎样的功能成分。每种类型都通过实例加以说明。从经验意义上来说,"性状—事物"类概念语法隐喻的一致式是关系小句,实现一个言辞,表达的意义是把某种属性赋予某个载体。经过语法隐喻之后,整个言辞浓缩为一个成分,由名词词组来实现,"性状—事物"充当名词词组的事物/中心词。这个包含语法隐喻的成分又进入新的言辞,从中承担各种功能,在不同的经验域中表达新的意义。

第六章是"性状—事物"类概念语法隐喻的经验意义变化。此章基于上一章的分析数据和名物化名词词组的经验结构分析,通过比较该类隐喻的一致式和隐喻式,进一步探讨名物化的语义生成力,建构了经验意义变化的分析框架,归纳出经验意义变化的主要和次要类型,并考察了各种类型的意义变化在语料中的分布规律,以及意义变化的词汇语法实现和语境控制因素。

第七章是对语法隐喻的人际意义和语篇意义变化研究的启示和初步思考,提出了探讨这两大意义变化的可选视角,并基于语料做了尝试性分析。

第八章是结论,总结了本研究的主要发现和贡献,同时指出本研究的不足和未来进一步研究的方向。本研究的主要发现包括以下几点。(1)从一致式到隐喻式的转变过程中,"性状—事物"类概念隐喻在经验意义上主要产生四种类型的语义变化:语义抽象、语义概括、语义特化和语义模糊。其中,语义特化又包含"获得技术性"和"增强技术性"两类;语义模糊分为"内在歧义"和"外在歧义"两种类型。(2)不同类型的经验意义变化在语料中呈现出一定的分布规律。语义抽象是普遍性的变化,其他类型为具体变化。语义特化的比例较高(44.82%),其中35.98%的实例属于在语境中获得技术性;19.09%的实例具有语义模糊,语义概括在10.35%的实例中有所体现。(3)经验意义的各种变化都有具体的词汇语法体现形式,并由语境因素控制。语义抽象源于语义交联,本研究提出了"过程+性状+事物"三种语义范畴融合的"三重交联";具有语义概括的事物由名词词组中不带任何修饰成分的中心词来实现,该类名词词组在小句中所承担的功能角色与一致式小句中"载体"的恢复程度有一定的相关性;语义特化所涉及的技术性与语境参数中的语场关系密切;语义模糊产生于性状本身的"梯度性"、隐喻化过程中的信息丢失、名词词组复合体的复杂性,可在语境中依据事物所在的名词词组的特征语、小句过程类型或其他评价型成分来消除歧义。(4)语法隐喻中的人际和语篇意义的变化可分别从评价意义和指称系统的视角进行初步探讨。本研究涉及语法隐喻理论的"意义"核心问题,对语法隐喻在意义上的变化做了较为系统的分析阐释,在一定程度上进一步完善了语法隐喻理论。本研究是对语言本体的语法研究,对语篇和会话分析,尤其是批评话语分析或积极话语分析有一定的实际价值,也对以语言为基础的学习理论的构建有一定的意义。由于研究时间和条件所限,本研究所涉及语料的数量和类型有所欠缺;本研究重点关注了"性状—事物"类概念语法隐喻在经验意义上的变化,篇幅所限,对人际和语篇意义的变化只做了初步探讨。此外,本研究选取了一类概念语法隐喻,在今后的研究中应囊括更多的语法隐喻类型。

本研究受教育部人文社科青年基金(项目编号:14YJC740017)和上海理工大学外语学院博士启动基金资助。

目 录 ///////////

Chapter 1

Introduction

This study aims to investigate the semantic change that takes place in the transference from a congruent form to a grammatically metaphorical form by focusing on the quality-thing ideational metaphor. An overview of this study will be given in this chapter. The research background, research rationale, research objectives and questions, and organization of this study will be introduced in sequence.

1.1 Research Background

Grammatical metaphor is a significant theoretical innovation in Systemic Functional Linguistics (hereinafter SFL). It is different from lexical metaphor in traditional rhetoric and conceptual metaphor in Cognitive Linguistics. Metaphor in the grammatical sense is "the wholescale recasting of the relationship between the grammar and the semantics" (Halliday, 1995/2007a[1]: 19). Grammatical metaphor has developed from a special grammatical phenomenon into a universal one in language use. It enriches the types of meaning and the modes of expression

---

[1] The literature quoted was originally published in 1995, and it was republished in 2007. The second version is used for reference in this book, so the source of the literature is written as 1995/2007a for a clear representation of the historical development of the quoted theory. References of this kind are quoted this way in this book.

by expanding the way human beings construe experience and the meaning potential of the language system. The past over-thirty years have witnessed its theoretical maturation and abundant applications. The theory of grammatical metaphor has gone through three developmental models since it was established by M. A. K. Halliday: the Functional Model (Halliday, 1985a, 1994; Halliday & Martin, 1993), the Stratified Functional Model (Halliday, 1998, 1995/2007a, 1996/2007b,1998/2007c; Thompson, 1996; Halliday & Matthiessen, 1999) and the Stratified Systemic Functional Model (Halliday & Matthiessen, 2004, 2014). Over the years, grammatical metaphor has gradually been well integrated into the framework of SFL. Grammatical metaphor was initially defined as the transference of processes and functional elements in lexicogrammar, but with the introduction of the notions of stratal-tension and fractal expansion and projection, some theoretical issues of grammatical metaphor, such as its typology, its working mechanism and the relationship between the congruent mode and the metaphorical mode, have been addressed.

The relationship between the congruent and the metaphorical modes, however, has not yet been fully explicated. Consensus has been reached that the two modes share certain "core meaning", and it is the basis on which they are related to each other. A single meaning can be expressed both congruently and metaphorically, but language is a meaning-making system and choice is meaning, and thus the two expressions are not totally synonymous (Halliday, 1985a, 1994; Halliday & Matthiessen, 1999). The differences in meaning realized by the congruent and metaphorical forms have aroused a wide concern of researchers, but so far most of the related studies have been confined to theoretical assumptions and generalizations for lack of thorough corpus-supported analyses as well as a systematic and comprehensive analytical framework. Therefore, it is of necessity to conduct research to work out the way meaning is changed in the process of grammatical metaphorization, the types of meaning that get involved and the causing factors of such changes.

1.2 Research Rationale

This study is theoretically based on SFL and employs Functional Grammar (hereinafter FG) as the analytical tool for grammatical description.

The fundamental dimensions in language (system, structure, stratification, metafunction and instantiation) proposed by SFL impenetrate the guiding principles of this study. In order to explore the changes in meaning in the process of grammatical metaphorization, questions in respect of the nature of meaning and the way meaning is realized should be firstly answered. The principles of metafunction and stratification come in for the answers. Language has three metafunctions: ideational, interpersonal and textual functions; "the basic functions of language, looked from another point of view, are simply different kinds of meaning" (Halliday, 1970/2007d: 176). In this sense, changes in meaning are in fact changes in metafunctions. The intrinsic functions of language have evolved into the three modes of meaning (see Chapter 3). Language is a stratified system; the stratum of semantics lies intermediately between the stratum of context and the stratum of lexicogrammar. The three strands of meaning are realized by specific lexicogrammatical systems (TRANSITIVITY, MOOD and THEME-RHEME) and simultaneously determined by the corresponding parameters of the context of situation (field, tenor and mode). By the same token, changes in meaning are not self-evident, but are realized by changes in lexicogrammar and at the same time controlled by corresponding contextual factors. Therefore, it is required to look for evidence of changes in meaning from both "bottom-up" and "top-down" points of view. Only by analyzing the differences both in grammatical configurations between the congruent and the metaphorical expressions and in contextual environments where the two modes work, can we discover the differences in meaning.

Why is one type of nominalization (quality-thing ideational metaphor) chosen as the subject for investigation? There are two reasons for this. In the first place, nominalization is studied under the umbrella of grammatical metaphor in SFL, and it is attributed a high value, because it is "the single most powerful resource for creating grammatical metaphor" (Halliday, 1994: 352) and "the predominant semantic drift of grammatical metaphor in modern English" (Martin, 1992: 406). Bussmann (1996/2000: 328) asserts in his dictionary that "virtually any word can be nominalized". It is this tendency towards "thing-ness" that makes ideational metaphors possible. In view of its special status in grammatical metaphor, nominalization becomes the primary choice of this study. In the second place, related literature review indicates that most of the studies on nominalization from various linguistic perspectives focus on the verbal-noun nominalization, with the other types of nominalization degraded into a less important position. Although, relatively speaking, SFL excels the other approaches in that it interprets nominalization in terms of both semantic and class shifts, its well-established theory requires empirical support with data of different kinds of nominalization other than the verbal-noun type. That is one of the primary reasons why this study focuses on the quality-thing ideational metaphor, a previously-ignored type, and more reasons will be given in Chapter 2, Section 2.3.5.

This study is characterized by centrality, comprehensiveness, contrastiveness and complementarity. By centrality, it means that this study deals directly with the nucleus of the theory of grammatical metaphor, because it is aimed at working out the semantic change in grammatical metaphor, which has long been a research gap. As for comprehensiveness, this study is built on the theory of SFL, with the five dimensions of language interacting to serve as the guiding principles of study, and changes in different modes of meaning will be thoroughly explored. In addition, this study adopts a contrastive approach in analyzing the congruent and the agnate metaphorical expressions respectively and comparing them in respect to grammatical configurations. The feature of complementarity in this study is revealed, on the one hand by the integration of the "top-down" view (from context to semantics) with the "bottom-up" view (from lexicogrammar to semantics), and on the other hand by the combination of qualitative and quantitative approaches. In this study, objective analysis of a good quantity of authentic data will be conducted, which will make up for the "theory-weighted" deficiency of the previous studies.

1.3   Research Objectives and Research Questions

This study is aimed to explore the semantic change in the transference from the congruent to the metaphorical by focusing on the quality-thing ideational metaphor. This study is intended to address the following questions by analyzing the grammatical status of the quality-thing nominalizations in the clausal transitivity configurations as well as the experiential structure of these metaphorical nominal groups①.

(1) What types of change in experiential meaning may take place while a quality is transferred into a thing?

(2) How is each type of experiential semantic change distributed in the data?

(3) How are the various changes in experiential meaning are related to their lexicogrammatical realizations and corresponding contextual parameters?

(4) What are the implications for the study of changes in interpersonal and textual meanings in grammatical metaphor?

1.4　Organization of This Study

This study falls into eight chapters. Chapter 1 serves as an introduction to this study. The background, rationale, objectives and questions of this study are presented, followed by the organization of this study.

Chapter 2 is the literature review. Studies from three aspects are included: developmental models of the theory of grammatical metaphor, studies on semantic change in grammatical metaphor and studies on nominalization from different linguistic perspectives.

Chapter 3 is theoretical foundations for this study. The five fundamental dimensions of language (structure, system, stratification, instantiation and metafunction) and "congruence", the basic concept of grammatical metaphor, are firstly introduced. And then the relations between form, function and meaning are clarified; important concepts of quality-thing ideational metaphor are discussed finally to build a comprehensive framework of guiding principles for this study.

Chapter 4 introduces the research methodology in detail. This study is data-based and adopts both qualitative and quantitative methods. This chapter begins with how the data are collected and processed, and then describes how the data are analyzed at the three ranks of word, group and clause by means of the statistical and analytical tools (Excel and UAM Corpus Tool 3.3h).

Chapter 5 focuses on the transitivity analysis of all the clauses containing quality-thing ideational metaphors under investigation. With a brief introduction

---

① In this study, a metaphorical nominal group refers to a nominal group in which the Thing is metaphorical—realized by a nominalization.

to the domains of experience and transitivity, the process types of these clauses are counted and analyzed, and the various functional roles that the metaphorical nominal groups play as both direct and indirect participants in the transitivity configurations are analyzed and counted.

Chapter 6 is concerned with the experiential semantic change in quality-thing metaphor. On the basis of the statistics from the previous chapter and analytical results of the experiential structures of those metaphorical groups, an analytical framework of change in experiential meaning is established. Four types of change are found out: one universal type (semantic abstraction) and three particular types (semantic generalization, semantic specialization and semantic obscuration) with their subtypes. All the metaphorical groups in the data are classified in terms of these change types, the number and percentage of each type are counted, and each type is illustrated and explained in detail with specific examples.

Chapter 7 provides some implications for the study of interpersonal and textual semantic changes in quality-thing metaphor. It is proposed that the interpersonal semantic change can be investigated from the perspective of Evaluation due to the specialty of quality-thing metaphor. Analysis can be conducted to find out what might happen to the congruent evaluation carried by qualities when they are metaphorized into things. The expansion in textual meaning can be discussed from the viewpoint of Reference by analyzing the functional elements (Deictic, post-Deictic and Epithet) in metaphorical nominal groups.

Chapter 8 summarizes the major findings of this study, points out its significance and limitations, and provides suggestions for future study.

Chapter 2

Literature Review

In this chapter, the developmental models of the theory of grammatical metaphor will be reviewed firstly to discover the theoretical problems that have not been fully solved in this area. Now that the semantic change in grammatical metaphor is still a "less-charted territory", previous studies on this aspect should be sorted out to find out the possible deficiencies. And finally research from different linguistic perspectives on nominalization, the most important device of ideational metaphor, will be taken into account to justify the choice of quality-thing ideational metaphor in this study.

2.1 The Theory of Grammatical Metaphor[①]

It should be clearly stated that it is for the convenience of theoretical description that the developing trace of grammatical metaphor from its commencement to maturation is divided into several stages, and there are no clear cuts between these stages (Zhang & Dong, 2014). They are successive and even overlapping, with one phase based on the contributions of the previous ones.

2.1.1 Early Studies (1970s – 1984)

---

① This section was published in *Foreign Language Teaching and Research*, 2014(1): 56-68.

In the 1970s, Halliday gave a special concern to the social attributes of language, and conducted a series of studies on registers and language variants in social contexts. It is in these studies that the metaphoricity of language was mentioned. In a paper entitled "Sociolinguistic Aspects of Mathematical Education", Halliday (1974/1978a) discussed the levels of technicality in mathematical language, stating that mathematical and scientific English demonstrates a high degree of nominalization, and further explained that the preference for nominal modes of expression is due to the fact that expressions with nominals have a greater syntactic and semantic potential for various information structures and the fact that nominalization obscures ambiguities. In another paper entitled "Antilanguages" (Halliday, 1976/1978b), the notion of metaphorical variants was brought forward. An antilanguage is generated by an antisociety which is built within another society as a deliberate alternative and resistance to it by taking the form of passive symbiosis or of active hostility. An antilanguage exists in the context of resocialization; it is a metaphor for an everyday language, since it is different from the norm language in terms of phonology, morphology, lexicon, syntax and semantics, and all these differences are called metaphorical variations.

As a response to the western metaphor-mania in rhetorical and cognitive senses, Halliday (1984/2005a) proposed a brand-new perspective on metaphor and coined the term grammatical metaphor in a conference paper "Grammatical Metaphor in English and Chinese". Halliday's notice of grammatical metaphor stemmed from his concern over the difficulty that Chinese-language learners encountered. He held the idea that metaphor is not only a lexical phenomenon, but involves grammatical transferences. Two types of metaphor were distinguished: (a) learned metaphors which are typical of written language, especially scientific or bureaucratic language and to which non-metaphoric equivalents can be found, and (b) everyday metaphors which have been automatized to become a natural mode of expression in the language system. Halliday pointed out that there is no sharp line between the two types, but they need to be treated differently in particular situations. Halliday highlighted the second type, and further divided it into interpersonal metaphors and ideational metaphors with sub-classifications. Table 2-1 summarizes this early classification with examples in both English and Chinese for comparison.

Table 2-1   Halliday's early classification of grammatical metaphor (Halliday, 1984/2005a)

	Type			Example
Grammatical metaphor	learned metaphors			English: the analysis of the process of social structuralchange requires a historical perspective
				Chinese: 社会结构变迁程序的分析需要历史上的观点
	everyday metaphors	interpersonal metaphor	modality & polarity	English: I think he's coming I don't think he's coming
				Chinese: 我想他会来 * 我不想他会来①
			mood	English: do that again and I'll clobber you
				Chinese: 你再这样做就会挨打
		ideational metaphor	possessive type	English: he has black hair
				Chinese: (no parallel)
			cognate type	English: have a bath, make a mistake
				Chinese: 洗澡、犯错误
			phrasal verb type	English: they called the meeting off

This classification is mostly based on the mode of language (spoken or written); the spoken mode and the context of language use are stressed. Halliday repeatedly emphasized the textual motivation of grammatically metaphoric structures. The three kinds of ideational metaphors in spoken language are all textually motivated to get the message organized in an appropriate way in the discourse.

Halliday's initial concern for grammatical metaphor is closely related to his study of language from the socio-semiotic perspective in the 1970s and the practical education-orientation in the 1980s, but a comprehensive theory of grammatical metaphor has not yet been established.

---

① The improper expression is marked by the asterisk*.

2.1.2　The Functional Model (1985 – 1994)

2.1.2.1　Establishment of the Theory

The establishment of the theory of grammatical metaphor starts with the publication of the first edition of *An Introduction to Functional Grammar* (IFG hereinafter) in 1985. Halliday pointed out that lexical choice is only one side of the lexicogrammatical selection, and "there is a strong grammatical element in rhetorical transference" (Halliday, 1985a: 320). While lexical metaphor involves the different meanings of a lexical item, grammatical metaphor is concerned with the variation in grammatical forms to express a certain meaning. The "literal" realization of a semantic configuration in the lexicogrammar is taken to be congruent. The congruent and the metaphorical are distinctive from each other but share a certain core meaning.

Halliday (1985a, 1994) proposed two main types of grammatical metaphor based on the model of semantic functions: ideational metaphor and interpersonal metaphor, and discussed grammatical metaphor in terms of the functions of the structural elements; therefore this phase is named as "The Functional Model" (see Table 2-2).

Table 2-2　The Functional Model of grammatical metaphor

Types of grammatical metaphor		Realization
Ideational metaphor		transference from clause complex to clause
		transference from process to thing
		transference between other functional elements
Interpersonal metaphor	Metaphor of mood	transference between different mood types
	Metaphor of modality	transference from implicit modality to explicit modality: from modal phrases / groups to projecting clauses

In the case of ideational metaphor, one process can be transferred to be another, a clause complex can be transferred to be a clause, and the related functional elements in each clause are correspondingly changed. Interpersonal metaphor is further divided into metaphor of modality and metaphor of mood. The former is realized by the changes in the types of mood; the latter involves transference from an implicit modality to an explicit one, which is realized by a projecting clause in the form of a proposition.

Based on ideas in IFG (1985a), the second edition of IFG (1994) makes some modifications in the following aspects.

(1) Lexical metaphor is differentiated from grammatical metaphor in terms of the two perspectives from which metaphor is viewed. Lexical metaphor is seen "from below" as to how a lexical item expresses various meanings, while grammatical metaphor is viewed "from above" as to how a given meaning is realized by different lexicogrammatical forms.

(2) Meaning construction and experience construal by means of language are foregrounded. In explaining the differences between spoken and written language in their patterns of metaphoric usage, Halliday (1985a: 329) states that "speech and writing differ in the kind of complexity that they typically display", but Halliday (1994: 349) rewords the idea as "they (speech and writing) have different ways of constructing complex meanings". Moreover, in discussing the function of modal auxiliaries, the two editions also display different wordings and thus different ideas. Halliday (1985a: 336) states that "the general function of the modal auxiliaries is to express degrees of polarity, this gives an idea of how all these four scales are semantically related", but Halliday (1994: 357) emphasizes the notions of construal and semantic space by stating that "the four types of modality...are all varying degrees of polarity, different ways of construing the semantic space between the positive and negative poles".

(3) "Nominalization" is introduced as an important type of ideational metaphor. It is further explicated that when clausal patterns are replaced by nominal ones, some information tends to be lost.

2.1.2.2   Main Ideas and Problems

In the Functional Model, some important ideas were put forward but failed to gain due attention.

(1) There is no clear cut between a congruent form and its metaphorical counterpart, and being congruent does not mean being better or more frequent or functioning as a norm. "There are many instances where a metaphorical representation has become the norm, and this is in fact a natural process of linguistic change" (Halliday, 1985a: 321).

(2) Metaphorical choice is in itself meaningful, which brings in extra semantic features. "A piece of wording that is metaphorical has as it were

an additional dimension of meaning: it 'means' both metaphorically and congruently" (Halliday, 1994: 353).

(3) The extent to which a metaphorical expression needs to be unpacked depends on specific study objectives. Sometimes a brief note to the effect of a metaphorical mode is what is needed, while in some cases, it is required to trace a "history" of intermediate steps linking the metaphorical form and the postulated "most congruent" expression.

(4) An important function of metaphorical interpretation is to explicate how an instance in a text is related to the whole language system. A text is an instantiation and actualization of the potential that constitutes the language system, and thus "text linguistics" cannot be detached from the study of the underlying grammar.

(5) Although ideational metaphor and interpersonal metaphor are distinctive in types, they can be found co-existing in one single clause, with the various kinds of metafunctions realized simultaneously in one clause.

There are also some unsolved problems in this model. First, the concept of congruence is not well-defined. Although the uncertainty of congruence has been acknowledged, the criteria for "the most typical way" of expression are not clarified. Second, the relationship between the congruent form and the metaphorical form in meaning remains to be answered. The two share a certain "core meaning", but they are not totally synonymous. The changes in meaning in metaphorization require further research. Third, the relationship between lexical metaphor and grammatical metaphor is not explicated. It is stated that the two are metaphors viewed from different perspectives, but it is also claimed that metaphorical forms often entail some lexical variations. Last but not least, grammatical metaphor is classified into ideational metaphor and interpersonal metaphor, with the exclusion of textual one, and consequently, the influences that grammatical metaphor has on the textual construction are not given sufficient emphasis. Nevertheless, researchers have made some complements in this aspect; for instance, Ravelli (1988) studies the functions of grammatical metaphor in textual construction in various genres by means of the interrelation between grammatical metaphor and the mode of communication.

2.1.3　The Stratified Functional Model (1995 – 2003)

The next developmental phase can be termed as Stratified Functional Model (see Table 2-3). Halliday and other scholars further modified the previous model by introducing the important concept of stratification, explaining the underlying motivation of grammatical metaphor in terms of language evolution, and defining grammatical metaphor as a metaphorical extension of the semantic system. In addition, the changes in meaning that occur in metaphorization as well as the relationship between lexical metaphor and grammatical metaphor were also explicated.

Table 2-3   The Stratified Functional Model of grammatical metaphor

Type of GM	Strata				Ideational function of metaphorical expressions
	Semantics		Lexicogrammar		
	congruent	metaphorical	congruent	metaphorical	
Ideational metaphor	sequence	figure, element	clause complex	clause, nominal group	semantic junction of relator, process and thing
	figure	element	clause	nominal group	semantic junction of process and thing
	element: quality	thing	adjectival group	nominal group	semantic junction of quality and thing
	process	quality, thing	verbal group	adjectival, nominal group	semantic junction of process and quality/ thing
	circumstance	process, quality, thing	prepositional phrase	verbal, adjectival, nominal group	semantic junction of circumstance and process/quality/ thing
	relator	circumstance, process, quality, thing	conjunctive group	prepositional phrase, verbal, adjectival, nominal group	semantic junction of relator and circumstance/ process/ quality/ thing
Interpersonal metaphor	Metaphor of mood				
	Metaphor of modality				

2.1.3.1 New Developments

(1) The notion of stratification is introduced to explain the working

mechanism of grammatical metaphor from the semogenic perspective. In fact, Martin (1993a: 112) expressed the same idea: "Grammatical metaphor can thus be seen to introduce a tension between grammar (a text's wording) and semantics (a text's meaning)." The necessity for the distinction between the stratum of semantics and the stratum of lexicogrammar is interpreted from the perspective of language evolution. In this vein, the concept of congruence is thus redefined as the "pattern of relationships between the semantics and the grammar in which the two strata initially co-evolved" (Halliday, 1998: 208). The realizational relationship between semantics and lexicogrammar is congruent when a sequence is realized by a clause complex, a figure is realized by a clause, and an element is realized by a group or phrase, because the grammatical units such as clause complex, clause, group or phrase have evolved to fulfill such functions. But metaphor occurs when there is realignment between the semantic units and their realizational grammatical units. Grammatical metaphor takes place out of the inter-strata tension between semantics and lexicogrammar; whenever the realizational relationship between the two strata is decoupled and recoupled, the realizational domains of semantic categories are expanded, and consequently the modes that human beings construe the experiential world are also expanded.

(2) The semantic changes in grammatical metaphor have been brought to the front by introducing two important notions: junction of semantic features and syndromes of grammatical metaphor. "The metaphorical version is not simply a meaningless (i.e. synonymous) variant of some more congruent form; it is 'junctional'—that is, it embodies semantic features deriving from its own lexicogrammatical properties" (Halliday & Matthiessen, 1999: 283). Grammatical expressions should not be taken as a group of different grammatical structures realizing the same meaning; choices on different lexicogrammatical structures definitely lead to variations in meanings that these structures realize. The meaning realized by a metaphorical form is a junction of the original congruent meaning and the newly-created meaning in the process of metaphorization. Studies on semantic junction will be reviewed in Section 2.2.

What is related to the junctional features is the idea of *syndromes*. Because the metaphorical process takes place in the grammar, any transformation in one grammatical element may lead to corresponding changes in others, and may have an influence on the whole clause or complex. Any displacement in rank or status inevitably involves a series of changes in others. "So grammatical metaphors tend to occur in syndromes: clusters of interrelated transformations that reconfigure the grammatical structure as a whole" (Halliday, 1998: 214). There are two kinds of syndromes: lower rank syndromes in which figures are reconstrued as if they were elements and higher rank syndromes where sequences are reconstrued as if they were figures. Based on the junction of elemental semantic categories, Halliday (1998) reclassified grammatical metaphor into 13 types (listed in Table 2-4).

Table 2-4　Types of elemental grammatical metaphors
(adapted from Halliday (1998: 209-210))

Type	Semantic element	Grammatical class
1	quality→entity	adjective→noun
2	process→entity	verb→noun
3	circumstance→entity	preposition→noun
4	relator→entity	conjunction→noun
5	process→quality	verb→adjective
6	circumstance→quality	adverb/prepositional phrase→adjective
7	relator→quality	conjunction→adjective
8	circumstance→quality	be/go+preposition→verb
9	relator→process	conjunction→verb
10	relator→circumstance	conjunction→prepositional / group
11	[zero]→entity	=the phenomenon of...
12	[zero]→process	=...occurs/ensues
13	entity→[expansion]	noun→[various](in env.1,2 above)

(3) The relationship between lexical metaphor and grammatical metaphor has been revisited. Halliday (1998: 191) theorizes lexical transformations as the "same signifier, different signified" and grammatical transformations as the "same signified, different signifier". In grammatical transformations, what varies is not the lexical item but the grammatical category. But Halliday & Matthiessen (1999) hold the idea that lexical metaphor and grammatical metaphor work with the same metaphorical mechanism in terms of semantic domain. "Lexical and grammatical metaphor are not two different phenomena; they are both aspects of the same general metaphorical strategy by which we expand our semantic

resources for construing experience" (Halliday & Matthiessen, 1999: 233). The main distinction between the two kinds of metaphor is one of delicacy. In a sense, lexical metaphor has grammatical implications because grammar and lexis are the two poles of a continuum of delicacy, and the co-occurrence of lexical metaphor and grammatical metaphor is not unusual. Another point that the two kinds of metaphor share is the junction of semantic features. Grammatical metaphorization is not simply an alternative way of expressing a certain meaning but a different process of construing experience. Similarly, in lexical metaphor, the transferred lexical item maintains the original "literal" meaning and meanwhile relates to the new semantic features created by metaphorization. Therefore, it should be admitted that the two kinds of metaphor work by the same principle, and that grammatical metaphor involves changes at the lexicogrammatical stratum as a whole, not just what happens to lexical items.

2.1.3.2 Major Problems

The first problem that can be found in this model is that the interpersonal metaphor has not been given as much attention as that is given to the ideational metaphor. It is obvious that all the 13 types in the modified typology of grammatical metaphor (Halliday, 1998) belong to the ideational category, so it might leave such an impression that grammatical metaphor refers to any phenomenon involving rankshift, yet the classification based on metafunctions is denied (Yan, 2003). In addition, the tension between semantics and lexicogrammar is also built on theoretical explorations in the ideation base, and thus interpersonal metaphor is ignored in a large measure.

The second problem is that the relation between stratal tension and semantic junction is not well clarified, so there seems to be ambiguity in the theorization and definition of grammatical metaphor according to the inter-stratal model (Halliday, 1998) and the intra-stratal model or semantic model (Halliday & Matthiessen, 1999). The inter-stratal model explains that grammatical metaphor derives from the realignment between semantics and its lexicogrammatical realization, while the semantic model bases the categorization of grammatical metaphor in relation to the junction of semantic categories. But in effect these two kinds of perspectives are closely related to each other because grammatical metaphors examined according to semantic junction can be taken as the result of transference or transcategorization of metaphors in the inter-stratal model

(Devrim, 2015).

2.1.4   The Stratified Systemic Functional Model (2004 – present)

The latest phase can be named as the Stratified Systemic Functional Model (see Table 2-5), which starts with the publication of the third edition of IFG (Halliday & Matthiessen, 2004). A systemic perspective has been added to the theoretical framework on the basis of the previously proposed ideas of stratification and semogenesis, and consequently, the important roles of logico-semantic relations in metaphorization and the textual effects exerted by grammatical metaphor have been affirmed definitely.

Table 2-5   The Stratified Systemic Functional Model of grammatical metaphor

Type of GM		Strata				Ideational function of metaphors	Interpersonal function of metaphors	Textual function of metaphors
		Semantics		Lexicogrammar				
		System	Option for metaphors	System	Option for metaphors			
Ideational metaphor	logical metaphor	expansion: potential options of sequence, sequence variants, figure, element	sequence variants, figure or element	clause complex (variants), clause, phrase	congruent clause complex, clause, phrase	transference of expansion or junction between expansion and process or thing	interaction confined to transference of figures and speech functions	figure as Theme and new information
		projection: potential options of sequence, sequence variants, figure, element	sequence variants, figure or element	clause complex (variants), clause, phrase	congruent clause complex, clause, phrase	transference of projection or junction between projection and process or thing	interaction confined to transference of figures and interactive subjects	the projecting as the single Theme, the projected as rheme and new information

(to be continued)

Type of GM		Strata				Ideational function of metaphors	Interpersonal function of metaphors	Textual function of metaphors
		Semantics		Lexicogrammar				
		System	Option for metaphors	System	Option for metaphors			
Interpersonal metaphor	experiential metaphor	transitivity: potential options of sequence, sequence variants, element	figure variants or element	clause (variants), phrase	congruent clause (variants), phrase	transference of process, junction between thing or circumstance	transference of interactive subjects, figure as interactive subject or object	figure as Theme or new information; transference between Theme and new information
	metaphor of mood	mood: potential options of figure, figure variants, sequence	figure variants or sequence	clause (variants), clause complex	congruent clause (variants), clause complex	transference from figure to sequence with logico-semantic relation of projection	transference between speech functions	transference between Theme and new information
	metaphor of modality	modality: potential options of element, figure	subjective or objective figure	adverbial phrase, modal verbs, projecting clause	variant of projecting clause	transference from element to figure with logico-semantic relation of projection	explicitness of modality	appraiser as Theme

The advent of this model reveals an evident change in the explanation of the relationship between semantics and lexicogrammar. First of all, text, as the largest semantic unit, has been added to the whole system so as to indicate the connection between individual texts and semantic system in that every single text is an instance of the semantic potential of language system. Secondly, all the meta-meanings including logical, experiential, interpersonal and textual meanings are rendered equal importance, which has made up for the shortcoming of the first two models. Thirdly, the working mechanism of grammatical metaphor is explained in terms of transgrammatical semantic domain, which helps to avoid the intra-stratal and inter-stratal contradiction. Semantic domains can transfer across different grammatical units, but these patterns realized by different grammatical units are not totally synonymous, since they have different values in the semantic system of language (Halliday & Matthiessen, 2004, 2014).

With an emphasis on grammatical metaphor's intrinsic effect on the expansion of meaning potential, the classification of grammatical metaphor in terms of metafunctions is retained in this model. The two fundamental means by which the meaning potential of language is expanded—expansion and projection, correspond naturally to the ideational and interpersonal metaphors respectively. In addition, the notion of cline is further foregrounded, stressing the degree of "metaphoricity" among a set of metaphorical variants. What's more, the third model lays special stress on the textual effects of grammatical metaphor (Halliday & Matthiessen, 2004, 2014), but the term textual metaphor proposed by some scholars (Martin, 1992; Thompson, 1996, 2014; Fan, 2001, 2007; He et al., 2015) is not accepted therein.

2.1.5   Summary

Having undergone these developmental stages, the theory of grammatical metaphor has gradually been anchored to the comprehensive framework of SFL. Up till now, relatively sound explanations have been provided in at least four aspects. First, the condition under which grammatical metaphor is created has been explicated with regard to semogenesis and stratification of the language system. Second, it has been systemically proved that there is a reversible cause-and-effect relationship between grammatical metaphor and the expansion of meaning potential of the language system. Third, the relationship between lexical metaphor and grammatical metaphor is clarified in a dialectical manner. Fourth, in line with the simultaneity of the three metafunctions, the ideational, interpersonal, and textual functions concerned with grammatical metaphor have been explicitly stated.

But the theory of grammatical metaphor has also invited some criticisms and challenges, which can be generally summarized as the following two points. (1) The fundamental concept "congruence" and the territory of grammatical metaphor are not clearly defined; it seems that grammatical metaphor can be taken as all-embracing with too many linguistic phenomena cast into its realm (De Beaugrande, 1991; Zhao, 2001; Fawcett, 2006, 2008; Wang, 2013). (2) The theory of grammatical metaphor emphasizes the congruent mapping between form and meaning, while underrating, to some extent, the semantic changes that take place in the process of metaphorization (Goatly, 1997; Zhu et al., 2004; He, 2008).

Meaning stands at the center of SFL; grammatical metaphor involves not only changes in grammatical forms, but more importantly semantic changes. However, as reviewed in this section, what is changed in meaning in the process of grammatical metaphorization is still a less-charted territory which deserves more attention and further investigation. In the following section, studies on the semantic aspect of grammatical metaphor will be reviewed.

2.2 Studies on Semantic Change in Grammatical Metaphor

Back to the 1970s, before the theory of grammatical metaphor took shape, in his study of antilanguage, Halliday (1976/1978b: 175) noticed the issue of semantic sameness between metaphorical variant expressions and their non-metaphorical counterparts: "The notion of a semantic variant is apparently contradictory: how can two things be variants ('have the same meaning') if their meanings are different? But this is the wrong way of looking at it". However, he dismissed the issue by stating that semantic variants are interpretable at the higher level of culture as an information system. The sameness in meaning between a congruent form and its corresponding metaphorical form, and the semantic change that occurs due to the cross-coupling between the stratum of semantics and the stratum of lexicogrammar are at the core of the theory of grammatical metaphor. Generally speaking, studies in these respects are not copious enough, but researchers have recognized the primary status of the semantic problems and carried out some studies. These studies can be roughly classified into the following five aspects according to their study questions, methods and results: (a) preliminary theoretical concern on the question of semantic change without sound interpretations, (b) studies on the addition of semantic features, (c) studies on the reduction of semantic features, (d) metafunction-related studies and (e) cross-disciplinary studies.

2.2.1 Preliminary Concern

When he proposed the theory of grammatical metaphor, Halliday (1985a:

321) mentioned the connection in meaning between congruent and metaphorical forms, stating that they are "systematically related in meaning, and therefore synonymous in certain aspects", and that metaphorical variations are not totally synonymous because "the selection of metaphor is itself a meaningful choice, and the particular metaphor selected adds further semantic features". Halliday's brief statement has been to some extent overlooked by readers or researchers, but it is nevertheless informative to acknowledge the equal status of the congruent and metaphorical realizations in the system of language, as well as their systematic relations and differences in meaning. While introducing the metaphor of transitivity, Halliday (1994: 344) pointed out again that "the different encodings all contribute something different to the total meaning" and a set of metaphoric variants "are potentially co-representational". Halliday (1994) went on to make an important point that a piece of metaphorical wording has an additional dimension of meaning, since it means both metaphorically and congruently. In discussing nominalization, Halliday (1994) discovered that when clausal patterns are replaced by nominal ones, there is a loss of information: for instance, the nominal construction *alcohol impairment* fails to indicate the semantic relation between Classifier and Thing, and may be agnate to a couple of transitivity configurations such as *alcohol impairs*, *alcohol is impaired* and so on. Although Halliday acknowledged the semantic connection among metaphorical variants and their co-representational potential, he offered no further investigation into how and in what aspects they are systematically synonymous; in addition, he made no specific surveys of the types of additional semantic features produced in metaphorization.

Ravelli (1988:137) also took into account the semantic change implied in grammatical metaphor, pointing out that it is not fully accurate to say that a congruent realization and a metaphorical one have "the same meaning", because the metaphorical "has a feedback effect into the semantics". A metaphorical alternative may select or omit some aspects of the semantic configuration realized by the congruent form, so that the congruent and metaphorical realizations may share some meaning content but differ in others. Ravelli (1988:138) refined Halliday's model, interpreting grammatical metaphor as "a combination of semantic features" or a "semantic compound" between a given meaning and some other meanings. Ravelli (1988:138) deviated from the traditional starting point of the "one single meaning" by admitting the semantic change in

21

metaphorization, but she didn't define and demarcate the "given meaning" and the "other meanings", because, as she indicated, it is almost impossible to make clear the exact nature of the semantic differences. To describe the stratum of semantics thoroughly, "it would be necessary to represent the level of semantics with system networks as for the lexicogrammar" (Ravelli, 1988: 138). Therefore, despite the theoretical power of Ravelli's model, it fails to be applied to practical description of metaphors, and Ravelli herself continued to follow Halliday's general perspective of "one meaning, different realizations".

As to the "same" meaning expressed by congruent and metaphorical modes, Thompson (1996: 165-166; 2014: 237) explained that "one of the fundamental assumptions of a functional approach is that it is not possible to separate expression and meaning in this simple way". The expression is the meaning; every single choice is meaningful, and the choice of a more metaphorical expression construes a different meaning from what is construed by the choice of a more congruent wording. Although both kinds of wording refer to the same state of affairs in the external material world, they clearly construe quite different meanings about that state of affairs. Many other scholars (e.g. Yan, 2000; He, 2008) also acknowledge that grammatical metaphor involves variations in both form and meaning, and the transference in lexicogrammatical forms is simultaneously a meaningful transference.

These studies have addressed the changes in meaning that happen in the process of turning a congruent form into a metaphorical one, yet none of them has gone further to come up with feasible approaches to solve the practical problems.

2.2.2 Addition of Semantic Features

Halliday (1995/2007a) pointed out that experience is transformed into meaning through grammar; the semogenic power of grammar lies in selection. Grammar selects patterns with experiential value and construes them into a multidimensional semantic space. The semantic space has the potential of expanding by means of grammatical metaphor. Although "congruent relations are those that are evolutionarily and developmentally prior, both in the construal of experience and in the enacting of interpersonal relationships" (Halliday, 2007e: 21), the grammar can also reconstrue experience by means of incongruent modes so as to create new semantic categories and expand semantic potential. Halliday

(1995/2007a: 16) illustrated the change of meaning in lexical category that occurs in metaphorization by exemplification: while *move* is nominalized into *motion*, happening is transferred into a different type of phenomenon, since it embodies the semantic features of both happening and thing. This transformation is due to the fact that the category of thing or entity which is congruently construed by a noun or nominal group in grammar is a class of meaning rather than a class of phenomenon in the real world. The grammar has initially construed this category, so when grammar reconstrues it in a different form, a new type of element which combines the category meanings of noun and verb comes into being. While *move* is taken as *motion*, the real world has not been changed in any way; what has been changed is the nature of our experience of the world. Here in effect, Halliday's statements have addressed two important ideas: first, the metaphorical mode has an extra semantic feature added to the congruent one, and the new semantic feature arises from the semantic nature of the category of thing; second, the congruent and the metaphorical modes are different ways of construing the experiential world, and they are related in that the real world remains the same despite the way it is construed.

Halliday (1998, 1996/2007b, 1998/2007c,1999/2007f) repeatedly mentioned the semantic problem of grammatical metaphor in various papers. It has been pointed out that the semantic density of the metaphorical form is higher than that of the congruent one, because its meaning is compacted or distilled (Halliday, 1998/2007c). What's more, a set of agnate variants differ in meaning in some measure, even if they are represented by the same experiential items. But there is no further explanation as to how and in what aspects these variants are semantically disparate.

Semantic junction[①] is the most frequently used term to refer to the semantic connection between the congruent and metaphorical forms. Discussions on this concept can be summarized as follows.

(1) Semantic junction as one of the means of grammar expansion. Grammar does not remain static; it grows by moving into new domains, by

---

① There seems to be some inconsistency in the interpretation of this term. Halliday (1996/2007b) exemplified that "junction" involves the integration of a lexicalized meaning with the category meaning of a grammatical class; whereas Halliday & Matthiessen (1999) and Halliday (1998) refer to it as the junction of two semantic elemental categories.

increasing the delicacy in its construction of existing domains or in the form of semantic junction brought about by grammatical metaphor. Due to its inherent metaphorical potential, grammar can reconstrue experience at a more abstract level, so that "a new meaning is synthesized out of two existing ones, (a) a lexicalized meaning and (b) the category meaning of a particular grammatical class" (Halliday, 1996/2007b: 397).

(2) Semantic junction implied in early technical terms. Some technical elements in scientific theories are originally metaphorical; for example, *heat* originates from Greek θερμον, θερμοτηζ, meaning "quality of being hot" or "measurement of how hot". Such kind of technical term is created as a semantic junction with a quality being construed as a thing, so it is in origin a complex that combines both features (Halliday, 1998/2007c).

(3) Semantic junction as a result of logical metaphors. Apart from nominalization, logical metaphors may also result in semantic junction. When the congruent relator is transformed into a verb or verbal group in the metaphorical form, a mixing of "logical relation construed as process" occurs (Halliday, 1998/2007c: 40; Halliday, 1999/2007f: 132). Halliday (1998/2007c) further explained the reason for the creation of semantic junction: it is a theoretical and metaphoric operation for the grammar to transform experience into meaning. The semantic junction is a meaning-creating process, because new semiotic entities emerge from it. However, these entities are created not by a pure semiotic operation but by a reconnection with the material world, and what matters in the arising of the new meaning lies in what the grammatical category means in the first place.

(4) Semantic "distillation" due to semantic junction. Semantic junction involves semantic condensation, which is termed as distillation by Martin (Halliday & Martin, 1993; Halliday, 1998; Halliday, 1999/2007f). The metaphorical form creates a new meaning through the cross-rank and trans-categorical semantic junction, while this meaning is not lexical but a fusion of the category meanings of both the congruent and the metaphorical forms. Grammatical metaphors "involve one category (a quality or a process) being presented as if it were another category (a thing/an entity)" (Martin & White, 2008: 150), so they involve the junction of category meanings, not simply word meanings, and in this sense semantic junction may serve to distinguish lexical metaphors from grammatical metaphors.

(5) The role of semantic junction. It is indicated that semantic junction is one of the four essential aspects of grammatical metaphor; "the effect of this semantic junction is to create virtual phenomena which exist on the semiotic plane" (Halliday, 2008: 95-96). These virtual phenomena such as virtual entities, virtual processes and the virtual class of a virtual entity are critical to the construction of theory. For instance, when *brake failure* takes the place of *the brake failed*, it is already, to some extent, a theoretical construct. Therefore, semantic junction "provides the resource for the two fundamental requirements of scientific discourse: technical concepts and reasoned argument" (Halliday, 1999/2007f: 107). Halliday (1999/2007f) also offered a sound explanation for what causes the semantic variation: metaphorical agnates are not simple tautologies, because they belong to different constructions of knowledge. Knowledge is experience transformed into meaning, and the meaning is located in some system, but the systemic environments of the grammatically congruent and metaphorical construals are likely to be different—the congruent one comes from commonsense or everyday knowledge, while the metaphorical one is mostly from scientific and technical knowledge.

The concept of semantic junction is repeatedly emphasized by Halliday & Matthiessen (1999). It is stated that the metaphorical form is not simply a meaningless or synonymous variant of certain more congruent form. Another term semantic hybrid is also used by Halliday (2007e: 22) to refer to the addition of semantic features in grammatical metaphorization. It can be concluded that the general effect of grammatical metaphor lies in the fact that "it construes additional layers of meaning and wording" (Halliday & Matthiessen, 2004: 626; 2014: 699); the metaphoric rewordings are actually remeanings, which are new ways of semanticizing human experience.

In addition to the above-mentioned discoveries of the addition of semantic features, there are lots of studies conducted by some other functional researchers. Derewianka (2003) insisted that the congruent expression is a semantic simplex representing the choice of a single semantic feature, while the metaphorical mode is a semantic complex representing the choice of a compound of semantic features. Young & Nguyen (2002) verified the multi-meanings created in nominalization by analyzing some science text books and classroom discourses in a high school. Fan (2001: 41) defined the meaning of nominalization as "participant meaning + process meaning", and further pointed out that one grammatical category realizes one semantic feature in the congruent form, but in the metaphorical one, one grammatical category realizes more than one semantic feature. For instance, as to experiential metaphors, their metaphorical meaning might include "participant meaning + process meaning", "process meaning + circumstantial meaning" and "participant meaning + circumstantial meaning" (Fan, 2001: 41-42, 99-100, 115-117). Yang (2007) assumed that grammatical metaphor is a kind of transcategorical rank shift or class shift, and this shift may certainly add complexity to the semantics of the metaphorical expressions. Zhao & Zhang (2009) proposed a mechanism of the semantic integration of verb-noun nominalization.

2.2.3 Reduction of Semantic Features

There is also a missing of information or reduction of semantic features in metaphorization, and the consequent ambiguity in meaning has remained a major concern for many studies. When interpreting the differences between spoken and written modes of meaning, Halliday (1987/2007g: 346) stated that the written medium distances the act of meaning from what is in the real world, and in the written language this distance is achieved symbolically by the use of grammatical metaphor, because "nominal constructions fail to make explicit many of the semantic relations that are made explicit in clause structure", and "written discourse conceals many local ambiguities of this kind, which are revealed when one attempts a more 'spoken' paraphrase". It is pointed out that discourses that are highly metaphorical are loaded with "distilled" or "condensed" technical terms, which may lead to ambiguity in meaning (Halliday, 1998/2007c: 48). Although the use of grammatical metaphor contributes to a gain in textual meaning, it is accompanied by a loss of ideational information, because the overuse of nominals may result in the absence of logical relation markers in the clausal structures, which in turn causes multiple ambiguities in meaning (Halliday, 1999/2007f). Halliday & Matthiessen (1999: 231) indicated that grammatical metaphor usually involves rankshift and there may be a loss of information in rankshifting, and exemplified that the degree of information-missing varies when a clause complex is transferred into a clause and a clause is further turned into a nominal group: "The principle would seem to be that, where the members of a pair of agnate wordings differ in rank, the wording that is lower in rank will contain less information." The issue of the semantic status of such agnate sets has been theoretically raised. Hita (2003) discussed ambiguity in grammatical metaphor in terms of the distinction between transitive and ergative analyses; Kong (2007) proposed that situational and cultural contexts should be taken into account so as to eliminate such kind of ambiguity in meaning. Apart from nominalization, logical metaphors also bring about obvious semantic ambiguities, that is, when a logical relationship is realized by a verb, ambiguities may arise (Halliday, 1998; Halliday & Matthiessen, 1999; Jones, 2010), and as the degree of metaphoricity increases, the semantic relations between elements and those between figures become progressively implicit (Halliday & Matthiessen, 1999).

It is worth mentioning that semantic ambiguity does not imply a shrinking of semantic potential. Halliday (1998) clarified that it seems as if there is a reduction in meaning potential in the metaphorical mode, but it is a misleading impression. "There is, certainly, a great deal of neutralization taking place when a figure is reworded as a nominal group; but the result is not loss of semantic distinction but ambiguity: the different possible meanings are still discrete" (Halliday, 1998: 227). Therefore, in metaphorization, there is no reduction in the total semantic scope; on the contrary, new meanings are created by the semantic junction across ranks and categories as discussed above.

The loss of semantic features is an important aspect of the semantic change in grammatical metaphor. The previous investigations have noticed this importance, but questions remain to be answered as to the specific semantic features to be reduced, the possibility of classifying the process of information missing and the effects that information missing may have on metafunctions.

2.2.4   Metafunction-related Studies

The influences that grammatical metaphor makes on the three metafunctions are also of vital importance. Halliday (1998/2007c) affirmed the contribution made by grammatical metaphor, nominalization in particular, to textual organization: a nominalization can package discourse information and take the thematic place, so that the logical progression of an argument is rendered discursively possible. However, he did not admit the effects grammatical metaphor might make on the ideational meaning. It seems that Halliday holds ambiguous or contradictory ideas as to whether or not grammatical metaphor can make differences in the ideational meaning. He assumed that since the congruent and the metaphorical forms construe the same state of affairs in the material world, they are experientially synonymous; but he pointed out that the construal and reconstrual of experience involve three successive steps of generalization, abstractness and metaphor, and each step has enlarged the meaning potential by adding a new dimension to the total model, so that the move from the congruent construal of experience to the metaphorical mode definitely makes a difference in the ideational meaning (Halliday, 1998/2007c). By analyzing the language of science, Halliday (1998) illustrated that grammatical metaphor is not merely regrammaticizing but also resemanticizing, and the reconstrual of experience stands for a new construction of knowledge, and consequently a new ideology. Put in metafunctional terms, ideationally, the nominalizing grammar creates a world of both things and relations between the things; interpersonally, it distinguishes itself as a discourse of experts with power and technocratic control. Therefore, the use of grammatical metaphor maximizes the distance between scientific knowledge and daily life experience.

Halliday & Matthiessen (1999) confirmed once again that agnate forms are not free variants and they are at the very least restrained by contextual parameters. Halliday & Matthiessen (1999: 238) posed the following question: "The question is not whether they differ but how, and why, they differ. What kind of meaning is being construed by the systemic contrast between them?" They discussed respectively the differences in ideational, interpersonal and textual meanings in grammatical metaphor, explained the reasons for the changes in ideational meaning, and summarized that the influences of grammatical metaphor lie in the fact that there is an increase in textual meaning, a loss of experiential meaning and a gain in the potential of experiential information. Halliday & Matthiessen (2004, 2014) made similar statements as to the metafunctional effects of grammatical metaphor.

Halliday (2008: 108-109) pointed out three features of grammatical metaphor: "oblique", "impersonal" and "ambiguous". These features correspond to the three metafunctions respectively: the metaphorical mode stands far away from experience, so that it is oblique in the experiential terms; the frequent omission of agents and other participants results in semantic impersonality and objectivity in the ideational meaning; and the absence of markers of syntactic relations among elements leads to logical and textual ambiguity. Martin & Rose (2007) also stressed the experiential effects made by grammatical metaphor due to its distance from the daily life experience. Tian (2017) discussed how such kind of objectivity in meaning is realized in both syntactic and semantic aspects.

Martin (1992, 1993b) put a special emphasis on the role of grammatical metaphor in textual construction, and he proposed the concept of textual metaphor. Hu (2004) reviewed Martin's opinions briefly, and some other researchers (Fan, 2001; Huang, 2002; Liu, 2008; Wei, 2008; Thompson, 2014; Yang, 2016) echoed the legitimacy of textual metaphor, though they differ in the specific identification and classification of textual metaphors. Dong & Zhang (2017), however, proposed a distinction between textual grammatical metaphor, which occurs within the grammatical unit of clause (or clause complex) and is realized by changes in lexical-grammatical structures, and texture metaphor, which takes place in the discourse-semantic stratum of the language system and is realized by non-structural cohesive devices.

Overall, the majority of the previous studies focus on ideational metaphors, and pay little attention to the semantic change in interpersonal metaphors. It has been advocated by Thompson (2013) that a complementary perspective should be adopted to study the changes in ideational meaning brought about by interpersonal metaphors; in order to comprehensively analyze the semogenesis of grammatical metaphor, both the experientialized lexicogrammar and the interpersonal meaning of interpersonal metaphors need to be taken into account.

2.2.5　Cross-disciplinary Studies

Researchers are going beyond the scope of SFL to search for cross-disciplinary approaches to the semantic problems of grammatical metaphor. For example, many Chinese researchers have conducted studies by drawing on the cognitive science. Xie & Peng (2004) found that meaning permeates into grammatical structures and grammatical metaphor reveals the conversion between the semantic and grammatical relations. Lin & Yang (2010) studied the semantic relations and rankshift directions from a cognitive perspective, finding that a congruent form and its metaphorical counterpart are metonymically related; they also found that situational contexts and communicative intentions control the meaning to be expressed, and the choice of meaning determines the direction of semantic mapping as well as the choice of expression mode, which in turn influences the direction of rankshift. Fan (2007) analyzed grammatical metaphor in Langacker's cognitive model of an individual's language, and pointed out that grammatical metaphor involves transference of grammatical units from one domain to another, and this transference attributes grammatical metaphor with dual-meanings. Drawing on the theories of image schema and metonymy from Cognitive Linguistics, Cong (2011, 2013) introduced the bidirectional mode of the Ideal Cognitive Model and re-categorized ideational grammatical metaphors based on semantic changes, concluding that nominalization involves meaning omission and verbalization involves meaning expansion. Liu & Zhang (2014) discussed the semantic relations between the congruent and metaphorical modes within a cognitive framework, proposing that grammatical form is the product of cognition. They stated that the transference between grammatical forms is what appears on the surface, while the real motive mechanism of grammatical metaphor lies in the transference of cognitive domains. Chen (2014) presented a pragmatic-cognitive account of grammatical metaphor: it is assumed that there is a natural link between a linguistic form and its communicative relevance, and the metaphorical expression is a unique way of achieving the optimal relevance and possesses special cognitive effects.

In recent years, there is an increasing contact between SFL and Legitimation Code Theory (LCT) (Tang, 2014). On the basis of Bernstein's Code Theory and the theory of knowledge structure, socialist Maton (2011, 2013, 2014) created LCT for the analysis of socio-cultural behaviors. LCT's principle of semantics originates from the functional theory of grammatical metaphor and the concept of technicality. The semantic codes of legitimation consist of Semantic Gravity which refers to the relevance between meaning and context and Semantic Density which indicates the density of meaning in socio-cultural behaviors. Semantic Gravity can be employed to define the metaphorical potential, and Semantic Density can be used to evaluate the degree of congruence and metaphoricity, so that the semantic wave is in consistency with the nature of grammatical metaphor (Luo & Jiang, 2015).

2.2.6 Summary

There are some obvious features and insufficiencies in the above-reviewed studies of the semantic change in grammatical metaphor.

(1) Most of the studies are scattered here and there in the literature of grammatical metaphor. Concentrated and systematic investigations which take the semantic problem as the single concern can hardly be found. Consequently, in

the absence of comprehensive theoretical and analytical frameworks, the previous studies tend to over-generalize their discoveries and fail to explore at length the various changes in meaning that occur in metaphorization.

(2) Most of the previous studies stay around the lowest rank, i.e.word. These studies focus on the semantic features like semantic junction of different category meanings realized by congruent and metaphorical lexical items. But few studies go further up along the hierarchy of ranks, so that studies on higher ranks (group/ phrase and clause) are not sufficient. Clause is the basic unit for functional grammatical analysis. It is in a clausal configuration that individual lexical items can take on functional roles. Therefore, the discussion on the changes in meaning in grammatical metaphor should take the whole clause into account. Studies which go beyond clauses are even scarcer. Most of the previous studies have focused on the loss or addition of information caused by metaphorization, while the new contexts in which nominalized wordings play their roles have been left largely unexamined.

(3) Some central questions have not yet been explicitly answered. For instance, what do the congruent and the metaphorical expressions share in meaning? Where do they part in meaning? How are these semantic disparities realized? Most of the previous studies seem to have isolated the study on meaning from the whole system of language by disregarding the fact that meaning is realized by lexicogrammar and meanwhile controlled by the context in which it occurs.

(4) Most of the existing studies are confined to theoretical assumptions due to a lack of empirical evidence. For example, Ravelli's (1988) modified model is of remarkable theoretical significance, but encounters difficulty in practical application. The theoretical framework of multi-layered semantics proposed by Fan (2001) is not specific enough to offer valid explanations for such complicated and diverse metaphorical phenomena. What's more, the reasoning in many studies is merely based on a couple of simple instances as examples, which are not scientific and convincing enough. Therefore, quantitative research involving a large number of authentic data should be conducted.

In order to avoid general and superficial theoretical assumptions, this study is designed to integrate theory with practical data analysis. One type of nominalization is chosen as the study subject for the sake of operability. It is quite necessary to include here the literature review on nominalization to reveal its status in linguistic studies.

2.3 Studies on Nominalization

Nominalization has long been standing as a focus of the Western linguistic research. The study on nominalization can be traced back to the Greek and Latin grammarians who were mainly concerned with the division of a sentence into the nominal part and the verbal part, the classification of word classes and the transference between them. The early Greek grammarians used and developed the transcategorizing potential of Greek derivational morphology, most notably the potential of derivational morphology to transform verbs and adjectives into nouns and the recursive potential of nominal phrases to incorporate clauses and prepositional phrases (Halliday & Martin, 1993).

"Nominalizations are the perfect prism through which to see modern grammar" (Roeper, 2005: 125). Koptjevskaja-Tarmn (1993) presented a nominalization typology with illustrations from seventy languages. This complicated language phenomenon has been studied within various mainstream linguistic frameworks, such as Structural Linguistics, Transformational Grammar, Cognitive Linguistics and SFL. In this review, the main works and ideas from each school will be briefly summarized for comparison.

2.3.1 The Perspective of Structural Linguistics

Jespersen (1924) is a pioneer in dealing with nominalization within his analytic syntactic framework. Jespersen (1924) stated that English word-classes or parts of speech are composed of substantives, adjectives, verbs, pronouns and particles, with adverbs, prepositions, conjunctions and interjections being grouped in the compass of particles. These word-classes are ranked: substantives are taken as primaries, adjectives as secondary (adjuncts) and adverbs as tertiary (subjuncts). There is certainly some degree of correspondence between the three parts of speech and the three ranks established. But meanwhile there are transferences between words of different classes, with their ranks being altered. For example, combinations of words (*utterly dark, judges severely*) with ranks II+III[1] can be turned into *utter* (II) *darkness* (I) and *severe* (II) *judges* (I).

---

① Ranks of words are given in Roman numbers.

Jespersen regarded nominalized words as a separate class of words, termed them nexus-substantives and further subdivided them into verbal nexus-words (e.g. *arrival*) and predicative nexus-words (e.g. *cleverness*), which corresponds to what are contemporarily called verb-noun and adjective-noun nominalizations. He took infinitives and gerunds into account while illustrating from a historical perspective how verbal substantives sometimes tend to discard some of the characteristics of substantives and to assume some of those verbal features. Additionally, he noticed the differences in meaning between nexus-substantives and their original verbs or adjectives from which they are derived. For instance, although *white* and *whiteness* are equally abstract, they are not absolutely identical in meaning; the two stand for different ideas, as can be seen from the verbs for collocation in the two cases: *being white = having whiteness*.

What happens to the syntax as a result of nominalization is "rankshifting", as is exemplified by Jespersen (1924: 137):

The Doctor (I) *arrived* (II) *extremely* (IV) *quickly* (III) *and examined* (II) *the patient* (I) *uncommonly* (IV) *carefully* (III); *she* (I) *recovered* (II) *very* (IV) *speedily* (III).

The Doctor's (II) *extremely* (III) *quick* (II) *arrival* (I) *and uncommonly* (III) *careful* (II) *examination* (I) *of the patient* (II) *brought about her* (II) *very* (III) *speedy* (II) *recovery* (I).

It can be seen that as the rank (II) verbs *arrived, examined* and *recovered* have been turned into the rank (I) substantives *arrival, examination* and *recovery*, the subordinate members are changed correspondingly, either upward or downward in rank, and mostly their forms are changed.

Jespersen also discovered the potential rhetorical effects caused by "rank-shifting". Firstly, nominalization simplifies the clause structure by affording us the power "of avoiding many clumsy expressions, because subordinate clauses would otherwise be necessary to render the same idea" (Jespersen, 1924: 136). Secondly, nominalization has the power of expansion: "The nexus-substantive is simply introduced to give us an easy means of adding some descriptive trait in the form of an adjunct which it would be difficult or impossible to tack on to the verb in the form of a subjunct" (Jespersen, 1924: 138). Thirdly, nominalization makes a difference in style between language of science and that of everyday life. The preference for nexus-substantives (nouns) in expression, which renders language more abstract and abstruse, is characteristic of scientific thinking.

Jespersen's study focuses not only on the forms of nominalization but functions, and it reveals an initial insight into the distinction in language style or genre. Due to his analytic syntax-oriented approach, the role of context on the macro-level of language use is not fully considered. Nevertheless, Jespersen's work is enlightening and contributive to the subsequent researchers, especially those of the Prague School.

Mathesius (1975/2008), founder of the Prague School, is particularly concerned with the nominal tendency of Modern English. He discussed nominalization (although the term was not used) by English-Czech comparison in terms of verbo-nominal predication and complex condensation. The former involves the re-match between grammatical element and syntactic function; the latter deals with the contributions of the verbal noun, the participle and the infinitive in syntactic condensation.

According to Mathesius (1975/2008), there are two broad categories of verbo-nominal predication in English. In the primary category, the action and its agent or patient in a sentence are not separately expressed by the grammatical predicate and subject, but rather blended in a synthetic expression functioning as the grammatical subject, and the finite verb only indicates the existence of the action. The action in each of the following examples quoted from Mathesius (1975/2008: 104-105) is presented nominally, either by the gerund (*buying and selling, coming and going*) or by the noun (*accumulation*). Mathesius also points out that one of the reasons why "there"- constructions are frequently used in English lies in its preference for nominal expression of verbal action, due to its tendency to take action as a mere fact.

The white dog was there before there was any <u>buying and selling</u> in the London market.

There was a steady <u>coming and going</u> of Stubland's aunts and uncles and of Sydenham's and Dolly's people.

There has been a constant <u>accumulation</u> of evidence showing how perfidious was the Balkan policy of Count Berchthold.

The second category of verbo-nominal predication involves no action-agent merging, and four subtypes are included (Mathesius, 1975/2008: 105-106): (1) possessive, (2) causative, (3) adverbial and (4) adjectival qualification. The fourth one has nothing to do with nominalization, so it is not considered here. The possessive type is represented by expressions such as *to have a walk* and *I have a great admiration for the performer*. The action is expressed by a noun, and is linked to the grammatical subject by the copula *have*. In the causative type, the action is also expressed by a noun which is tied to the subject by verbs of the meaning "to do, to perform", for example, *you do the cooking and I do the shopping*. The adverbial type differs from the previous two types in that the nominalized action is construed as a prepositional phrase, for example: *The Democratic Party is now in full control of the nation*.

In the discussion of "complex condensation", Mathesius (1975/2008) illustrated the various condensed syntactic types with the verbal noun, the participle and the infinitive, which can all be conceived as forms of nominalization in a broad sense. More importantly, he noticed the bi-character (both nominal and verbal) of the verbal noun. The nominal character of the verbal noun can be revealed by its taking the article, or by its modification through an adjective (or a pronoun) or through the genitive of a noun, as illustrated by the following examples: *(the) having him for an unbidden companion in such a solitary place much increased her nervousness; hurried reading of all sorts of books is simply waste of time*[1]. The English verbal noun displays a much more verbal character, and in this sense it is known as gerund.

In the upper half of the twentieth-century, a group of descriptive structuralists led by Bloomfield applied the philosophy of Behaviorism to linguistic study. They held the idea that the criterion for demarcating word-classes and grammatical categories does not lie in word-meaning, but in the filling-roles words play in grammatical structures. Word-classes and grammatical categories carry no meaning until they work in specific language structures. Therefore, those scholars did not propose the concept of nominalization, but classify words by means of "immediate constituents analysis". Nominalization can be formed by a base word of derivation or a subordinate endocentric structure with a Head. For example, *employment* and *insightfulness* can be further decomposed structurally into *employ + ment* and *insight + ful + ness*. In this way, nominalization is only taken as a grammatical element which is a hole-filler in a grammatical structure, and it

---

[1] These examples are quoted from Mathesius (1975/2008: 150).

is meaningful in the syntactic system. It is believed that the agnate sentences *the bomb exploded at night* and *the explosion of the bomb occurred at night* are identical in meaning. But *explode* and *explosion* differ in word-class and serve as different grammatical items in syntactic structures.

Descriptive structuralists tend to take the form of a word as their sole focus; their analysis of a word's surface structure is separated from the word's meaning and function. As a result, nominalization is indistinguishable from ordinary nouns. For instance, they tend to identify *the doctor's arrival* with *the doctor's house*, failing to clarify the relation between *doctor* and *arrival* and that between *doctor* and *house*, and thus cannot reveal the deep meaning of these structures.

2.3.2　The Perspective of Transformational Grammar

Transformational Grammar proposed by Chomsky (1968/2006) makes a distinction between surface structure and deep structure. It is stated that the grammar of a language, English, for example, generates a deep structure for each sentence, and the grammatical transformation mechanism indicates the relation between this deep structure and its surface structure. The process of nominalization can be stated only in terms of deep structures. It is a very general property of English that "nominal phrases exist corresponding to sentences that are very close in surface form to deep structure, but not corresponding to such sentences that are remote in surface form from deep structure" (Chomsky, 1968/2006: 93-94). This point can be illustrated by the following examples: the sentence *John is certain that Bill will leave* corresponds to the nominal phrase *John's certainty that Bill will leave*, because the surface form of the sentence is close to its deep structure; while there is no such a nominal phrase as *John's certainty to leave* corresponding to the sentence *John is certain to leave*, because the surface structure of the sentence is remote from its deep structure.

The notions of closeness and remoteness can be made precise to explain why nominalizations exist in certain cases but not in others; "nominalizations must reflect the properties of deep structure" (Chomsky, 1968/2006: 94). Although deep structures are real mental structures and play a central role in the grammatical processes in producing and interpreting sentences, the role that surface structures play in determining semantic interpretation is also asserted by Chomsky. The process of nominalization is one of mental transformations; while the deep structure is transformed into surface structure by means of mental operations, the meaning of deep structure is revealed and the structure is simplified simultaneously.

In the earliest work on transformational grammar, Lees (1960) took a transformationalist position, stating that nominalization is an essential part of syntax; a nominalized expression is transformed from a core sentence, and they are agnate in relation. Whether the lexis under concern in the core sentence is retained in the nominalized form is a criterion for this agnation. But Chomsky (1970) adopted the lexicalist position whereby the transformational component is simplified, and the base rules are extended to accommodate the derived nominals directly. Chomsky's *Remarks on Nominalization* (1970) might be taken as the first argument for the existence of deep structure. Chomsky (1970: 187, 214) classified various nominal expressions into three types in this work: (1) the gerundive nominals like *criticizing* in *John's criticizing the book*; (2) the derived nominals like *criticism* in *John's criticism of the book*; and (3) the mixed forms with some peculiar properties as illustrated by examples like *John's accepting of the proposal* and *the expanding of the plant*.

Chomsky (1970: 187) explained the differences among these types in three aspects: "the productivity of the process in question, the generality of the relation between the nominal and the associated proposition, and the internal structure of the nominal phrase." Gerundive nominals involve a free grammatical transformation from propositions of subject-predicate form (i.e. a sentence-like structure), and the semantic relation between the nominal and the proposition in the deep structure is rather straightforward and regular. Additionally, a gerundive nominal does not have the internal structure of a noun phrase, so that *John's* in *John's criticizing the book* cannot be replaced by any determiner such as *the* or *that*, nor can the nominal be modified by adjectives or numerals.

Derived nominals are quite different from gerundive nominals in all of these respects. As to productivity, there are many restrictions on the formation of derived nominals, since the transformational rules which work well in forming gerundive nominals fail to serve in cases of derived ones. For example, the structure underlying the sentence *John is certain to win the prize* is transformed into the gerundive nominal in *John's being certain to win the prize*, but not into the derived nominal in *John's certainty to win the prize*. Meanwhile, transformational "rules" are both morphologically and semantically weak in the formation of derived nominals. For example, the suffix *-ter* which can be added to *laugh* to form *laughter* possesses no generative power to derive other words, and no rules suffice to explain the discrepancy in meaning between the derived nominal *revolution* and the base verb *revolve*. Therefore, the semantic relations between the derived nominal and the related proposition are varied and idiosyncratic; the range of variation and its accidental feature are characteristic of lexical structure, which confirms Chomsky's lexicalist position. Additionally, the derived nominal, coming from the lexicon directly, has the internal structure of a noun phrase. Determiners or adjectives can be inserted in derived nominals like those in *the proof of the theory* and *John's deliberate criticism of the movie*. Many derived nominals can pluralize, for example, *a couple of John's proofs of the theory*, and derived nominals cannot contain aspect which is a grammatical feature of verbs. These properties of derived nominals are in line with a lexicalist perspective.

Chomsky (1970) also admitted that it is not clear whether the lexicalist hypothesis can be extended to cover the mixed forms of nominals. These forms seem to have the internal structure of noun phrases, so it is permissible to replace the possessive subject with a determiner, but the insertion of adjectives might be unnatural. And since not all verbs can be turned into such forms, such kind of construction is limited. Chomsky (1970: 214) declared that "there is an artificiality to the whole construction that makes it quite resistant to systematic investigation". Structural ambiguity also poses a problem. From the lexicalist perspective, it is supposed that both *tomatoes grow* and *NP grows tomatoes* are base forms of *the growing of tomatoes*.

Chomsky (1970) intended to elaborate linguistic theory to incorporate both syntactic transformations and lexical features. He proposed to adopt a common abstract syntactic notation, X-bar theory, to represent both the structure of nominalizations and that of sentences. But the transformational approach fails to make a comprehensible explanation of the diversified cases of nominalizations due to a lack of generalized rules. Chomsky's approach is extended in "The Minimalist Program" (1995), in which the distinction between deep structure and surface structure is abandoned, and the entry condition of a lexical item into a sentence is defined by "broad transformation" that assimilates the lexicon into syntax. This minimalist theory has initiated other efforts in this field. Bouchard (1995) introduced the analysis of semantic structure. In his analysis of the nominalized verbs of the mental type, he discovered that a key factor in nominalization lies in the intentional feature of the possessive claimer. The claimer must be an entity, and work as the agent of the event. This discovery explains the infeasibility of *John's easiness to please*, because in the underlying sentence *it's easy for you to please John*, the possessive claimer of the mental verb *please* is not *John* himself. Bouchard's study is enlightening yet tentative, and its universality awaits further test. It is also clear that in Chomsky's framework, nominalization is discussed with respect to transformations in syntactic and lexical structures; the close relation between natural language and its context of use is none of its concern.

2.3.3   The Perspective of Cognitive Linguistics

Cognitive linguists also adopt the derivational perspective that nouns are often derived from words of other classes. Certain properties of nominalization are taken by them to demonstrate the autonomy of grammar as well as the distinction between syntax and lexicon. A primary concern of cognitive grammar is to describe the conceptual import of grammatical constructs, and cognitive semantics identifies meaning with conceptualization. Nominalization involves a conceptual reification, and its characters can be clarified in respect to the notional definitions of the noun and verb classes. According to the prototypical description, physical objects are prototypical for the class of nouns, and their interactions are prototypical for verbs. In the schematic sense, a verb profiles a process, and a noun profiles a thing. Langacker (1991/2004: 22-50) discussed three fundamental aspects of nominalization: the types of nominalization, periphrasis and predictability. Langacker's classification of nominalization (see Table 2-6) is based on two parameters.

Table 2-6   Langacker's classification of nominalization

Parameter	Kind		Example
Facet of the underlying relational predication selected for reification and profiling	Alternate profiling	verb-nominal profile shifting	*complainer, advisee, rocker, painting, diner*
		episodic nominalization	take a *walk*, have an *argument*
		-ing derived nominalization	*Walking* is very good for one's health.
		abstract noun	*fear, anxiety, freedom*
		quality-designating noun	Williams' *walk* is peculiar.

(to be continued)

Parameter	Kind		Example
The internal organization of the relational predication	Type vs. Instance nominali- zations	action nominalization	Zelda's signing of the contract
		factive nominalization	Zelda's signing the contract
		that-clause nominalization	That Zelda signed the contract is simply false.

The first parameter is the facet of the underlying relational predication selected for reification and profiling, and the second one lies in the internal organization of the relational predication. The first broad kind is termed as alternate profiling with five subtypes. (a) Nominalization can be simply caused by shifting the profile of a verb to some nominal entity. The profiled element can be the verb stem's trajector (i.e. its internal subject), for instance, words like *dancer* and *judge*. What is profiled can also be the verb stem's landmark—its internal object (e.g. *advisee, choice*), an instrument (e.g. *rocker*), a product (e.g. *painting*) or certain setting or location (e.g. *diner*). (b) A second type is episodic nominalization, which means that a nominalization designates a single episode of the process profiled by a perfective verb, for example, *take a walk* and *do an imitation*. Such nominalizations are count nouns. (c) Another type is also derived from perfective verbs by adding *-ing*, but functions as mass nouns. For instance, *walking* in *walking is very good for one's health* has no independent material existence, but is manifested by means of the occurrence of a process. (d) Abstract nouns such as *fear*, *anxiety* and *freedom* represent abstract substances and are characterized in respect to certain region in the emotive domain. (e) Another type of nominalization includes nouns designating the style or manner in which the activity in question is initiated. For example, *walk* in *Williams' walk is peculiar* designates the style of the process rather than the episodic process itself.

The second broad kind is termed as type vs. instance nominalizations with three subordinate types: (a) action nominalization (e.g. *Zelda's signing of the contract*) wherein the preposition *of* appears between the nominalized verb and its notional object; (b) factive or gerundive nominalization (e.g. *Zelda's signing the contract*) in which the preposition *of* is absent; (c) that-clause nominalization (e.g. *That Zelda signed the contract is simply false*). Action and factive nominalizations differ in both grammatical properties and the level of organization where the nominalizing operation takes place. Action nominalizations are similar in structure to ordinary nominals, but factive nominalizations have the internal structure of a clause. On the basis of semantic function, "an action nominalization derives from a process type, a factive nominalization from an ungrounded instance of the type; and a that-clause nominalization from a grounded instance" (Langacker, 1991/2004: 33).

The grammatical markers ('s, of, by) of a nominalization are also examined. They are assumed to be semantically empty by transformational linguists (Lees, 1960; Chomsky, 1970), whereas taken to be periphrastic and attributed distinctive meanings within the cognitive framework. These periphrastic variants are different when they are applied to certain cognitive domain. The preposition *of* designates the intrinsic relationship between its trajectory and landmark; nominal periphrasis with *by* identifies its object as the trajectory of the nominalized verb and meanwhile reveals its active role; possessive inflection is employed to specify the trajectory of the process (e.g. *Zelda's signing of the contract*) or its landmark (e.g. *Lincoln's assassination*).

In terms of the predictability of nominalization, Langacker (1991/2004) stated that there are patterns to be discerned. Like any schematic symbolic unit, nominalization can also be described along such parameters as specificity, entrenchment and symbolic complexity. Accordingly, a sequence of statements have been made: patterns vary in their degree of productivity; many nominalized expressions have unpredictable semantic properties; nominalizing patterns fulfill the dual missions of both characterizing established expressions and permitting the computation of new instantiations; the morphological aspects of nominalization are seldom consistent with the semantic aspects.

Apart from the pure cognitive perspective, some researchers start to try a novel and synthetic method. One of the representatives is Heyvaert (2003) who adopts a cognitive-functional approach to nominalization, combining concepts and theories from both Cognitive Linguistics and SFL. Heyvaert presented a systematic account of the constructional mechanisms that underlie deverbal nominalization, asserting that nominalizations are functional re-classifications of verbal predicates into nominal constructions. She emphasizes the integration of both clausal and nominal properties in nominalized constructions in terms of the functional categories of type specification, instantiation, quantification and grounding, and took categorization by means of schema as the cognitive mechanism of nominalization. By discussing in detail a number of nominalization systems, Heyvaert (2003) proposed the major steps to analyze nominalization: identifying the level of assembly from which the nominalization derives; determining whether the reclassification involves rank shift; recognizing the exact nominal strategy; and finally integrating the internal lexicogrammatical features with external functional behavior of the nominalized construction.

Heyvaert's work has aroused the attention of many researchers (Zhang & Wang, 2004; Liu & Wang, 2005). Plemenitaš (2015) also discussed the complementarity between cognitive approach and systemic functional approach to nominalization in respect of features of nominalization, levels of entrenchment, reader processing and the global textual function of nominalization.

The cognitive approach describes precisely the conceptual reification, so that the social and cultural factors in play are beyond its scope. For the past decades, theoretical discussions of nominalization have wrestled with the issue of whether this phenomenon is best accommodated in the syntax or in the lexicon. Studies conducted from the perspective of SFL can craftily avoid the controversy. Related ideas and studies in SFL will be reviewed in the next section.

2.3.4　The Perspective of Systemic Functional Linguistics

Nominalization is discussed under the heading of grammatical metaphor in SFL, which is quite different from the traditions of other schools in both methodology and research scope. A nominalization denotes a reified process or quality (Halliday & Matthiessen, 2014); it is a phenomenon "whereby any element or group or elements is made to function as a nominal group in the clause" (Halliday, 1994: 41). In this section, the relationship between nominalization and grammatical metaphor, the typology and functions of nominalization will be reviewed.

Halliday (1994) and Halliday & Matthiessen (2004, 2014) spare a particular space for ideational metaphors and nominalization, and the term nominalizing metaphor is used. Nominalization is thus usually taken as a kind of ideational metaphor: for example, the verbal nominalization (*press > pressure*) and the adjectival nominalization (*hot > heat*) are instances of "ideational metaphors where processes and qualities are construed as if they were entities" (Halliday & Matthiessen, 2014: 710). But nominalization is more properly defined as a device for producing grammatical metaphor. It is the major resource for the grammar to "turn a range of non-participant meanings into participant-like ones"

(Martin, 1992: 138). Therefore, grammatical metaphor presents predominantly a "nominalizing" tendency (Halliday & Matthiessen, 1999: 269). However, "it would be wrong to equate grammatical metaphor with nominalization" (Halliday, 1998/2007c: 39). Nominalization is predominant in the sense that most metaphoric shift is channeled into a nominal group, but not all of the metaphorical cases go that way. There is a general tendency of grammatical drift (see Figure 2-1) from the congruent elements to entities, qualities, processes and circumstances. Compared with the other types of metaphoric drift, the dominant status of nominalization is quite obvious to be seen, but there exist verbalization and other transformations (Zhu, 2006).

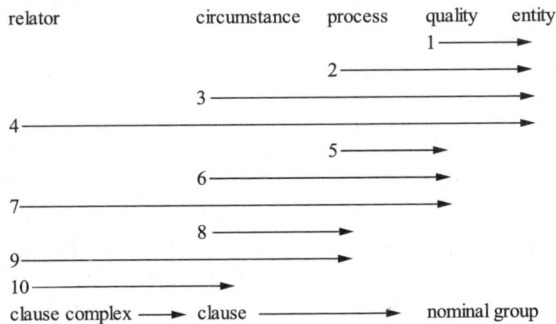

Figure 2-1   The general drift of grammatical metaphor (Halliday, 1998: 211)

Some scholars have also noticed the rankshifting involved in nominalization. Thompson (2014: 241-242) pointed out that "nominalization is not merely a process of transforming a verbal class into a noun, but in fact a shift from a clause to a nominal group. Nominalization involves a realignment of all the other elements of the message." Fowler (1996: 82) found that a nominal group entails a verb and certain related participants, for example, the noun *plan* actually amounts to *someone planned for me*.

In SFL, the classification of nominalization is characterized by a broad coverage and comprehensiveness. As indicated and exemplified in Table 2-7, nominalization involves not only class shift, but also corresponding semantic shift.

Table 2-7 Function-based typology of nominalizations in SFL (adapted from Derewianka (2003: 197))

No.	Semantic shift	Class shift	Example
1	quality > quality: thing	adjective > noun	unstable > instability
2	process > process: thing "doing" process > "doing" process: thing "sensing" process > "sensing" process: thing "saying" process > "saying" process: thing "relating" process > "relating" process: thing	verb > noun verb > noun verb > noun verb > noun verb > noun	transform > transformation imagine > imagining declare > declaration has > ownership
3	phase of process > phase of process: thing	phase > noun	going to > prospect
4	conation > conation: thing	conation > noun	try to > attempt
5	modality of process > modality of process: thing	modal > noun	can > possibility may/must > permission/necessity
6	circumstance > circumstance: thing minor process > minor process: thing	adv. group/prep. phrase > noun preposition > noun	how quickly? > rate [of growth] with > accompaniment
7	relator > relator: thing	conjunction > noun	so > cause, proof

Semantically, there are seven major types of shift: the shift from quality, process, phase of process, conation, modality of process, circumstance or relator to thing or entity; grammatically, the lexical classes that realize such meanings as adjective, verb (including modal verb and verbal group representing phase and conation), adverb, preposition and conjunction are turned into the class of noun. This classification is based on the functions of elements within a clause. But a whole clause can also be nominalized. Halliday (1994) covers the following kinds.

(1) The thematic equative whereby the nominalization serves a thematic purpose. For example, *what the duke gave to my aunt* in *what the duke gave to my aunt is a teapot* (Halliday, 1994: 41).

(2) That-clause as Head of a nominal group. For example, *that you're sorry* in *that you're sorry isn't enough* (Halliday, 1994: 242).

(3) Embedded factive that-clause. For example, *it is obvious that Caesar was ambitious*, and *the reason why Caesar was killed is that he was ambitious* (Halliday, 1994: 266).

(4) That-clause in impersonal projection, turning a fact into a noun. For example, *it is said that...*, and *it seems that...* (Halliday, 1994: 271).

What functions nominalization can fulfill is also a major concern of systemic functional linguists. The textual effects produced by nominalization are most frequently discussed. Halliday (1988/2007h: 147-148) discovered two important discoursal effects of nominalization by analyzing Newton's work: "packaging a complex phenomenon into a single semiotic entity" and "rhetorical function". Eggins (2004) also found that nominalization contributes to rhetorical organization and increased lexical density in written texts. Thompson (1996: 167-168) emphasized the function of "encapsulation". Colombi (2006: 153-154) summarized the functions of nominalization as turning actions into things, "removing people" and creating conceptual objects.

As the most important type of grammatical metaphor, nominalization is also a key word in almost every discipline-based study and studies of texts of various registers. These studies are briefly summarized as follows: texts of science (Halliday & Martin, 1993; Halliday, 1995/2007a, 2007i; Martin & Veel, 1998; Banks, 2003, 2008), texts of history (Martin & Wodak, 2003; Coffin, 2006), texts of social science (Wignell, 2007), texts of arts (Ravelli, 1998), texts of medicine (Galve, 1998), texts of institution (Martin, 1993a; Iedema, 1995) and texts of language development (Painter, 1993, 2003; Derewianka, 1995, 2003; Schleppegrell, 2008; Christie & Martin, 2007; Martin, 2007; Pankova, 2010). There are also studies of other languages other than English, and some studies are concerned with comparison between languages (Steiner, 2002; Astiga, 2002; Yang, 2007; Byrnes, 2009).

2.3.5 Summary

Nominalization is included as an important type or device of ideational metaphor in SFL, so it is not merely treated as the formal transformation of lexical items from one grammatical class to another. Instead, both the semantic shift and class shift involved in nominalization are taken into account, and the relationship between shifts in meaning and shifts in form is well explained in terms of the realizational principle of stratification. Meanwhile, the functions of nominalization in discursive flow are explored at great length. What's more, the range of studies on nominalization in SFL is much wider than that from other approaches. Apart from the most frequently discussed verbal-noun nominalization, the other types are also brought into attention; for example, the nominalizations of phase, conation and modality of process are particularly singled out, and the nominalizations of circumstances and relators are covered as distinct categories. The typology of nominalization has illustrated that it is theoretically possible that any element in a clause or even a clause itself can be transformed into a noun or nominal group, and it is this thing-ness that serves as the underlying principle of nominalizing ideational metaphor.

However thorough the classification of nominalization is, up till now, related studies in SFL and other linguistic approaches tend to take verbal-noun nominalization as a primary concern, failing to accord the other types an equal status. Some researchers even equate nominalization with verbal-noun nominalization, defining nominalization as "the use of a nominal form to express a process meaning" (Thompson, 2014: 241). Therefore, there seems to be a controversy over the legitimate status of the other types of nominalization illustrated in Table 2-7. For instance, Halliday (1998) and Derewianka (2003) acknowledged the transformation from quality to thing as an independent type of nominalization, while Thompson (2014) took it as an ensuing result of the nominalization of process. Thompson (2014: 241-242) justified his idea on the grounds that process is central in a clause, and if a process is nominalized, "it has an inevitable knock-on effect on these other elements". According to him, a quality is construed as the Attribute in a relational process, and it is the nominalization of the process that induces the change from quality to thing. There is no problem with the centrality of the process in a clause, but it is in effect the quality-thing nominalization that leads to the missing of the congruent relational process, not vice versa.

This study focuses on quality-thing ideational metaphor in an effort to change the current over-emphasis on the process-thing type. Studies on process-thing nominalization have been substantially conducted, but quality-thing nominalization hasn't gained due attention. This study will take it as a window to explore the semantic change taking place in grammatical metaphor.

The mere focus on quality-thing type in this study does not in the least devaluate the significance of other types of nominalization. The reason of this choice lies in the fact that the quality-thing metaphor is more typical and has an advantage over the other relatively minor types in number. In terms of realizational forms, qualities are realized by adjectives which are located at the open lexical end of the lexicogrammar continuum; whereas phase, conation and modality of processes, circumstances as well as relators are realized by more closed grammatical items, and thus there might be difficulty in unpacking these metaphors (phase of process-thing, conation of process-thing, modality of process-thing, circumstance-thing and relator-thing) in that the congruent expression and the metaphorical expression bear no resemblance in lexicogrammatical forms. In addition, the lexical realizations of phase of process-thing, conation of process-thing and modality of process-thing have been covered in discussions on nouns of projection and nouns of fact (Halliday & Matthiessen, 2014: 536). For example, the phase of process realized by *going to* can be metaphorized to be a thing realized by a noun *prospect* and the conation of process realized by *try to* can be changed into a thing realized by a noun *attempt*; these two nouns can be followed by embedded projected clauses: "*that* + indirect indicative", "*of* + imperfective" or "*to* + perfective". The lexical realizations of modality of process, such as *possibility* and *necessity*, belong to fact nouns, i.e. nouns of modalization (chances) and nouns of modulation (needs) respectively. A fact noun serves as the Head/Thing of a nominal group with a projected clause as Postmodifier/Qualifier.

The circumstance-thing or minor process-thing is "one of the less clear-cut categories to identify" (Derewianka, 2003: 203), and we can hardly notice the existence of grammatical metaphor unless we analyze the instances intentionally. For example, the noun *accompaniment* seems far from the congruent Circumstance realized by a prepositional phrase introduced by the preposition *with*, and it is more likely to be unpacked as a process realized by the circumstantial verb *accompany* which may occur in a circumstantial identifying clause. The large gap between the congruent and the metaphorical is also presented in the following examples from the data of child language collected by

Derewianka (2003: 204): *This gave us an idea of the distance it would be (this gave us an idea of how far it would be), but a large ovalic one on the bottom in resemblance to a head (but a large ovalic one on the bottom look like a head).* In these two metaphorical instances, the congruent expressions realized by the adverbial phrase *how far* and the prepositional phrase *look like* are changed into abstract things realized by nouns *distance* and *resemblance*. But difficulties arise in unpacking such kind of metaphor, because lexical items like *distance* are usually taken as dead metaphors viewed synchronically and *resemblance* corresponds more to a congruent verb *resemble* realizing a process.

As to the relator-thing whereby a relator realized by a conjunction is metaphorized into a thing realized by a noun, the problem lies in the inherent degree of metaphoricity; that is, there are various intermediate forms in between the most congruent and the most incongruent forms. As illustrated by Halliday & Matthiessen (2014: 673), from the congruent paratactic clause complex *she didn't know the rules, so she died* to the metaphorical relational clause *the cause of her death was her ignorance of the rules*, there are a couple of intermediate forms on the cline: *her ignorance of the rules caused her to die; through ignorance of the rules, she died; her death was due to ignorance of the rules; her ignorance of the rules caused her death.* And the metaphorical relational clause can be further metaphorized into a nominal group *her death through ignorance of the rules.* Therefore, in unpacking the relator-thing metaphor into the congruent relator, there are a few steps to go through, and thus the relationship between the metaphorical and congruent forms is somewhat obscured.

Chapter 3

Theoretical Foundations

This study is based on the theories of SFL, so in this chapter the five fundamental dimensions of language proposed by SFL are firstly introduced. And then "congruence", the basic yet controversial concept in the theory of grammatical metaphor, is discussed in detail as to its early appearance, the reasons for controversy and the approaches that should be taken to deal with this notion. Since this study is designed to seek evidence for changes in the stratum of semantics from the lexicogrammatical and contextual strata, the relations between form, function and meaning need to be clarified. Finally, important concepts of quality-thing ideational metaphor, such as the definitions and classifications of quality and thing, as well as the distinctions between grammatical metaphor and transcategorization, are discussed. Based on these theoretical considerations, a comprehensive framework of guiding principles for this study is constructed.

3.1 The Dimensions in Language

This study is theoretically grounded on the five dimensions (forms of order) in language proposed by SFL; they are "the basic concepts for the study of language" (Halliday & Matthiessen, 2014: 20). When the grammar of a language is explored in functional terms in respect of how it creates and expresses meaning, dimensions (structure, system, stratification, instantiation and metafunction) get involved simultaneously. Since languages are not artificially designed, but evolved systems, they can only be explained from a comprehensive or systemic perspective rather than the traditional compositional one. These dimensions work together to define the architecture of language, so that whatever is observed about one aspect is to be located in the whole picture with reference to other aspects, and meanwhile discussion on any single aspect contributes to the entirety of language. Following this line, this study of the quality-thing ideational grammatical metaphor adopts the systemic theory, with these inter-woven dimensions sustaining the whole theoretical and analytical foundations.

It has been discussed in the previous chapter that grammatical metaphor arises from the decoupling and recoupling between the strata of semantics and lexicogrammar, and that it is stratification which appeared in language evolution that makes grammatical metaphor possible. Language system is a meaning potential; both the congruent and metaphorical modes of expression are choices made out of the language system, and thus they realize different meanings, i.e. metafunctions. Since changes in meaning are abstract, it is necessary to seek for evidence of semantic change from the stratum of lexicogrammar and that of context in view of the realizational stratal relationship. Lexicogrammatical structures also derive from systems. In this study, analysis of the lexicogrammatical realization of experiential meaning, that is, transitivity structure, will be conducted. Specific transitivity configurations composed of various processes and elements come from choices in transitivity system, and systemic grammatical analysis serves as basis for the revelation of systemic semantic change. This study involves analysis of a large quantity of authentic instances. Instances and system are complementary to each other; what happens to instances will, in some sense, have a feedback effect on the language system. Therefore, this study is well anchored on these dynamically integrated dimensions in language. The five dimensions and their ordering principles (see Table 3-1) will be firstly introduced in this section.

Table 3-1 The dimensions in language and their ordering principle
(Halliday & Matthiessen, 2014: 20)

No.	Dimension	Principle	Order
1	structure (syntagmatic order)	rank	clause ~ group/phrase ~ word ~ morpheme [lexicogrammar]; tone group ~ foot ~ syllable ~ phoneme [phonology]

(to be continued)

No.	Dimension	Principle	Order
2	system (paradigmatic order)	delicacy	grammar ~ lexis [lexicogrammar]
3	stratification	realization	semantics ~ lexicogrammar ~ phonology ~ phonetics
4	instantiation	instantiation	potential ~ subpotential / instance type ~ instance
5	metafunction	metafunction	ideational [logical ~ experiential] ~ interpersonal ~ textual

3.1.1   System

Language sets up relations on both paradigmatic and syntagmatic axes. Syntagmatic relations are modelled as relations of structure (which will be discussed in Section 3.1.5), and paradigmatic relations are modelled in SFL as relations of system. System is the first dimension to be introduced here because different from Saussure, Hjelmslev and Firth's tradition that the two axes are given equal status, SFL foregrounds paradigmatic relations by taking system as "the fundamental concept" (Halliday, 1970/1976a: 26) and "the underlying principle of organization" (Matthiessen & Halliday, 2009: 9). "Systems can be treated as primary and structures can be 'derived' from terms in systems by means of realization statements" (ibid.). Since language is a network of relations, one item is defined according to its relation to the other related items, and language is polysystemic. "It is the pattern of systemic relations which grounds the discussion, with respect to strata, rank and metafunction" (Martin, 2013: 11).

Compared with syntagmatic relations, paradigmatic relations are more abstract, because they are relations between an element and what could have taken its place but did not. "A system is thus a representation of relations on the paradigmatic axis, a set of features contrastive in a given environment" (Halliday, 1966/2007j: 110). Meaning is choice; meaning-making is choosing among options available in the environment of other alternatives. As stated by Lyons (1977: 33), one of the most fundamental principles of semantics is "the principle that choice, or the possibility of selection between alternatives, is a necessary, though not a sufficient, condition of meaningfulness". "The power of language comes from its paradigmatic complexity" (Halliday, 2007e: 9), and this is the meaning potential of language, which is theorized by means of system networks designed to present a holistic picture of a language. A system network can be visualized graphically by using the conventions developed by Halliday in the 1960s. A system network has a horizontal dimension and a vertical dimension. The vertical dimension specifies the possibilities of combination among the constitute systems and their features, whereas the horizontal dimension is ordered in delicacy whereby entry into one selection relies on another.

3.1.2 Stratification

The higher order consciousness engendered in the process of human evolution is semiotic consciousness which transforms experience into meaning. Higher order consciousness relies heavily on two essential steps by which language evolved: metafunction and stratification. Stratification is theoretically defined as the "global dimension ordering language in context into subsystem according to the degree of symbolic abstraction" (Matthiessen et al., 2016: 205).

As is illustrated in Figure 3-1, context is a stratum above language; the linguistic system is organized into three strata: semantics (the system of meaning), lexicogrammar (the system of wording) and phonology or graphology (the system of sounds or graphics); the stratum of phonetics or graphics is the substance of linguistic expression. These four strata are grouped into the content plane and the expression plane.

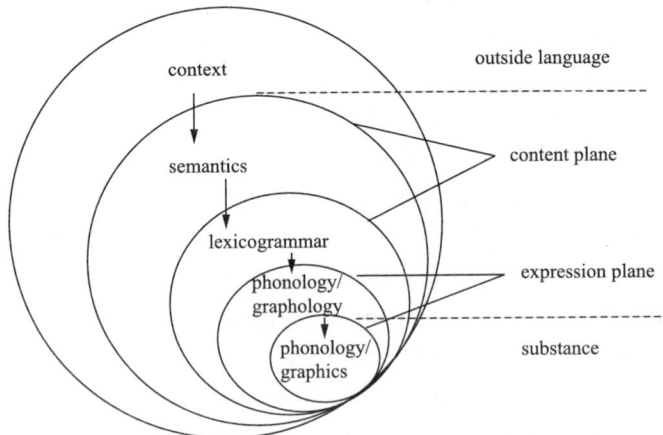

Figure 3-1　Stratification

The primary semiotic systems like those of other species or the protolanguage are not internally stratified, but when the primary semiotic evolved into a higher order semiotic, a space was created where meanings could be organized as a purely abstract network of interrelations. This space is referred to as the stratum of lexicogrammar located between the meaning and the expression (Halliday, 1992/2007k; Halliday & Martin, 1993; Halliday, 2007e). It is the appearance of grammar that renders possible the metafunctional organization and the phenomenon of grammatical metaphor. The effect of this stratification is that it has transformed a closed, meaning-bearing system into an open, meaning-creating one which is not only semiotic but semogenic (Halliday, 2007e). It is worth noting that lexis and grammar constitute the single one stratum of wording, because lexis can be defined as the "most delicate grammar", and they form a cline of delicacy (Halliday, 1961: 267; Halliday et al., 1964: 35; Hasan, 1987: 184; Halliday & Webster, 2009: 73).

These different strata are related by realization (indicated graphically by ↘). Realization is the relationship of symbolization (Matthiessen, 1995); it is not a casual relation, but a redundancy one: "It is not that meaning is realized by wording and wording is realized by sound, but that meaning is realized by the realization of wording in sound" (Halliday, 1992/2007k: 357). The notion of metaredundancy proposed by Lemke (1984) "formalizes the strata principle in semogenesis" and explains "the semiotic principle of realization" (Halliday, 1992/2007k: 357).

As stated by Halliday (2005b: xxviii), his notion of semantic stratum took shape in his cooperation and interaction with Lamb (1964, 1966/2004) and Bernstein (1971), but "it was not until the 1980s that it started to get fleshed out, with Hasan's work in semantic variation, Martin's work in discourse and genre, Matthiessen's experience in text generation" and his own explorations into grammatical metaphor (Matthiessen, 1983, 1988; Hasan, 1989, 1992/2009; Martin, 1992, 1993b; Halliday, 2005c).

But now that meanings are construed and enacted in the lexicogrammar, is it necessary to build in semantics as a separate stratum? There are two valid explanations for the necessity of this stratum. One is offered by Halliday & Webster (2009: 83): "Semantics is the transformation of the ecosocial environment into a meaning potential in terms of the topological domains of experience and social interaction. Lexicogrammar is the organization of these into linguistic form (grammar and lexis) in terms of metafunctionally related 'typological' networks of grammatical and lexical features." This explanation draws on the topological and typological views that were originally depicted by Martin & Matthiessen

(1991/2010). The other answer is provided by Halliday & Matthiessen (1999) in respect to language system evolution: If the congruent pattern had been the only form of construing experience, it would not be necessary to distinguish semantics from grammar; they would be the two facets of the content plane. But as "the system continued to evolve beyond that point, enriching itself (i.e. engendering a richer model of experience) by forcing apart the two 'facets' of the sign so that each could take on a new partner" (Halliday & Matthiessen, 1999: 237). Therefore, the potential for metaphor arises when language evolves to be stratified and the realignment between semantic categories and grammatical categories becomes possible.

3.1.3 Instantiation

A language is an open dynamic system which is not autostable, but metastable (Lemke, 1984); it persists "only through constantly changing by interpenetration with their environment" (Halliday, 1992/2007k: 358). So the concept of instantiation comes in to give a dynamic interpretation of the language system. The system of a language is its underlying potential as a meaning-making resource, and it is instantiated in the form of a text; meanwhile, a text created in a language gains semiotic recognition by reference to the system of the language. Halliday (1992/2007k, 2008) and Halliday & Matthiessen (2004, 2014) explained the relationship between language as system and language as instance by the analogy of the relation between climate and weather. System and instance are by no means two distinct phenomena, but the same phenomenon viewed by different observers from different standpoints. "The system is the pattern formed by the instances, and each instance represents an exchange with the environment" (Halliday, 1992/2007k: 359). Each instance can have some or even minute effects on the probabilities in a system and change the system to certain extent. Although one single instance may not make a big difference, but when the same thing occurs repeatedly with numerous instances, the system might be changed in one way or another, and finally our experience of the world might be reshaped as a whole.

Instantiation is the cline between potential and instance, and it "emerges when instances of potentially symbolic behavior become systemic" (Matthiessen et al., 2016: 136). When the cline intersects with the strata differentiation between context and language, an instantiation-stratification matrix is produced (see Table 3-2).

Table 3-2   Cline of instantiation in context and language (Matthiessen et al., 2016: 137)

	Potential	Subpotential	Instance type	Instance
Context	context of culture (cultural potential)	institutional (subcultural) sites	situation types	contexts of situation
Language	language system (meaning potential)	register	text types	texts (acts of meaning)

Between the two poles of potential and instance, there are some intermediate patterns. In terms of context, specific contexts of situation are instances of the underlying context of culture. As to the study of language, we can start with a single text, and then collect other similar texts with certain criteria, so that the patterns that all such texts share can be identified in terms of a text type. Text types are actually ways of using language in various contexts, which are termed as registers viewed from the system pole of the cline. Register here refers to a functional variety of language (Halliday et al., 1964; Hasan, 1973; Halliday, 1978c; Matthiessen, 1993; Ghadessy, 1993; Lukin et al., 2008), and can be viewed as a setting of systemic probabilities. For instance, the relational type of clause is more likely to appear in scientific reports than it is in recipes.

The importance of the cline of instantiation also lies in our scientific engagement with language in that it offers a guiding principle of methodology. Following SFL, we study phenomena of language by observing and analyzing instances (texts) in specific contexts of situation. On the basis of this analysis, we can then go further up the cline by making generalizations about the text samples, based on which we can obtain a text type or register or gain insights into the potential itself. Therefore, the use of corpus, a large collection of instances according to certain criteria, contributes to the study of language, but language researchers are required to shunt between the perspective of system and the perspective of instance to observe, analyze and describe what the corpus can reveal, and finally generalize and theorize about the system.

3.1.4   Metafunction

Gregory (1987) traces the development and status of metafunctions in systemic linguistics. Before the appearance of the term metafunction, Halliday (1969: 81-82) mentioned four components in the organization of grammar, i. e.

"the components of extra-linguistic experience, of speech functions, of discourse organization and of logical structure". Halliday (1970/2007d: 144) further introduced these components as "functions of language", which are "simply different kinds of meaning" and labeled them as ideational, interpersonal and textual, but left out the logical components due to its specialty in its realizations. Halliday (1970) introduced linguistic ontogeny, stating that "the link between function and structure is seen most clearly in the language of the child" (Halliday, 1970: 322), and his ideas were further elaborated in other papers (Halliday, 1973, 1975/2004a). "Language is as it is because of the functions in which it has evolved in the human species" (Halliday & Matthiessen, 2014: 31). The evolutionary process from microfunctions to metafunctions will be discussed in Section 3.2.2; this section only focuses on the concept of metafunction.

Metafunctions are the modes of meaning. The two basic modes are experiential function—meaning as construal of both the external and internal experience, and interpersonal function—meaning as enactment of roles and relations between speaker and listener. But the effective operation of these two modes is inevitably linked to the third brand of meaning: textual function, whereby language is text and is related to itself and the contexts in which it is used. Textual function is an enabling function, without which any use of language is impossible. What's more, there is a fourth functional component—the logical function, embodying systems that build logical-semantic relationships between clausal units. Experiential and logical functions are grouped under the heading of ideational function because they are close in meaning viewed from above.

As revealed by the principle of stratification (see Table 3-3), meaning is realized by the stratum of lexicogrammar and resonates with the semiotic parameters (field, tenor and mode) of the stratum of context. The three modes of meaning are simultaneously configured by different structures in one clause. Generally speaking, the experiential meaning is realized by the lexicogrammatical system of transitivity, the interpersonal meaning is realized by the system of mood and modality and textual meaning is realized by the system of theme-rheme. Meanwhile, choices in metafunctions are determined by the corresponding contextual parameters.

Table 3-3   Repercussions of metafunctional principle

Context of situation	Realized by	Metafunction	Realized by	Lexicogrammar
field	↘	ideational	↘	transitivity
tenor	↘	interpersonal	↘	mood/modality
mode	↘	textual	↘	theme-rheme

3.1.5 Structure

Structure is the dimension in the organization of language along the syntagmatic axis; it is termed as constituency: constructing larger units out of smaller ones. The guiding principle is rank, which is also a functional one. A structure should be distinguished from a syntagm. A structure is an ordered set of functions, for example, "Mood + Residue"; whereas a syntagm is a linear sequence of classes, such as "nominal group + verbal group + prepositional phrase". Units of different ranks have distinct functions in the system of language. The principle of rank is essential to the stratum of lexicogrammar and the stratum of phonology/graphology. In grammar, clause is the rank that assumes the major responsibility of integrating various choices in metafunctions into a single frame. A clause is composed of elements of lower rank, such as phrase/group, word and morpheme. Every rank has its own structural configuration, and each rank can be characterized by iteration; clauses combine to form clause complex, and by the same token, there are phrase/group complex, word complex and morpheme complex. A complex is not higher in rank than the original single unit; clause and clause complex belong to the same rank.

"All these compositional hierarchies are ultimately variants of a single motif: the organization of meaning in the grammar" (Halliday & Matthiessen, 2014: 22). As noted earlier, the experiential, interpersonal and textual meanings can be realized as configurations of elements that can be mapped onto each other; for instance, the same nominal group might function as Actor, as Subject and as Theme simultaneously. But it should be noted that structures of the clause complex, that is, the logical structures realizing expansion and projection do not match this kind of multidimensional mapping. Another possible problem of structure is the fact that although the constituency model works well for experiential meaning, the interpersonal and textual meanings are not ideally realized by constituents of a structure, because interpersonal meanings are often construed prosodically and textual meanings periodically, and these meanings need to be construed with the discursive flow (Halliday, 2005b).

3.2 Form, Function and Meaning

3.2.1 Form and Meaning

Form here is used to refer to the formal organization of grammar, lexicogrammar to be precise—the wordings in contrast with the meanings being encoded. Meaning is a property of the lexicogrammar as a whole; it is of grammatical systems as much as lexical items (Halliday, 2005b). These two terms *semantics* and *meaning* are interchangeable in this study, because what is under discussion is natural adult language, that is, the higher-order semiotic system which can not only carry meaning but also create meaning. Meaning is "the key property of semiotic systems. In language (as opposed to protolanguage and other primary semiotic systems), meaning is organized within the semantic stratum" (Matthiessen et al., 2010: 136). The meaning-creating power of language dwells in the stratification of its content plane into the stratum of meaning (semantics) and the stratum of wording (lexicogrammar); whereas primary semiotic systems are not further stratified, so that they can only carry, yet not generate meaning in specific contexts.

Halliday (1973: 98) states that "grammar is the level of formal organization in language; it is a purely internal level of organization…but it is not arbitrary… The grammar itself has a functional basis". The relation of grammar to semantics is natural rather than conventional, and both of them are abstract systems of coding, so that "there is no clear line between semantics and grammar, and a functional grammar is one that is pushed in the direction of the semantics" (Halliday, 1994: F45). And he further adds that "the higher-rank choices in the grammar can be essentially choices in meaning without the grammar thereby losing contact with the ground" (Halliday, 1994: F45). It can be inferred from these statements that FG still resides in the lexicogrammatical stratum, without going beyond the formal plane; it is not incorporated to be part of the stratum of semantics no matter how close it is to the semantics. FG is well defined by the way it is named: it is a functional one, which means that it is based on meaning, while it is essentially a grammar, indicating that it interprets linguistic forms, and any distinction recognized in grammar contributes to the way wording is presented. Therefore, FG is not a semantic grammar, but a grammar that interprets formal categories through meaning. The relation between form and meaning is one of realization: meaning is realized by grammar, and to put it in a precise way, meaning is realized by the realization of wording in sound or writing.

In view of the symbolic relation between form and meaning, it is inappropriate to say one determines the other. Diachronically the wordings and the meanings emerge simultaneously, and semantics and grammar evolve together in all three senses of semohistory (Halliday & Matthiessen, 1999). Now that we are adopting the constructivist view by following the European linguists Hjelmslev and Firth, we presume that grammar construes experience, and meaning is constructed out of grammar. The experiential reality is beyond what we can work out, but our construals of reality, that is, meanings, are what we surely know. As put by Halliday & Matthiessen (1999: 17), "meanings do not 'exist' before the wordings that realize them. They are formed out of the impact between our consciousness and its environment." The meaning of a linguistic item is encoded in the wording as an integrated whole. Apart from the single item, all the other possible variables such as its location in the syntagmatic structure, its collocation with some other items, and its internal organization need to be taken into account. It is in this integration that grammar exerts itself to assign specific semantic functions to these variables, and the underlying systemic principle works.

3.2.2   Function and Meaning

The function of language is defined as "property of language as a whole: principle of organization manifested throughout the system" (Matthiessen et al., 2016: 114). The functionality of language is due to the fact that language co-evolves with its eco-social environment and develops in the individual in this environment. "In principle, language is as it is because of the functions it has evolved to serve" (Halliday, 1970/1976a: 26). Functionalism in this sense stems from Malinowski's approach in anthropology and the functional notion developed by the Prague School. As a technical term, function involves two senses (Halliday & Hasan, 1985/1989; Martin, 1991; Martin, 1993c): extrinsic and intrinsic functionality. The former refers to the use of language, while the latter means the internal organization of language. In SFL, function is used to refer to the intrinsic one, with the exception of discussion about the earliest stage of language development. In the intrinsic sense, function is employed in two distinct yet closely related senses: function refers to the overall organization of language in the successive phases of evolution in terms of modes of meaning, which is termed by Matthiessen et al. (2016: 115) as "the spectrum of different modes of meaning", and function refers to the local organization of the structure of a unit. The senses and types of function are presented in Figure 3-2.

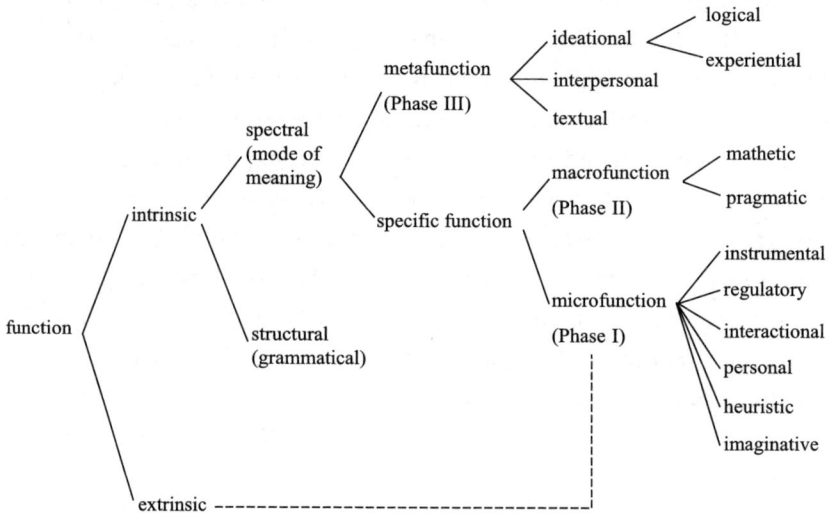

Figure 3-2   Senses and types of function (adapted from Matthiessen et al.(2016: 116))

As indicated by this figure, the spectral organization of language into modes of meaning is composed of metafunctions and specific functions, and specific functions include macrofunctions and microfunctions. These are the phases of language development; the developing process of the child's emergent language system is in some sense analogous to the stages of language evolution (Halliday, 1973). In Phase I, function is the same thing as use; the microfunctions such as instrumental and regulatory functions are what the child does with language, which in turn determine the linguistic structures the child employs. In the transition from Phase I to Phase II, the original discrete social functions are generalized into "a basic opposition between 'language as learning' and 'language as doing'" (Halliday, 1975/2004a: 28). The mathetic function is for learning, and the pragmatic one for doing. In the transitional Phase II, function is no longer synonymous with use; "the notion 'function of language' splits into two separate notions: that of 'use of language' and that of 'component of the linguistic system'" (Halliday, 1975/2004a: 51). It should be noted that there is a difference in using the term macrofunction between Matthiessen et al. (2016) and Halliday (1973). Matthiessen et al. (2016) use it to refer to the mathetic and pragmatic functions in Phase II, while Halliday (1973) takes it as a provisional term which is not different from metafunction in Phase III: These macrofunctions "are the highly abstract linguistic reflexes of the multiplicity of social uses of language" (Halliday, 1970/1976b: 19; Halliday, 1973: 36). These metafunctions (ideational, interpersonal and textual) are complementary modes of meaning, and they are structured simultaneously by distinct modes of expression. Figure 3-3 sketches out the functional development from the child's language into the adult language.

Phase I →	Phase II →	Phase III→	
functions = uses (each utterance one function)	functions = generalized types of use (functions coming to be combined)	functions = abstract components of grammar (each utterance plurifunctional)	uses = social contexts (each utterance in some specific context of use)

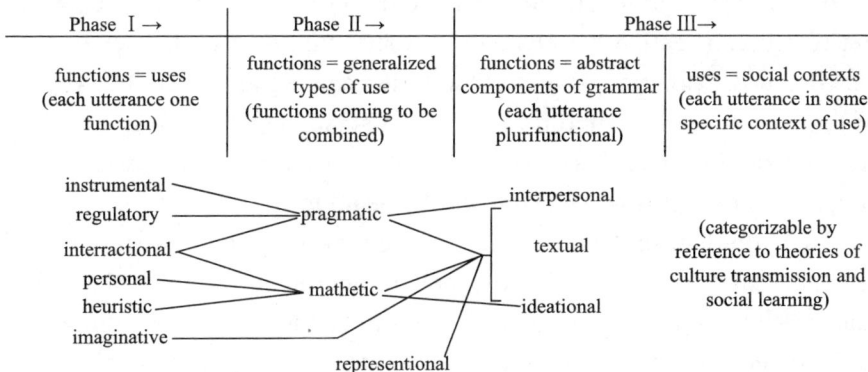

Figure 3-3　Functional development (adapted from Halliday (1975/2004a: 52))

In Phase I, functions are equated with various uses of language; in Phase II, functions are generalized into two major types of use, and grammar (a level of linguistic form) is added intermediately between content and expression. When the progression from Phase II to Phase III is completely finished, functions become abstract components of grammar, and adult linguistic system is built on a functional plurality. But it does not mean that the original functions in Phase I have disappeared; they have become the generalized social contexts of language use. Therefore, function is meaning in terms of metafunction, because function is defined here to refer to the function of the whole system of language, that is, the meaning potential of the ideational, interpersonal or textual elements in language.

Now the discussion will be shifted to the other sense of function: function refers to the role that an element plays in a grammatical structure, for example, Actor, Goal, Subject, Predicate, Theme and Rheme, and each function makes a contribution to the organic whole of the unit. Here grammar is interpreted via the relation between form and meaning. In this sense, in terms of the functional elements of grammar, function is a relational concept; it is a medium that relates meaning and form in that grammatical form is explicated by means of its relation to meaning in functional theory (Zhang, 2012). Dik (1989) states that in FG the most important position is assigned to function or relation rather than category, and uses function to refer to the relation between an element and the whole structure that it is part of. But Hjelmslev (1954) defines function as a relation between the stratum of expression form and that of expression content from the perspective of his semiotic theory. The function of a structural element lies in the fact that it can realize the element in a structure of a higher level. When we are working at the function of a structural element, we are in effect exploring the way it realizes meaning. Therefore, function stands between form and meaning; functional structure serves as a kind of relation between formal structure and meaning structure, but it is pushed towards meaning in SFL.

In functional grammatical analysis, every item in a structure is given both a class label and a functional label, indicating its grammatical class and grammatical function. In addition to the word classes that are traditionally called "parts of speech", every grammatical unit can be classified, so that there are classes of morpheme, classes of group and phrase and classes of clause. The class label indicates generally the possible grammatical functions that an item may serve, but it fails to show the specific role played by the item in certain structure, so that the functional label is required. Halliday & Matthiessen (2014: 76) state that "the functional categories provide an interpretation of grammatical structure in terms of the overall meaning potential of the language". The metafunctions of language are manifested in the grammatical structures in the language system. Grammar is "the inter-functional hookup" that integrates the various functional components into a unified structural form (Halliday, 1970/1976b: 24). A clause shows simultaneously and compatibly the three metafunctional dimensions of grammatical structure.

To further elaborate on the relation between grammatical function and meaning, we shall take the ideational function and its realizational structure as an example. In these grammatical structures, elements are recognizable as elements in our construal of the world experience. For instance, the simple clause *Jack built this house* is structurally represented as a configuration of the functions "Actor" (*Jack*), "Process: doing: creative" (*built*) and "Goal: resultant" (*this house*). Such categories as Actor, Process, Goal and their sub-categories are categories of our experience, reflecting our construal of the material world. The function that language is serving in this context of construing experience determines the structural realizations. As stated earlier, our construal of reality is meaning, so in this sense, meaning determines the grammatical functions that elements play in a structure. And the categories of grammatical functions do not appear arbitrarily somewhere outside of language; "it is the internal structure of language, the grammatical organization as we find it, empirically, which leads us to analyze the clause in this way—though, of course, once we identify the underlying functions this may lead us to select one rather than another of a number of possible structural interpretations" (Halliday, 1970/1976b: 20). Grammatical functions are of significance in relation to the meaning potential of the various metafunctional elements in language.

　　To summarize, we have in the first place distinguished two senses of function in SFL: (a) the overall organization of language in terms of general modes of meaning or meaning potential, and (b) specific structural or grammatical functions in a unit. In the first sense, function is meaning in that the various components of meaning are derived from the diverse functions of language. In the second sense, grammatical function is a bridge linking meaning and grammatical form. But the inter-connections between these two senses of function should be recognized. The grammatical functions do not arise from nowhere; they also stem from the social functions that language serves, and thus they are deeply rooted in meaning. Grammatical functions come from meaning and realize meaning. Halliday (1985b: 4) inherited "the semantics basis of grammar" from the Chinese linguist Wang Li. FG is meaning-oriented. As stated by Butt (1996: xv), "A grammatical description is functional when it is organized around the tasks language fulfils in human interaction and when the categories of description themselves are arrived at on the basis of the semantic consequences of each element of a clause or sentence."

3.3 *The Concept of Congruence*

The concept of congruence is of paramount importance to the theory of grammatical metaphor, because it is critical to evaluating the metaphoricity of a relevant expression. "The often professed ideal of 'plain, simple English' would seem to imply something that is in general what we are calling congruent" (Halliday, 1985a: 329). Halliday (1985a: 321, 343, 345) defines a congruent expression as "the most typical way of saying a thing", "the most straightforward coding of the meanings selected", and "the typical way in which experience is construed". Thompson (1996: 164) states that "'congruent' can be informally glossed as 'closer to the state of affairs in the external world'. In simple terms, nouns congruently encode things, and verbs congruently encode happenings". But none of these definitions suffice for theoretical and empirical operations due to their subjectivity and vagueness. The Chinese linguist Hu (2000) summarizes five criteria for congruence proposed by Halliday and his associates: age, naturalness, lexical density, diachronic order and mode of communication, according to which the congruent forms are those that frequently occur in the speech of pre-adolescence children, that are iconic to the world in the most natural way, that package less information in its lexicogrammar, that appear at an early stage in semohistory and that are typical of spoken rather than written mode of communication. But all these criteria have invited challenges and criticism because of their inconsistency and the difficulty in being formalized, so more explicit interpretations of the concept of congruence are still in need.

This section aims to clarify this fundamental yet controversial concept in terms of both its theoretical groundings and new developments; the purpose is not to work out specific definitions and criteria for this concept but to interpret its intrinsic nature. The discussion includes the following aspects: firstly, the meanings of congruence in earlier works by Halliday and Robin Fawcett will be reviewed in order to bring into picture the general background against which the notion of grammatical metaphor emerged; secondly, insights into this concept will be taken forward by the lexicogrammar-semantics inter-stratal relation and the three dimensions of semogenesis in SFL; thirdly, features of indeterminacy, ineffability, cline and complementarity will be explored to account for the contingent nature of congruency; lastly, a systemic perspective will be adopted to explicate the relation between the congruent and the metaphorical.

3.3.1   The Concept of Congruence in Earlier Works

Even before the theory of grammatical metaphor was systemically introduced by Halliday (1985a), the concept of congruence had made sporadic appearance in the earlier works by Halliday and Fawcett, and had been understood differently in these various contexts.

3.3.1.1   The Early Works by Halliday

"Grammatical Categories in Modern Chinese" (Halliday, 1956/1976c) is the first paper in which the term congruent made its debut. In his description of the various kinds of grammatical structures in Chinese, Halliday found that there might be alternative forms for a basic structure, and he defined the likelihood of occurrence of every form as a probability value. Four degrees of probability were recognized: even, likely, almost certain and certain; they were symbolized by ½, ½+, 1- and 1, with the complementary negative degrees ½-, 0+ and 0. "A grammatical structure which reflects a contextual structure (by matching it with maximum probability)" is referred to be "congruent" (Halliday, 1956/1976c: 42). In this sense, congruence is related to markedness and frequency; the congruent form is one that is most frequently used for a given grammatical structure.

In the paper "Language Structure and Language Function" (Halliday, 1970/2007d), Halliday employs the term incongruent to explain the correlation between grammatical types and the functions they realize. It is stated that the three major types of transitivity roles (process, participant and circumstance) in most cases correspond respectively to the three major word or group classes (verb, noun and adverb), but "there are also incongruent forms of expression, with functions of one type expressed by classes primarily associated with another type" (Halliday, 1970/2007d: 180). This statement can be taken as the predecessor of "congruence in status" put forward by Halliday (1999).

The concept of congruence also appears in studies of language in social contexts. Halliday (1978c) points out that linguistic variants are symbolic expressions of the hierarchical social structure. The use of high variants by a speaker in formal contexts and low variants in informal contexts is called "the congruent pattern" which is defined by the contexts as the norm (Halliday, 1978c: 156). If a speaker uses a language variety in a context where it is not the norm, he/she uses it incongruently. But the incongruent use carries social meanings, since it produces a foregrounding effect. Halliday also stresses that the variation is limited, and it cannot go beyond the degree of intelligibility. In "Antilanguages" (Halliday, 1976/1978b), the concept of congruence is related to the notion of metaphor. An antilanguage is a metaphorical variant of "the regular patterns of realization" of the standard everyday language (Halliday, 1976/1978b: 177). Halliday (1976/1978b: 172) asserts that there are both continuity and tension between language and antilanguage, "reflecting the fact that they are variants of one and the same underlying semiotic. They may express different social structures: but they are part and parcel of the same social system".

Another paper "Language as Code and Language as Behavior: A systemic-functional interpretation of the nature and ontogenesis of dialogue" (Halliday, 1984) also involves the concept of congruence. This paper is concerned with the relationship between system and process in the interpersonal component, especially the actualization and refinement of systems in dialogues. Halliday stresses the role congruence plays in such a relationship by referring to the adult interpersonal systems and the ontogenetic development of language. In describing the levels of the basic interpersonal systems: context (move), semantics (speech function), lexicogrammar (mood) and the connection between these strata by means of realization, Halliday indicates the need for the concept of congruence. "A congruent realization is that one which can be regarded as typical—which will be selected in the absence of any good reason for selecting another one" (Halliday, 1984: 14). And there is a connection between incongruence and increased delicacy of the language system; "many of the more delicate distinctions within any system depend for their expression on what in the first instance appear as non-congruent forms" (Halliday, 1984: 14). As to the ontogenetic development of language, it is believed that a child's language evolves from a system which composes some apparent congruent options into a more complicated adult system where incongruent realizations carry an equal weight and there are hardly clear distinctions between congruent and incongruent ones.

The early descriptions of congruence by Halliday are summarized in Table 3-4. As can be seen from the above discussion, in the earlier works by Halliday, the concept of congruence is most frequently related with markedness (Halliday, 1956/1976c, 1985a), probability (Halliday, 1956/1976c), typicality (Halliday, 1976/1978b, 1985a, 1984/2005a) or norm (Halliday, 1974/1978a). But such terms are matters of scale which can hardly be explicitly measured; and some descriptive words like *regular, plain, simple, straightforward* are not objective enough to define congruence.

Table 3-4 Halliday's early descriptions of congruence

(adapted from Taverniers (2003: 28))

Congruence	
congruent form = **unmarked** form	Halliday (1956/1976c: 42)
"a grammatical structure which **reflects a contextual structure** (by matching it with **maximum probability**)"	Halliday (1956/1976c: 42)
"the **regular** patterns of realization"	Halliday (1976/1978b: 177)
" he (the speaker) may also use the forms (variants of language) incongruently: that is, **outside the contexts which define them as the norm**"	Halliday (1978c: 156)
"that one which can be regarded as **typical**—which will be selected in the absence of any good reason for selecting another one"	Halliday (1984/2005a: 14)
"the most **typical** way of saying a thing"	Halliday (1985: 321)
"the often professed **ideal of 'plain, simple** English'"	Halliday (1985: 329)
"that (structure) which would be **arrived at by the shortest route**"	Halliday (1985: 345)
"the most **straightforward** coding of the meanings selected"	Halliday (1985: 345)
Incongruence	
"incongruent means 'not expressed through the most **typical** (and **highly coded**) form of representation'"	Halliday (1976/1978b: 180)

3.3.1.2 The Early Works by Fawcett

Fawcett (1980) designs a congruence network (see Figure 3-4), which is the first system network for semantics.

In Fawcett's theory, Halliday's interpretation of the strata relationship between semantics and lexicogrammar is reinterpreted in that the system network is regarded as the semantic stratum and the syntagmatic structure is moved to the domain of syntax (constituting the lexicon). The congruence network involves a systemic representation of nominalization which later turns to be the most powerful resource of experiential metaphor in Halliday's account.

Examples of realization

referent (viewed as linguistic input) → CONGRUENCE →

- regarded as situation
  - *straightforward — *Ivy quickly refused his offer*
  - as "possessed" situation — *Ivy's quickly refusing his offer*
  - as quasi-thing — *Ivy's quick refusing of his offer*
- regarded as thing
  - *straightforward — *Ivy/the girl/Ivy's refusal*
  - identified by role in process — *what Ivy refused*
  - *simple — *Ivy*
  - bound by minimal relationship — *straight to Ivy*
- regarded as quality
  - of situation — *very quickly*
  - of thing — *very quick*

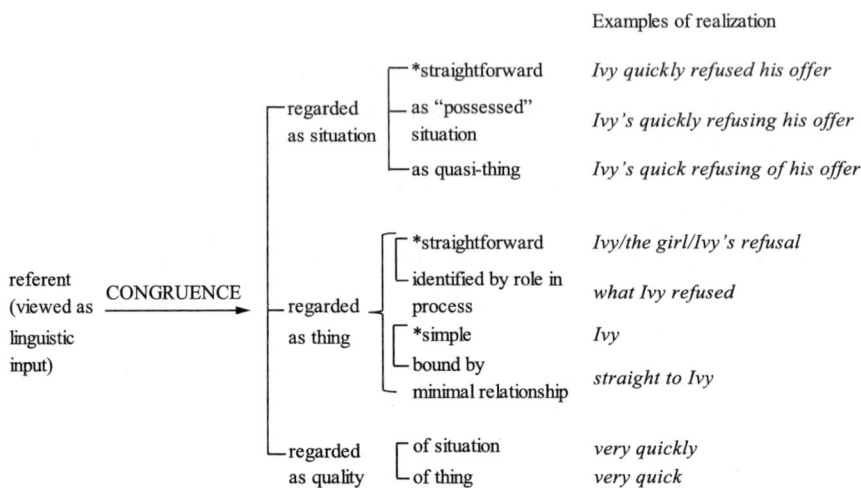

Figure 3-4　Congruence network by Fawcett (1980: 93)

Fawcett (1980: 91) suggests that the congruence network is the initial entry condition in other systemic grammars, and it is designed "to handle the complex range of possible relationships between the referent as a raw input to the linguistic system and the input to the various system networks". The entry condition of the congruence network is termed as referent, with two primary types (referent situation and referent thing) and an extended one (referent quality). The referent is "a mental construct in the performer's mind" (Fawcett, 1980: 89), so that it is used at the mental referential level, and consequently at the semantic level, differing from the real life situation or thing. Fawcett (1980) justifies his preference for the term referent situation over other established ones by stating that the term process used by Halliday (1970/2007d) does not refer to the pre-linguistic referent situation itself, but to its interpretation in the experiential component of the semantics, and the terms proposition and predication are associated with formal logic. The units in English which typically realize referent situations and referent things are clauses and nominal groups; another unit that typically expresses the quality of a referent situation or thing is termed by Fawcett as the quantity-quality group. This is where the term congruence stands out; it "provides an apt label for the system network in which we decide whether or not to use the typical set of semantic options—and so the typical syntactic unit—for a referent" (Fawcett, 1980: 92). If the untypical choice is made, what has originally been constructed as a referent situation is regarded as if it were a referent thing, and nominalization occurs. For example, as indicated in Figure 3-4, the "straightforward" (marked with an asterisk) construal of the referent situation is *Ivy refused his offer*, while the "quasi-thing" *Ivy's refusing of his offer* is the result of expressing the situation within the semantic features that lead to a nominal group. Reversely, a referent thing can be identified by "role in process"; as in *what Ivy refused*, the referent thing (*the thing that Ivy refused*) is processed as a clause. Therefore, due to the semantic nature of the congruence network, there is no one-to-one relationship between the features and the realizational units.

The system network formalizes another fundamental concept in SFL: choice; an incongruent expression is a meaningful choice. In Fawcett's study, incongruence happens at the level of the speaker's cognition of the world. Fawcett's system network representation is still heuristic and adopted in later research, such as in natural language generation (Teich, 1999).

3.3.2   Further Insights into the Concept of Congruence

The deepening of the understanding of congruence is in line with the gradual development of the theory of grammatical metaphor. In the late 1980s and the 1990s, Halliday and other researchers (Halliday, 1998, 1995/2007a, 1988/2007h, 1997/2007l; Halliday & Martin, 1993; Halliday & Matthiessen, 1999) focused on the grammar of scientific language and the role of grammar in construing and reconstruing experience, leading to a great breakthrough in the study of grammatical metaphor. Congruence is, therefore, redefined in terms of two crucial and interwoven notions in SFL—stratification and semogenesis.

3.3.2.1   Inter-strata Relation

Three core semantic categories in the ideational base have been established: sequence, figure and element; they refer to the phenomena of experience in the order of complexity (Halliday, 1998, 1999/2007f; Halliday & Matthiessen, 1999). These semantic categories are congruently realized in lexicogrammar by clause complex, clause and group/phrase respectively. It has been stressed repeatedly that these grammatical categories do not appear out of nowhere; they evolve when they are transforming experience into meaning, and thus semantics and grammar evolve together. As put by Halliday (1999/2004b: 364), "Grammar evolved, in one of its aspects, in the construing of human experience; the framework of clauses, clause complexes, and groups of words sorted out the phenomena of experience into figures, with the figures organized into sequences and made up of various lunds of elements. [...] Let me refer to this pattern of construal as the congruent pattern. However, as technology advances, knowledge comes to be restructured; so experience is reconstrued by the grammar in significantly different ways. "

Halliday (1999/2007f) summarized the general pattern of congruence between the grammatical and the semantic categories, with congruence in rank and congruence in status (elements) as indicated in Table 3-5 (＼ indicates realization). Stratification involves mapping meanings onto lexicogrammatical forms; it also allows remapping and cross-coupling between them. A stratified system has an inherent metaphoric power, and incongruence arises from inter-stratal tension.

Table 3-5 Congruence between semantic and grammatical categories (adapted from Halliday (1999/2007f: 110))

Congruence in rank		Congruence in status (elements)	
semantic	grammatical	semantic	grammatical
sequence ＼ figure ＼ element ＼	clause complex clause group / phrase	entity ＼ quality ＼ process ＼ circumstance (1) ＼ circumstance (2) ＼ relator ＼	noun (nominal group) adjective [in nominal group] verb (verbal group) adverb (/ adverbial group) prepositional phrase conjunction

3.3.2.2 Semogenesis

The process by which meaning is created is called semogenic process, and grammar is the powerhouse generating the semiotic transformation of experience. The priority of the congruent expressions in semohistory has been explained in terms of the three temporal frames (Halliday & Martin, 1993; Halliday & Matthiessen, 1999): phylogenetic (the evolution of human language), ontogenetic (the development of the individual speaker) and logogenetic (the unfolding of the act of meaning itself, that is, the construction of meaning in a text which is a real instance). The congruent forms evolve earlier in the language; children go through three critical steps (generalization, abstractness and metaphor) in their language development, and they master congruent forms before they move on to the metaphorical. As to logogenesis, the derivational priority due to the loss of information is obvious. For example, *she announced that she was accepting* appears earlier in a text than *the announcement of her acceptance*, because the latter causes ambiguity in meaning with the missing of information about the Sayer, the tense and so on. "Even the most abstruse scientific text is ultimately based in the grammar of the mother tongue, and depends on the primary construal of experience that that embodies" (Halliday, 1997/2007l: 198).

Halliday & Martin (1993) adopt two terms: the doric and the attic to refer to the congruent and the metaphorical. The doric style of everyday, commonsense discourse is featured by a high degree of grammatical intricacy, and it represents a dynamic mode; whereas the attic style of the emergent languages of science shows a high degree of lexical density, which characterizes a synoptic mode. But the two are not on equal terms, with the dynamic mode being phylogenetically and ontogenetically prior. It is also pointed out that it is the development of writing that brings language to our consciousness and offers a new synoptic perspective on experience.

Therefore, the semogenesis theory is important for our understanding of congruence and grammatical metaphor. Without the three diachronic dimensions, it would be impossible to talk about the ordered relationship between a set of metaphorically agnate wordings, and there would be no inherent priority accorded to any of them. Only if we view them historically or dynamically, can we find out which one evolves first along the three lines and thus discover the principle underlying congruence. This explains why the concept of congruence involves a sense of human intuition. Congruence is established with regard to our common sense and the accepted way that speakers of a language view the world; it reveals the relationship between language and reality. "Once we conceive of reality in semiotic terms, it can no longer surprise us that language has the power to construe it, maintain it, and transform it into something else" (Halliday & Matthiessen, 1999: 547). Experience is originally construed clausally, and only later it is reconstrued in nominalized forms, so grammar can be taken as the trace left over by the human use of language.

3.3.3　The Ineffability of Congruence

The implicitness of the concept of congruence inevitably invites criticism, but this kind of ineffability is an inherent feature of congruence. This abstract concept fails to be concretized or formalized, and it is even harder to work out universally recognized criteria for it. Because the objective material world is indeterminate, the grammar of the language system which construes the experiential world is correspondingly indeterminate. Indeterminacy is "a normal and necessary feature of an evolved and functioning semiotic system"; "it is something that should be built in to our ways of representing and interpreting language: part of the background, rather than the foreground, to our account of the construal of experience" (Halliday & Matthiessen, 1999: 547). Lots of grammatical categories display no fixed boundaries or criteria of membership, as indicated by Halliday (1994: F52):

> "There are many categories in English grammar that I do not 'know' the meaning of—that is, to which I could give no adequate gloss which would relate them to the categories of my conscious experience. Even those of which we have some conscious understanding, however, cannot be fully defined—that is, glossed in exactly equivalent wordings. They have evolved in order to say something that cannot be said in any other way; hence, they are strictly ineffable. The best one can do is to display them at work, in paradigmatic contexts, so as to highlight the semantic distinctions they are enshrining."

Halliday (1984/2007m) explores the reasons of the ineffability of grammatical categories. First of all, language, as a discipline of science, takes natural language as both its study objective and metalanguage, so natural language is explicated by means of itself, that is, "language turned back on itself" in Firth's words. Additionally, all social-semiotic systems are "dynamic open systems" which are metastable in that they persist and renew themselves through constant change by means of interaction with their environment. The system of natural language is certainly no exception; it exists because it is open and constantly changing. Therefore, it is of difficulty to define explicitly linguistic categories by using natural language.

The second reason lies in the cryptogrammar of natural language. Halliday draws on the American anthropologist Whorf's (1956) distinction in grammatical categories between overt categories (phenotypes) and covert categories (cryptotypes). In contrast to the overt categories such as reflection marks, function words and word sequence, covert ones are those whose meanings are complex and difficult to access, and can only be put under attention till reactances are discovered through the analysis of expressions in relation of agnation. The concept of agnation was introduced by Gleason (1965) to describe different structures "with the same major vocabulary items"; "the relation in structure is regular and systematic… it can be stated in terms of general rules" (Gleason 1965: 202). These general rules are termed as reactances, and it is by means of the reactances that cryptotypic grammar can be revealed. Many aspects of the grammar of clause and clause complex, for example, the transitivity patterns, tenses, aspects, grammatical metaphors and so on, are basically cryptotypic. As stated by Halliday (1994: 353), "in most instances of contemporary discourse it is only when we start to analyze that we become aware of the grammatical metaphors involved." In modeling the process of reflecting on natural language, Halliday (1987/2007n) classifies four levels of consciousness: Level 0—motifs, Level 1—words, Level 2—phenotypes and Level 3—cryptotypes. Level 0 is concerned with meaning, while the other three are at the lexicogrammatical level. The features of cryptogrammar are hidden motifs which function below the usual level of consciousness. The reality-generating power of cryptogrammar might be incompatible with explicit logical reasoning: "When we start reflecting on them (features of the cryptogrammar), bringing them up to our conscious attention, we destroy them. The act of reflecting on language transforms it into something alien, something different from itself—something determinate and closed" (Halliday, 1987/2007n: 125). Now that grammar is cryptotypic, the realizational relation between semantics and grammar is certainly more covert, which can hardly be explicated. What makes the matter more complicated is the fact that congruence represents the natural realizational relation between semantics and grammar in the language system, that is, the relation between meaning and wording in the natural spoken language, so that it is not a specific category, but an abstract category which functions to describe the deeply-hidden features of the language system.

All in all, the implicitness of the concept of congruence has to be acknowledged, and the failure to provide a definite definition by Halliday shouldn't be taken as a kind of neglect, but a solution with no other alternatives.

3.3.4 Approaches to Congruence

Now that we have admitted the implicitness and ineffability of congruence, we need to introduce the concept of cline and adopt complementary views in discussing metaphoricity.

3.3.4.1 Cline

"There is no very clear line to be drawn between what is congruent and what is incongruent. Much of the history of every language is a history of demetaphorizing: of expressions which began as metaphors gradually losing their metaphorical character" (Halliday, 1985a: 327; 1994: 348). Like any other phenomenon of language, congruence is thus a matter of degree. The simple dichotomy between congruent and metaphorical cannot be retained; a cline or continuum should be proposed instead, with one end of it being metaphorical and the other congruent, so that "the metaphorical relationship is not a symmetrical one: there is a definite directionality to it" (Halliday & Matthiessen, 1999: 235).

Figure 3-5 is an example indicating the degree of metaphoricity; the agnate expressions ranging from a to e form a continuum with the metaphoricity declining gradually. These expressions are systematically related to one another. Clause complex a (α ^ ×β) which is composed of a dominant clause and an enhancing dependent clause is the most congruent one among them, since it is most iconic to the happenings in the real experiential world. In Expression b, the original dependent clause is downgraded to serve as the circumstantial element of the clause; Expression c is a circumstantial type of relational clause with the two original clauses being downgraded to be nominalized elements, and the process is a causal verb; Expression d is more metaphorical in that the causal verb in c is also transformed into a nominal group; Expression e is a nominal group which is of the highest metaphoricity, because the original α clause has become the Thing in the nominal group, followed by a Qualifier (prepositional phrase with nominalization), and lots of information has been condensed in this process.

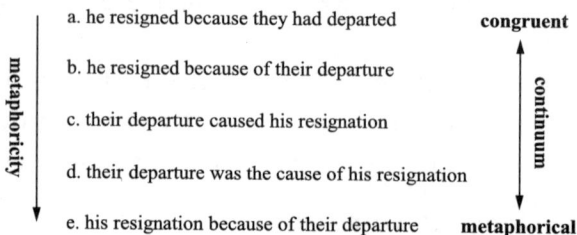

metaphoricity

a. he resigned because they had departed — **congruent**

b. he resigned because of their departure

c. their departure caused his resignation — continuum

d. their departure was the cause of his resignation

e. his resignation because of their departure — **metaphorical**

Figure 3-5　Degree of Metaphoricity: paradigmatic complexity

Therefore, unpacking a grammatical metaphor may also involve several intermediate steps before reaching the most congruent expression. As to the question of how far one should pursue in the analysis of grammatical metaphor, there is no universally valid answer; it depends on the purpose of analyzing. But there seems to be certain criterion for stopping short in the process of unpacking. Halliday & Matthiessen (1999) argue that if a further step of unpacking introduces a new textual metaphor or causes the incongruent distribution of textual information, it should be discarded. They exemplify this point: the metaphorical expression *in times of reduced loading* can be unpacked into the congruent one *(when) the load was reduced*, but it is not necessary to unpack it further into *(when) less freight was being carried*. This further unpacking does not alter its status as a figure; it simply smashes and redistributes the semantic features within the scope of the figure.

As indicated by Figure 3-6, the semantic feature of (1) is ((carry + goods): fewer), which construes the message in a congruent way with *the goods carried* as the point of departure and *fewer* as the new information in the culminant position; whereas in (2), the semantic feature is bracketed as ((goods + fewer): carry), which gives newness to *carry* rather than *fewer*, thus distributing the information in a less congruent way.

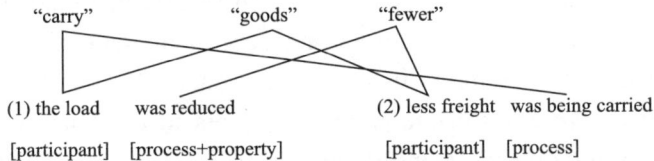

Figure 3-6   Redistribution of semantic features of two forms of unpacking
(Halliday & Matthiessen, 1999: 285)

3.3.4.2 Complementary Perspectives

(1) Dynamic/ Synoptic Complementarity

As discussed earlier, in the three dimensions of semogenesis, the congruent has an obvious temporal priority over the metaphorical: it evolves earlier in the language; it appears earlier as children develop their first language; it comes at an earlier point in the unfolding of a particular text. But if a set of metaphorical agnates are viewed statically or synoptically, each one is metaphorical from the standpoint of the other. What's more, semogenesis is distinct from biological evolution in that unlike the replacement of the previous species by the new one in the biological systems, grammar retains its earlier historical features; the occurrence of metaphorical forms does not deny the existing congruent forms, and both are kept in the language system as equal and meaningful choices. Children do not discard the commonsense grammar of daily life after they move on to the grammar of education or of the workplace; similarly, the clausal mode of expression does not vanish from the language system when the nominal mode dominates. Both the congruent and metaphorical expressions are lexicogrammatical forms to be chosen in the language system network: they are independent realizations of a core meaning. As Halliday (1985a, 1994) argues, neither congruent nor metaphorical is in nature "better", "more frequent", nor more of a norm than the other. Therefore, it should be noted that "more metaphorical wordings are inherently neither better nor worse than more congruent wordings: they are simply doing different jobs" (Thompson, 1996: 166). Halliday (1985a: 324;1994: 344) also states that "in most types of discourse, both spoken and written, we tend to operate somewhere in between these two extremes. Something which is totally congruent is likely to sound a bit of flat, whereas the totally incongruent often seems artificial and contrived." There are some correlations between the type of metaphorical wordings and discourse type. For instance, in scientific writing, the nominalized objectivisation is highly valued, whereas in oral narratives, some interpersonal metaphors play a significant role. The choice of more congruent or metaphorical forms depends to a large extent on the contexts in which they occur. We need to recognize the equal status of congruent and metaphorical forms in the language system, and meanwhile acknowledge the semohistorical priority of the congruent over the metaphorical.

(2) Syntagmatic / Paradigmatic Complementarity

From the perspective of syntagmatic structure, the congruent and metaphorical expressions represent different semantic configurations realized by correspondingly different grammatical configurations, but from the perspective of paradigmatic relation, they constitute a system network of agnates, occupying different topological positions in the expanded semantic space. The total semantic potential is not reduced by the lowering of congruence and the increasing of metaphoricity; instead it is expanded because the grammar creates new meanings.

Table 3-6 and Table 3-7 give examples of the transitivity analysis of a congruent form and its metaphorical expression.

Table 3-6   Example of syntagmatic analysis: transitivity (congruent)

he	resigned	because	they	had departed
α		×β		
Actor	material process	Relator	Actor	material process
pronoun	verbal group	conjunction	pronoun	verbal group

Table 3-7   Example of syntagmatic analysis: transitivity (metaphorical)

his		resignation	because of	their	departure
Deictic		Thing	Qualifier		
determiner		noun	prepositional phrase		
			preposition	nominal group	
				Deictic	Thing
				determiner	noun

By comparison we can find that the two are widely apart from each other in their syntagmatic structures. The logical relation between two clauses is transferred to be one within a nominal group. Syntagmatic contrast mainly focuses on distinctions, while paradigmatic clustering emphasizes both similarities and differences. According to Fawcett's (1980) congruence network, the referent in the first example is "regarded as situation" (*he resigned, they had departed*), whereas in the second example, the referent is "regarded as thing" (*his resignation, their departure*). When the process becomes thing, a great deal of neutralization takes place, which leads to semantic ambiguity, and more possible meanings are added to the semantic system. Therefore, when the metaphorical agnates are viewed typologically, they represent discrete semantic structures realized by different grammatical structures, but when scrutinized topologically, they are systematically related in meaning.

(3) Inter-stratal/ Intra-stratal Complementarity

As discussed earlier, stratification is the working mechanism underlying grammatical metaphor. It is the inter-stratal tension between the stratum of lexicogrammar and the stratum of semantics that causes grammatical metaphor. There are congruent realizations of semantic categories by the lexicogrammatical categories; when these categories in the two strata are decoupled and recoupled, the principle of congruence is broken. Meanwhile, grammatical metaphor can also be considered as an elaborating relation (a token-value type relation) between semantic configurations: "An identity is set up between two patterns, a sequence and a figure, a figure and a participant, and so on. In this identity, the metaphorical term is the 'Token' and the congruent term is the 'Value'" (Halliday & Matthiessen, 1999: 288). And thus the relation is intra-stratal instead of inter-stratal: the identity is held between different meanings rather than between meanings and wordings. Grammatical metaphor involves relating distinct semantic domains of experience; for instance, the domain of sequence is construed in terms of the domain of figures, and the domain of figures is construed via the domain of participants, and so on. "It is the fact that metaphor multiplies meanings within the semantic system that opens up the possibility of metaphorical chains, with one congruent starting-point and another highly metaphorical end-point" (ibid.).

Therefore, we should view the concept of congruence from both inter-stratal and intra-stratal perspectives. "The principle of congruence depends on the association among the three dimensions of rank, metafunction and stratification. It is important because of the potential for departing from it, which is a way of adding to the overall meaning potential" (Halliday, 2003: 20). As illustrated by Table 3-8, going through from the most congruent to the most metaphorical involves moving down the rank scale, narrowing down the grammatical realizational domains of semantics as well as shifting in metafunctions. Congruence not only represents the relation between different forms, but also the relation between form and meaning, which reveals the changes in meaning that occur in grammatical metaphor.

Table 3-8　Co-working dimensions in metaphoricity

Domain	System	Metafunction	Example	Metaphoricity
clause complex	hypotaxis	logical	He resigned because they had departed.	low
clause	causation	logical + experiential	Their departure caused him to resign.	medium
	circumstantiation	experiential	He resigned because of their departure.	
	relational process		Their departure caused his resignation.	
			Their departure was the cause of his resignation.	
nominal group	qualification		His resignation because of their departure.	high

The above discussion on the concept of congruence is largely confined to the language system itself, but the relation between language and the outside experiential world should also be taken into consideration to give a better interpretation of the concept. Halliday (1995/2007a) gives a "neither-both" answer to the question: does human experience determine the form of grammar, or the other way round? The form that is taken by grammar with its categories (nouns, verbs and so on) is shaped by human experience, and meanwhile, the form that is taken by human experience with its categories (happenings, things, qualities or circumstances) is shaped by grammar. Now that SFL adopts the tradition of objectivism, it is presumed that language reflects the experiential world. If there is a direct correspondence between linguistic expressions and the objective phenomena in reality, the language used should be taken as the congruent form. For example, if a happening or process in real life is realized by a verbal group grammatically, it is construed congruently; if it is realized by a nominal one, it is reconstrued incongruently. That is to say, a congruent expression encodes the objective world as it is, while an incongruent one departs from the objective reality by taking advantage of the second-order nature of language.

3.4   Quality-Thing Ideational Grammatical Metaphor

3.4.1   Thing and Quality

3.4.1.1   Defining and Classifying Thing

Halliday & Matthiessen (1999) put forward the semantic units of the ideation base of language: sequence, figure and element. Figure is the basic unit of an experiential phenomenon. The component parts of a figure are elements which in turn are classified into process, participant, circumstance and relator. Participants can be interpreted as expansions of things: things with added qualities. Participants are grammatically realized by nominal groups, and in terms of the experiential structure of the nominal group, the dividing line between qualities and things lies between the Classifier and the Thing.

The example in Table 3-9 shows the different types of functions and grammatical classes of components in a nominal group. Semantically, the Thing realized by the substantive noun is construed as a thing or entity, while all the other components such as Deictic, Numerative, Epithet and Classifier realized by determiner, adjective and numeral respectively are different types of qualities. What follows the Thing is Qualifier which is usually realized by a prepositional phrase or downward rankshifted clause.

Table 3-9　The multivariate structure of the nominal group (Martin et al. , 2010: 166)

Example	those	famous	first	two	dreadful	long	maths	sums	in the exam
Function	Deictic	Post-deictic	Numerative	Numerative	Epithet	Epithet	Classifier	Thing	Qualifier
Class	determiner	adjective	ordinal	cardinal	adjective	adjective	noun	noun	prep. phrase

Compared with other elements, things are relatively stable in time and space, and are more complex in their semantic make-up. Things can assume a variety of functional roles in figures of all types. A thing can be defined by reference to the particular role it is playing in a figure. Roughly speaking, there are fourteen functions (Actor, Goal, Behaver, Senser, Phenomenon, to name a few) that a thing can take on directly in various figures and eleven roles that it can play in an oblique way; for example, a thing can work as Recipient, Client, Scope, Initiator, Attributor and so on (Halliday & Matthiessen, 2014). But a quality only serves as Attribute, a process works as Process, and a circumstance only plays certain circumstantial role in a figure. In some cases, these elements become parts of things by grammatically entering into the structure of the nominal group, which further indicates the complexity of things.

As to the classification of things or entities, there are two typical models. Halliday & Matthiessen (1999) provide a preliminary taxonomy of simple things (see Figure 3-7). They take consciousness as a starting point, distinguish in the first place human beings with higher-order consciousness from things with no consciousness, and then draw a line between things in material world and those in semiotic world. The most important message conveyed here is that "it is in the category of thing that the grammar captures to the greatest measure the complexity of the elemental phenomena of human experience" (Halliday & Matthiessen, 1999: 193). The various kinds of participant along with different types of figure highlight the fact that experience is in nature both material and semiotic, made out of the constant interaction between entities and meanings.

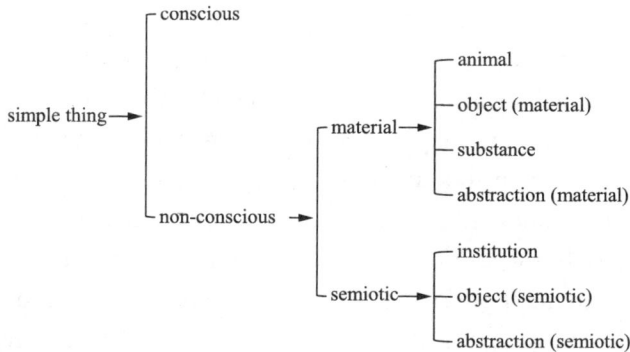

Figure 3-7   Taxonomy of simple things (Halliday & Matthiessen, 1999: 190)

Martin & Rose (2007) classify things or entities in line with the ontogenetic dimension of semogenesis: the process of language development that an individual goes through from generalization, abstraction to metaphorization (see Table 3-10). There is some overlapping between the two models of classification, but by comparison, Martin & Rose (2007) go further to include metaphoric entities which are transferred from processes or qualities, while Halliday & Matthiessen (1999) take metaphoric things as macro-things which are not included in this scheme.

Table 3-10   Classifications of entities / things (Martin & Rose, 2007: 114)

Indefinite pronoun		some, any, no thing, body, one
Concrete	everyday	man, girlfriend, face, hands, apple, house, hill
	specialized	mattock, lathe, gearbox
Abstract	technical	inflation, metafunction, gene
	institutional	offence, hearing, applications, violation, amnesty
	semiotic	question, issue, letter, extract
	generic	color, time, manner, way, kind, class, part, cause
Metaphoric	process	relationship, marriage, exposure, humiliation
	quality	justice, truth, integrity, bitterness, security

3.4.1.2 Defining and Classifying Quality

According to Halliday & Matthiessen (1999), as a semantic category, a quality stands along a cline between things and processes. A quality is the attribute or state that is ascribed to a thing, so that a quality is dependent on a thing. A quality needs to be construed together with a thing, taking the thing as the standpoint of reference; a quality has no independent status in the referential space and thus cannot be tracked down discursively. Qualities are not obligatory components, because a thing may or may not be endowed with certain qualities.

Both qualities and things are construed as participants, but they are not participants of different kinds. They play different roles in the same structure of a participant. It is the typical case that a quality combines with a thing to constitute a participant in a figure. The only context where a quality can take on a participant role independently is serving as Attribute when it stands in intensive relation to the other participant. There are two specific cases: in a figure of being, the other participant is Carrier to which the quality is ascribed (e.g. *the plate is dry*[①]); in a figure of doing, the participant is Actor or Goal and quality is the result of the doing (e.g. *the plate is wiped dry*). Attribute is not a prototypical participant, since it cannot work as the interpersonal Subject. But it can be interpreted as a participant if the noun or the substitute one is added to the nominal group, for example, *that is a heavy truck or that is a heavy one*. It has been further validated that a quality does not construe a different kind of class of thing, and the class can be presumed from the context. Therefore, a quality is grammatically realized by an adjective and typically construed either as Epithet to describe a participant or as Attribute to ascribe certain attribute to a participant; a quality is participant-like in this sense. But qualities have an intermediate status; some qualities are process-like or circumstance-like (Halliday & Matthiessen, 1999). In the clause *the dog wet the floor*, *wet* is construed as a verb, and the quality is not repeated as an Attribute, but it may reoccur with an intensifier (e.g. *very wet*). Some qualities may appear as depictive Attribute in a figure of doing and happening (e.g. *he came in drunk*), which is agnate with a Circumstance of manner (e.g. *he came in drunkenly*).

Compared with qualities, things display obvious temporal stability and experiential complexity. Things are extensible in time and can represent the junction of several different dimensions, but qualities are less stable in time, and only represent values on a single dimension such as age, size, weight and color. These values can be classified into three types: binary (e.g. *dead, alive*), scalar (e.g. *happy, sad*) and taxonomic (e.g. *wooden, plastic, stone*). That is to

---

① This example and the following examples in this paragraph are from Halliday & Matthissen (1999: 207-208).

say, qualities represent single properties, but things stand for combinations of properties (Bhat, 1994; Frawley, 1992). Halliday & Matthiessen (1999) suggest a tentative classification of qualities (see Table 3-11).

Table 3-11 Tentative classification of qualities (Halliday & Matthiessen, 1999: 211)

Qualities of					Taxonomic type	Agnate figure		Example
						Epithet (Classifier)	Thing	
Proj.	as sensing:	as assessment:				figure of sensing: Process	Senser/ Phen.	
	emotive	attitude (evaluation)			scalar	rejoice, grieve		happy, sad, delightful, tragic; good, bad
	cognitive	probability			scalar	suppose, believe, know		doubtful, sure; likely, certain
	desiderative	modulation			scalar	like, want, desire		willing, keen; desirable, necessary
		usuality			scalar			usual, common
Exp.	elaboration	attribution				figure of being		
			class	national	taxonomic			Thai, Burmese
				material				plastic, wooden
				etc.				...
			status	life	binary	Attribute	Carrier	alive, dead
				sex				female, male
				marital				single, married
				etc.				...
			sense-measure	visual: colour & shape	taxonomic			red, blue, pink; round, oval, square

(to be continued)

Qualities of					Taxonomic type	Agnate figure		Example
						Epithet (Classifier)	Thing	
Exp.	elaboration	attribution	sense-measure	weight	scalar	Attribute	Carrier	heavey, light
				texture				rough, smooth
				age				old, young
				etc.				...
			prop-ensity	(behav. qual.)	scalar [dynamic]			skilful, naughty
			quantity	inexact	scalar			few, many
				exact	taxonomic			one, two, three
		identity			scalar	Process: be, resemble	Carrier, Token	same, similar, analogous, different
	extension				taxonomic	Process: accompany, replace, be instead		additional, alternative, contrasting
	enhance-ment	temporal			taxonomic	Process: be before, after, at		previous, precedding, subsequent
		spatial			taxonomic	be above, within, outside		interior, external, anterior, posterior
		causal						consequent, resultant, conditional, contingent

Qualities are distinguished with regard to the fractal types of projection (sensing and attitude) and expansion (elaboration, extension and enhancement). Qualities of projection and qualities of expansion are fundamentally different in their agnate figures. Qualities of projection are agnate with processes in figures of sensing; for instance, *sad* in *the sad man* (or *the man is sad*) is agnate with *grieve* in *the man grieves*. Whereas qualities of expansion are usually agnate with processes in figures of being and having; for example, *similar* and *different* in *his idea is similar to / different from ours* are agnate with *resembles* and *differs* respectively in *his idea resembles / differs from ours*.

3.4.2   Grammatical Metaphor and Transcategorization

The transference from quality to thing is grammatically realized by a change from an adjective into an entity noun, so there might be some difficulty in distinguishing grammatical metaphor from grammatical transcategorization. Halliday & Matthiessen (1999) point out that new semantic features arise in the process of metaphorization, involving the semantic junction between the original meaning and the metaphorical meaning; for example, *failure* is process construed as thing, causing the semantic junction of "process + thing". Unlike grammatical metaphor, transcategorization refers to the derivation of one grammatical category from another. The transcategorized element loses its original semantic feature; for instance, when the noun *mouse* realizing thing is turned into the adjective *mousy* realizing quality, it merely means *like a mouse* due to the disappearance of the initial meaning of thing. Halliday (1998) illustrates the distinction between grammatical metaphor and transcategorization by giving some prototypical examples from ancient Greek (see Table 3-12).

Table 3-12   Prototypical examples illustrating grammatical metaphor and transcategorization (Halliday, 1998: 199)

(1) verb: active(Actor)noun	(2) verb: passive (Goal)noun
"one who /that which ...-s"	"that which is ...-n"
Ποιέω make: *ποιητής* maker	be made: *ποίημα* thing made
Πράσσω do: *πράκτωρ* doer	be done: *πρᾶγμα* thing done, deed
(3) verb: middle (Medium)noun	(4) adjective: noun of quality / degree
"...ing" (abstract)	"being..., how...?"
make: *ποίησις* making	*Μέγας* big: *μέγεθος* size; greatness
do: *πρᾶξις* doing, action	*Βαθύς* deep: *βάθος* depth; deepness, altitude

The first two kinds of nouns which are derived from verbs indicate concrete or perceivable things. Type (1) is typically a person, serving the role of Actor in a process; Type (2) is usually the product or outcome of a process. But the nouns in Type (3) and Type (4) do not represent things; what happens is that some process or some quality is construed as if it were a stable and measurable thing which can participate in some other processes. It can be seen that the first two types are not concerned with grammatical metaphor because they are merely entities defined by processes, but they do not contain any semantic feature of process. The other two types are demonstrations of grammatical metaphor in that the original semantic features of process and quality are retained and crosslinked with the newly-emerged semantic feature of thing.

Not all cases of grammatical transcategorization can be classified as grammatical metaphor; grammatical metaphor not only entails transcategorization but also creates junction of semantic features. Grammatical metaphor is a variant of a congruent expression both in formal and semantic senses, so the single formal feature does not suffice to be the criterion for grammatical metaphor. Grammatical metaphor should be valued in terms of function or meaning, because language is a system of meanings and relations (Halliday, 2015), and as stated earlier, in FG, the notion of category is less prominent than functions or relations (Dik, 1989). Grammatical classes are mutable, but what matters is the change of grammatical function (Halliday, 1995/2007a). In the following examples, *fitness*, *similarity* and *efficiency*, viewed from the perspective of grammatical categories, are nouns that are derived from the original adjectives *fit*, *similar* and *efficient*; however, analyzed in terms of grammatical functions and meanings, they are Classifiers of the Things (*function*, *parameter* and *indicators*) in the specific nominal groups, and none of the three nouns realizes a Thing. Classifiers are qualities of the class type, and they are different from things in that they have no independent existence; they cannot be established in referential space and re-identified in a running discourse. Therefore, such kind of grammatical transcategorization cannot be equated with grammatical metaphor.

(3-1a) We also note that properties aside from those evaluated in this work can also be included <u>in the fitness function</u> and optimized as long as they can be accurately computed, including the synthetic accessibility. (Text 1)

(3-1b) For each pair of functional groups, the calculated Tanimoto coefficient was used to determine whether the pair was similar or dissimilar using <u>a similarity threshold parameter</u>. (Text 1)

(3-1c) … operationalized through the "Three Red Lines" policy, which sets targets for total water use, the establishment of water use <u>efficiency indicators</u>, and the need for water quality standards to be achieved up to 2030. (Text 4)

3.5   *Summary*

This chapter starts with the five dimensions in language proposed by SFL, and then the relations between form, function and meaning are well explained. The fundamental concept in the theory of grammatical metaphor, congruence, is also discussed at length; it is put forward that the notions of cline and complementarity should be adopted in understanding congruence. Finally, the main ideas of quality-thing ideational grammatical metaphor are introduced. These theoretical foundations serve as the guiding principles of this study as presented in Figure 3-8.

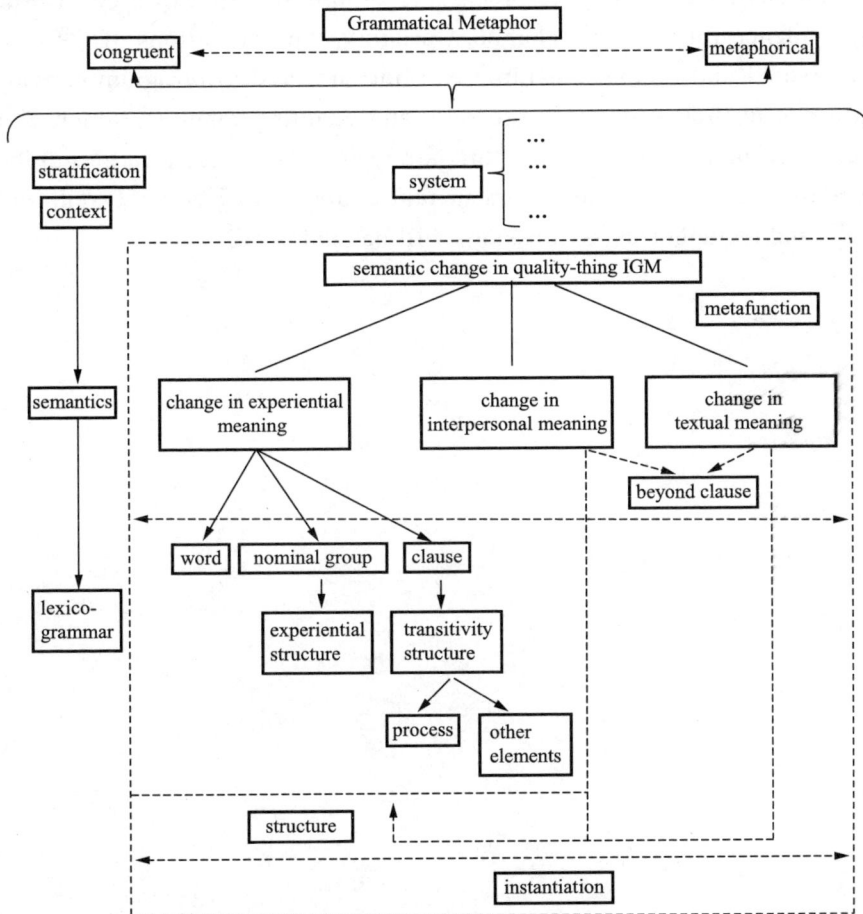

Figure 3-8   Guiding principles of this study

The semantic change in quality-thing ideational metaphor refers specifically to the change in the three metafunctions: experiential, interpersonal and textual meanings, and the various changes are systemic, so that there should be systems for change in each line of the three meanings. The semantic change is determined by the context and realized by the lexicogrammar, so both the contextual factors and lexicogrammatical realizations need to be taken into consideration. The lexicogrammatical analysis will involve different ranks of word, group and clause. To explore the experiential semantic change, the lexical items that realize quality-things will be accounted for, the experiential structure of metaphorical nominal groups should be analyzed, and the transitivity configuration of the clauses embodying quality-thing metaphors should also be explored in order to provide evidence for semantic change. Certainly, the realizations of the changes in interpersonal and textual meanings are not confined to the grammatical unit of clause due to their respective prosodic and enabling features, which is not a major concern of this study. Since this study is data-based, a large number of instances of quality-thing metaphors in real contexts will be analyzed, and the congruent and metaphorical expressions will be compared.

Chapter 4

Research Methodology

Different from most of the previous studies which are confined to theoretical assumptions, this study is designed to be an empirical one that is data-supported, by integrating the qualitative research method with the quantitative approach, and the real clausal contexts in which instances of quality-thing ideational metaphors play their functional roles will be thoroughly investigated. This chapter focuses on some essential aspects of the methodology. It starts with description of the data resources, and then introduces the procedures for data processing, and finally deals with the analysis and annotation of the data.

4.1 Data Resources

The sample texts in this study are thirty-five original scientific research articles randomly chosen from ten well-known scientific journals which are available online in the electronic journal resources Elsevier Science Direct and Springer Link. Texts of technology and science[①]are selected because the language of science is prominently characterized by grammatical metaphor. Volume 5 in the "Collected Works of Halliday" (2007i) is particularly dedicated to the language of science, and it is in this volume that the theory of grammatical

---

① "Science" here is used in the narrow sense, referring to natural science in contrast to the humanities.

metaphor is fully explicated.

These selected articles (about 164,300 words in number) are published in 2015 and 2016. The majority of them are from two popular journals—*Science* and *Nature*. The other eight journals are *Science of the Total Environment, Forensic Science International, Engineering Science and Technology—an International Journal, Chemical Engineering Science, International Journal of Mechanical Sciences, International Journal of Computer Vision, Physical Review Letters* and *Sleep Medicine* (see Appendix I for further information). "There is of course no single register of science" (Halliday, 2007i: xxiii). There are numerous scientific discourses, covering various disciplines and sub-disciplines. These articles have a wide range of coverage in disciplines, so that this study may be universally meaningful.

This study is purely concerned with language itself; the other modalities of semiotics such as formulas, tables, figures, charts, images and their captions are not taken into account. And only the main body of each article is taken as data for analysis; the abstract, references, appendix and acknowledgements are not covered.

4.2 Data Processing

These selected texts were further processed according to the following procedures.

The texts were firstly converted from the pdf format to the doc format via the software Abbyy FineReader 11 for the convenience of marking and numbering. Proofreading was conducted to avoid misprint or failure in word recognition. And then all the texts were studied thoroughly to find out all the instances of quality-thing ideational metaphor. These instances and the clauses where they are located and even wider contexts (if necessary for precise comprehension) were sorted out and numbered. Instances from the same original text were filed together, so there are thirty-five files named after the original sources: Text 1, Text 2… and Text 35. Because grammatical metaphor is distinct from grammatical class shift as discussed in the previous chapter, there are certain criteria for judging whether a case of adjectival nominalization is quality-thing ideational metaphor, according to which some cases are excluded from this study. There are five types of ruled-out instances.

(1) A nominalized adjective realizing a quality rather than the Thing in the nominal group. As stated in Section 3.4.3, a nominalized adjective may still realize a quality, such as Classifier or even Epithet, instead of the Thing in the nominal group. In the following examples, *stability* is a noun which is derived from the adjective *stable*, but it is working as the Classifier of the Thing *test* in the first example and of the Thing *scales* in the second example, so it is not an instance of quality-thing grammatical metaphor.

(4-1a) After **stability** test, the elemental distribution is still similar to the initial state. (Text 5)

(4-1b) We will show that some of our azotosome candidates have high decomposition energies relative to the cryogenic environment, resulting in very long **stability** time scales. (Text 3)

(2) A nominalized adjective followed by or modified by an exact number, serving as a measurement which cannot be unpacked. In the following examples, *conductivity* and *thickness* have become technicalized modes of measurement.

(4-2a) The 0.9-mm-thick glassy graphene film has a sheet resistance of 1.075 kilohm per square and a **conductivity** of 10,335 S/cm. (Text 7)

(4-2b) The fabricated patch was peeled off the glass slide to produce a freestanding patch with a **thickness** of 19.06 ± 3.36 mm, as determined by scanning electron microscopy (SEM) (Fig. 1C), in comparison to 12.10 ± 2.07 mm for unmodified chitosan films. (Text 8)

There is another excluded case where, as indicated in the following example, the nominalized adjective realizes the Thing in the experiential structure, but is preceded by a Numerative functioning as Head in the logical structure (see Table 4-1).

(4-3) If we assume that all the faces are rigid and the structure can only fold along the edges, this periodic structure will have three degrees of **freedom** identified by the angles a1, a2, and a3. (Text 2)

Table 4-1   Nominal group with Numerative as Head

	three	degrees	of	freedom
Experiential structure	Numerative			Thing
Logical structure	Premodifier	Head	Postmodifier	

(3) The nominalization of qualities of probability and modulation which are subtypes of qualities of projection (see Table 3-11). Adjectives such as *able, capable, possible, probable, certain, uncertain* and *necessary* belong to this category. Tucker (1998: 155) terms them as "situation-oriented quality". According to the typology of nominalization in SFL (see Table 2-7), the nominalization of these kinds of adjectives is classified as "modality of process" transferred into thing, which is distinguished from the quality-thing type. Nominalizations *ability, probability, uncertainty, possibility* and *necessity* in the following clauses provide good examples (congruent forms are given in brackets).

(4-4a) Among the conductive materials used in bioelectronics, conducting polymers (CPs) have attracted much attention over recent years because of their **ability** to conduct both electronically and ionically, to be processed into scaffolds, and to be rendered biodegradable. (Text 8)

(**Congruent**: conducting polymers (CPs) are *able* to conduct...)

(4-4b) The optimization statistics are generally very good, and applying MOFF-GA five times will only sample a fraction of the total search space while having a high **probability** of recovering the topper forming structures. (Text 1)

(**Congruent:** it is highly *probable* that the topper forming structures will be recovered.)

(4-4c) The dependence of the time scale on ΔE is exponential, so the **uncertainty** in the time scale will be greater than the underlying **uncertainty** in the energy barrier. (Text 3)

(**Congruent:** the time scale is more *uncertain* than the energy barrier.)

(4-4d) The achievable resolution suggests the **possibility** of retrieving even humidity and temperature profiles. (Text 14)

(**Congruent:** it is *possible* to retrieve even humidity and temperature profiles.)

(4-4e) The **necessity** of significantly increasing domestic agricultural production is a priority if food security is to be achieved. (Text 4)

(**Congruent:** it is *necessary* to significantly increase domestic agricultural production.)

Although Martin (1993b: 239) categorizes the nominalization of modal words, for example, from *capable* to *capability*, as quality-thing ideational metaphor, he takes it as a transitional stage in unpacking *capable* further into *can*. Therefore, he admits, at least, in an indirect way, the legitimate status of the nominalization of modality of process.

(4) Nominalization in stretched verb construction. This kind of verb phrase refers to such expressions (e.g. *make an accusation against somebody*) which can be seen as a stretched version of a simpler verb phrase (e.g. *accuse somebody*) (Allerton, 2002). Actually, a stretched verb construction is "a lexically empty verb" combining with "the following nominalization to express the process" (Thompson, 2014: 242). "The lexical verb serving as the Event of the verbal group functioning as Process tends to be fairly general, and the lexical content is represented by the noun serving as Thing in the nominal group functioning as Range in the clause, or in the prepositional phrase serving as Place" (Halliday & Matthiessen, 2014: 418). Although some of these constructions can be congruently represented by an attributive relational clause, they are not instances of quality-thing ideational metaphor; they can be taken as nominalization nested in verbalization.

Two examples are given to illustrate this point. The first example involves a combination of "Process + Range" (see Table 4-2); it can be congruently expressed as an attributive relational process: *lipid membranes <u>are important</u> as a very early evolutionary step in creating life on Earth*. And the second example involves the combination of "Process + abstract circumstance of Place" (see Table 4-3), which can be congruently expressed by an attributive relational process: *a new EU Directive <u>became effective</u>*.

(4-5a) This supports a "lipid world" hypothesis, in which lipid membranes <u>played an important role</u> as a very early evolutionary step in creating life on Earth. (Text 3)

Table 4-2   Stretched verb construction: "Process + Range"

lipid membranes	played	an important role	as a very early evolutionary step in creating life on Earth
Medium	Process	Range	Circumstance

(4-5b) On 2002 January 01, a new EU Directive <u>came into effect</u> on product noise emitted by construction and commercial lawn care equipment[①].

Table 4-3   Stretched verb construction: "Process + abstract Circumstance"

a new EU Directive	came	into effect
Actor	Process	Place

(5) An adjective with the specific Deictic *the*, referring to a general type of things. Although this form is used to represent a certain kind of thing, equivalent to the function of a nominal group, it involves no change in the grammatical category. The adjective, for example, *negative* in the following clause, remains to be unchanged in form. It is the combination of *the* with the adjective as a whole functions like a nominal.

(4-6) The authors also argue that all cultures have something positive that must be recognized and promoted, while identifying <u>the negative</u> as well. (Text 35)

With the exclusion of the above-mentioned five types of "fake" quality-thing nominalization, there are 900 clauses embodying quality-thing ideational metaphor that have been obtained in the data (see Appendix III). In view of the complexity of the real environments where these metaphors occur, both the ranking clauses and embedded/rankshifted[②] clauses are taken into consideration. In addition to the most common single clauses, a lot of ranking clauses are dependent clauses that enter into certain logico-semantic relationships in clause complexes. In the following examples, different types of clauses are demonstrated: non-finite Hypotactic elaboration, finite Hypotactic elaboration (non-defining relative clause), non-finite Hypotactic enhancement (cause: purpose) and non-finite Hypotactic extension (addition: adversative).

(4-7a) Despite having a similar pore size, as well as a higher amine density, a significant decrease in CO_2 uptake was observed, **<u>demonstrating</u> the <u>complexity</u>** <u>involved when tuning an MOF's properties via functionalization</u>. (Text 1)

---

① Lang, W. W. Global versus local issues in noise control policy [J]. *Noise Control Policy*, 2003(2): 17-22.

② Following Halliday & Matthiessen (2014: 382), "embedded" is used here as an alternative term synonymous with "rankshifted".

(4-7b) In addition, China increasingly imports oilseeds, soybeans, edible oils, and dairy products, which **may also bring uncertainty** in global markets. (Text 4)

(4-7c) Here, **to improve** synthetic **viability**, we have developed a GA that will be used with experimentally realized structures; this GA focuses only on optimizing the functionalization of materials. (Text 1)

(4-7d) Furthermore, the gas template of ammonium nitrate is successfully introduced in the gelatin-metal frameworks without **affecting** the **homogeneity**, and it enlarges the surface area of the carbon catalysts nearly six times. (Text 5)

Embedded clauses are also very important environments where such kind of metaphor dwells. "Embedding is a semogenic mechanism whereby a clause or phrase comes to function as a constituent within the structure of a group, which itself is a constituent of a clause" (Halliday & Matthiessen, 2014: 491). The most typical functions of an embedded element are working as Postmodifier of Thing in a nominal group and serving as Head/Thing in a nominal group. In the following illustrations, embedded clauses are marked by [[ ]]. Here are examples of embedded clause as Postmodifier in a nominal group, including both non-finite clauses and finite defining relative clauses.

(4-8a) In addition to the need to address future food security(excluded as quality)issues, the Chinese leadership has recently proposed an ambition [[of achieving environmental **sustainability**]] as part of an "ecological civilization" as presented at the18th Plenary Congress of the Communist Party of China. (Text 4)

(4-8b) Although polymers [[derived from transition metal macro-cyclic compounds]] are effective precursors [[to alleviate the **inhomogeneity**]], these compounds are generally expensive, even comparable to Pt/C catalysts, which significantly hinders their scalable production. (Text 5)

(4-8c) Still, curli have the characteristic cross-b hydrogen-bonded structure of amyloids [[commonly associated with proteinaceous fibers [[having outstanding **stiffness** and **strength**]]]]. (Text 9)

(4-8d) There is a need [[to develop a sustainable agricultural system [[that advances multiple goals—crop **productivity**, resource stewardship, health, social well-being, farm income, and rural development]]]]. (Text 4)

The following is an example of embedded clause as Head / Thing in a nominal group.

(4-9) [[Increasing **transparency** in the decision-making process]] would shorten the time to response and ensure that policies were equitably and consistently implemented. (Text 4)

When all the instances of quality-thing metaphor were confirmed, they were clearly numbered and marked. The following two examples are used to illustrate the way of marking. The angle bracket is used to denote a clause; for example, <C-1> means that it is the first selected clause in this text. The verb or verbal group realizing Process is italicized; the adjectival nominalization is presented in bold, and the bracketed number following it indicates its sequence and occurrence; for example, (2*1) means that the lexical item *selectivity* is the second instance of quality-thing metaphor and it is the first time it occurs in this text. The nominal group where the nominalization dwells is underlined.

(4-10a) MOFs have garnered significant attention for a wide range of applications, such as gas separation and storage, catalysis, and proton-conducting membranes. <C-1> The **breadth** (1) of applications *is largely due to* their highly tunable nature. (Text 1)

(4-10b) For example, Deng *et al.* synthesized an MOF-5 variant with three different functional groups and found it <C-2> *to have* a 400% increase in **selectivity** (2*1) for CO_2 over CO when compared to the unfunctionalized parent MOF. (Text 1)

4.3   Data Analysis

Now that the data are ready to be analyzed, the first step is to unpack all the metaphorical nominal groups under investigation into congruent clauses for comparison, and then further analyses at different grammatical ranks will be conducted by means of annotation and statistical tools.

4.3.1   Unpacking Metaphor

The congruent form of a metaphorical quality-thing nominal group is an Attributive intensive relational clause where quality is construed as "Attribute: Carrier + Process + Attribute" (Matthiessen, 1995), because there is "a deeper sense in which relational clauses are nominal: they construe the same range of relations as those of modification within the nominal group: the house was old: the old house" (Halliday & Matthiessen, 2014: 262), and "the grammar only allows attributes to be generated in relational clauses, although they sometimes occur in certain material ones as well, either as conditional or resultative" (Matthiessen, 1995: 212). For instance, the quality-thing nominal group *the breadth of applications* in the clause *the breadth of applications is largely due to their highly tunable nature* is agnate to the clause: *applications (of MOFs) are broad*. It is clearly revealed that when the Attribute realized by an adjective in the relational clause is nominalized into the Thing in a nominal group, the Process disappears because of the downward rankshift from a clause to a group; meanwhile the Carrier of the relational process is changed into the Qualifier of Thing in the group. The transformation from quality to thing leads to the changes of other elements in grammatical functions, which forms a syndrome of grammatical metaphor. In order to ensure the correctness in dealing with such syndromes, in case of indeterminacy in the process of unpacking, the British National Corpus (BNC) is resorted to for help. In the following example, the metaphorical nominal group *a high solubility in polar solvents* is embedded as the Postmodifier of the Thing *resource*; when it is unpacked into the congruent form, *solubility* is changed into *soluble*, and consequently the Epithet *high* should be turned into an intensifier of the adjective. If the collocation of *highly + soluble* remains in doubt, authentic instances from BNC can help to make it certain.

4.3.2   Analysis at the Ranks of Word and Group

The data analysis starts with the lower rank of word and group in order to find out some prominent features of the nominalized adjectives and the nominal groups with the nominalization as Thing or Head. First of all, all the adjectival nominalizations in the 900 clauses and their frequencies are counted. For example, the noun *presence* whose congruent form is an adjective *present* occurs 62 times in the data. The results will be statistically presented by Excel. These nominalized lexical items will be classified and described to reveal the characteristics they share. Secondly, all the nominal groups characterized by quality-thing metaphor in the data are sorted out, and their experiential structures are carefully analyzed and presented by Excel in order to discover the semogenic power of nominal groups, so that the addition and loss of information in the grammatical transference can be figured out.

4.3.3   Analysis at the Rank of Clause

All the files composed of the selected clauses were converted from the doc format to the txt format via Microsoft Word 2010 for further annotation and analysis. The corpus tool used in this study is UAM Corpus Tool 3.3h for both annotation and data analysis. Manual annotation is conducted by employing self-designed annotation schemes in this study. There is indeterminacy in language use and language description, and some verbs realizing processes are difficult to classify, so that personal judgement and interpretation may get involved in analyzing the data. The data are annotated by the author with intra-coder reliability analysis, and the indeterminate cases are discussed and checked by three other doctoral candidates majored in SFL.

The annotation in this study involves two aspects.

(1) The process type of each selected clause

When the congruent attributive relational clause is transferred to be a nominal group, it enters as a participant into a new process. The type of the process should be explored to make clear the new environment where the quality-thing metaphor works. The annotation system for process type is grounded on the transitivity system in functional grammar (see Figure 4-1).

With regard to the experiential function, the clause is "a mode of reflection, of imposing order on the endless variation and flow of events" (Halliday & Matthiessen, 2014: 213). The experiential meaning is realized by the grammatical system of transitivity. Transitivity is the encoding of our experience of process. "The system of transitivity provides the lexicogrammatical resources for construing a quantum of change in the flow of events as a figure—as a configuration of elements centered on a process. Processes are construed into a manageable set of process types" (ibid.). There are six major types of process with their subtypes. The distinct models of different processes for construing particular domains of experience will be discussed in detail in Chapter 5. Figure 4-2 provides examples for annotation by means of UAM Corpus Tool 3.3h.

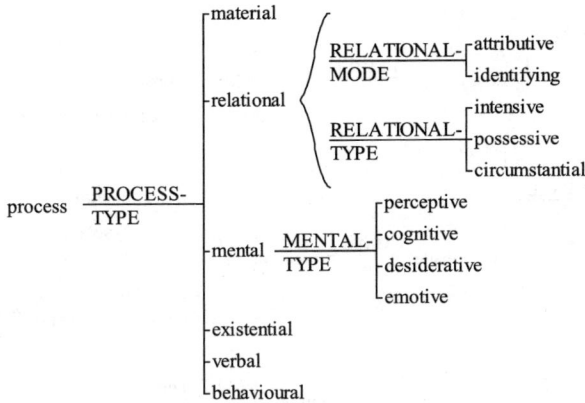

Figure 4-1　Annotation system for process type

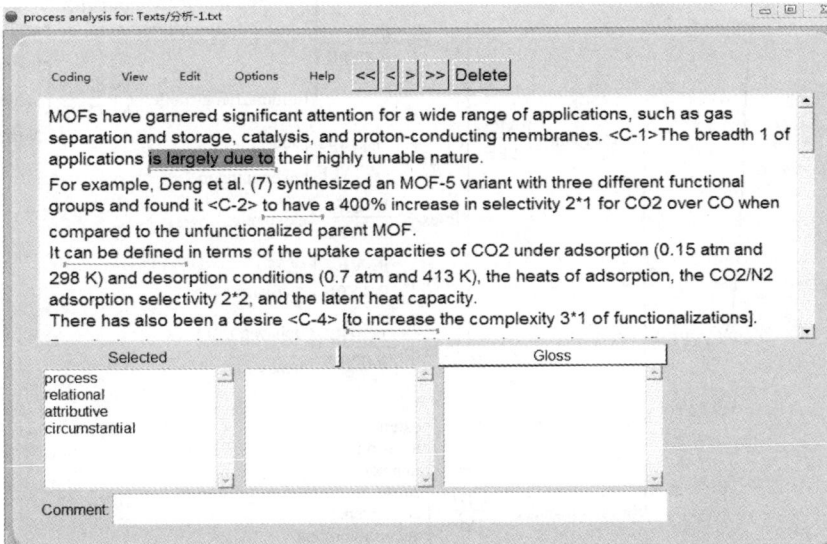

Figure 4-2　Annotation of metaphorical process type

(2) The functional roles played by the metaphorical nominal groups in the new processes

The self-designed annotation system with the entry condition "functional-element" embraces three simultaneous systems: rank, status and types (see Figure 4-3). In the system of rank, the feature "group" means that the metaphorical group remains at the group rank, and the feature "below group"

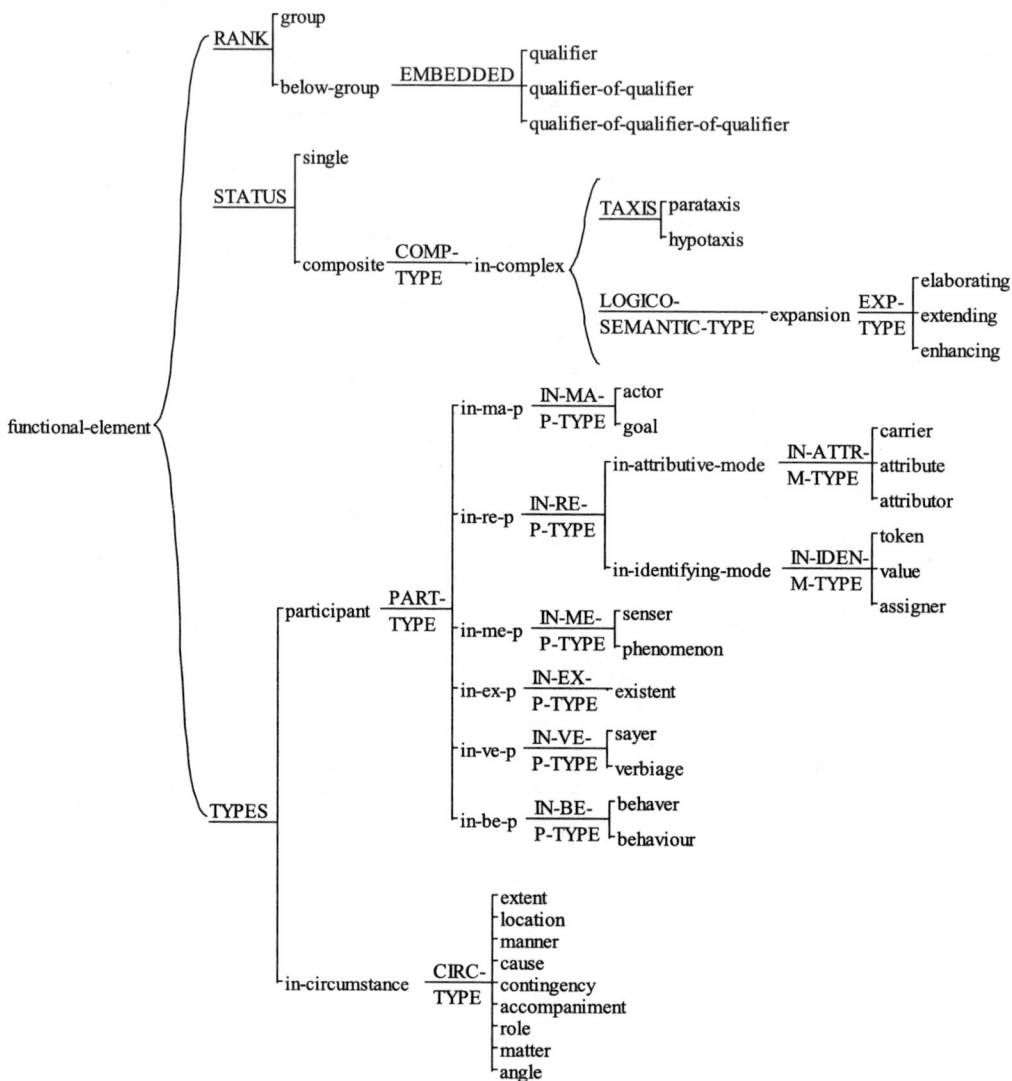

Figure 4-3　Annotation system for functional elements

means that the metaphorical group is embedded/rankshifted as Qualifier or even rankshifted further to be Qualifier of Qualifier. In the system of status, the feature "single" means that the metaphorical nominal group stands on its own, while "composite" means that it enters into a group complex with other nominal groups. In the system of "types", features are chosen with reference to whether the metaphorical nominal group serves as a direct participant in the new clause or as an indirect participant located in circumstances. Participant roles vary according to the types of process. There are roughly nine categories of circumstances (Halliday & Matthiessen, 2014: 313-314).

Figure 4-4 demonstrates the way of annotating such functional roles.

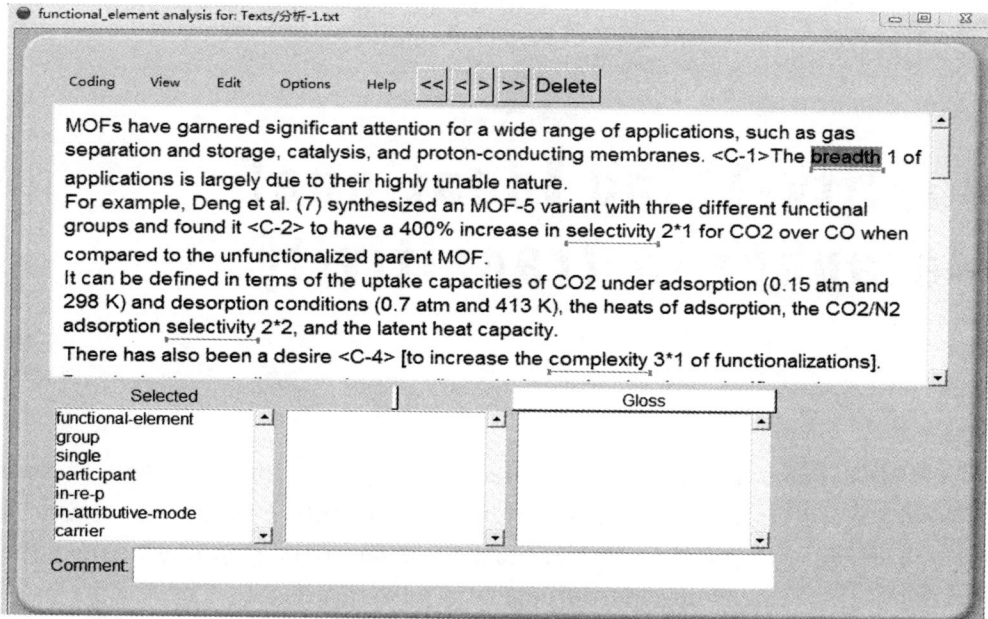

Figure 4-4   Annotation of functional roles played by the metaphorical nominal groups

Chapter 5

Quality-Thing Ideational Metaphor in Transitivity

What happens in quality-thing metaphorization is the fact that a figure of being/ascribing realized by an intensive, attributive relational clause is metaphorized into an element realized by a nominal group. And then the metaphorical element may participate in a new figure. Most of the previous studies stop at this point without going further to explore the inner components of the metaphorical group at the micro-level and the new environments where it works at the macro-level. This study aims to take a further step. In this chapter, the focus will be shifted onto group as an organic whole from the perspective of experiential meaning realized by transitivity in grammar. The following questions will be answered: When the element realized by the nominalized group becomes a participant in a new figure, what types of processes can it enter? What kind of functional roles can it play? And in what manner does it function in the new environment?

5.1 Domains of Experience and Transitivity

5.1.1 The Grammar of Experience: Types of Process

The experiential meaning of the clause is realized by the system of transitivity. Transitivity "is a notion to be applied to the entire clause" (Fontaine, 2013: 74). As defined by Halliday & Matthiessen (2014: 213), "the system of Transitivity provides the lexicogrammatical resources for construing a quantum of change in the flow of events as a figure—as a configuration of elements centered on a process". The world of experience is construed into a manageable set of process types; each process type constitutes a distinct model for construing a particular domain of experience as a figure of a particular kind. Figures categorize experience into particular types or domains. There are four primary domains of experience: the outer material world, the inner world of consciousness, the world of abstract relations and the world of symbolization[①] (Halliday & Matthiessen, 1999). Correspondingly, there are figure of doing and happening, figure of sensing, figure of being and having, and figure of saying; such figures are realized grammatically by material, mental, relational and verbal processes, and other borderline processes (behavioral and existential). The six process types with their subtypes constitute the basis for the annotation scheme in this study (see Figure 4-2 in Chapter 4). Among the process types, mental and relational clauses have subtypes. Under the umbrella of mental clauses, there are four subtypes: perceptive, cognitive, desiderative and emotive. Relational clauses are of particular complexity; the English system operates with three major types of relation (intensive, possessive and circumstantial), and each of them takes on two modes of being (attributive and identifying). Figure 5-1 illustrates the realizational relationship between the systems of experiential meaning and the lexicogrammatical systems of clauses with different process types.

The process types discussed above are built on the typological perspective on meaning, but one kind of process is by no means prior over another. Viewed from the complementary topological perspective, these process types are ordered and form a continuum. What is important is that the continuum is not between two poles but represented in the form of a circle or spectrum. This topological perspective on meaning demonstrates the general motif of indeterminacy, by which we can see the probabilistic nature of the semantic system and how regions

---

① Halliday & Matthiessen (2014: 213-216) mentioned three major domains of experience with the exclusion of "the world of symbolization". There is no fundamental distinction between the two versions; the experiential world of symbolization is realized by verbal processes that lie on the borderline between mental and relational processes.

of meaning overlap (Halliday & Matthiessen, 1999). Since indeterminacy is inherent in experience itself, only a system of fuzzy grammar can accommodate this nature. In construing experience, the grammar offers "a flexible semantic space, continuous and elastic, which can be contorted and expanded without losing its topological order" (Matthiessen, 1995: 516). Figure 5-2 represents the major process types and the clines between pairs of them.

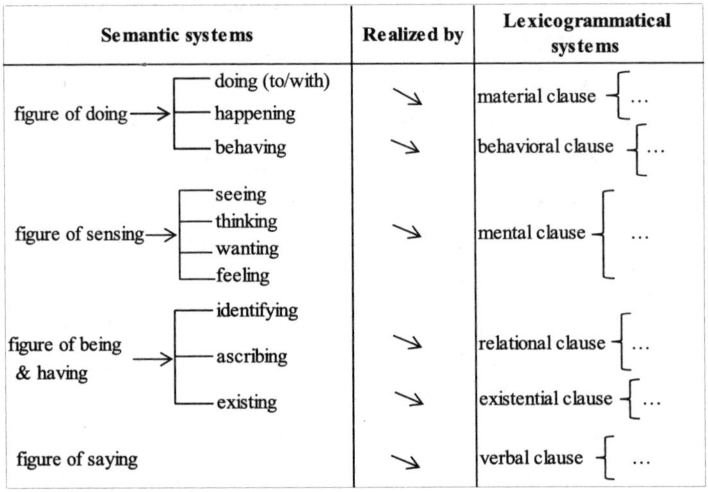

Figure 5-1   Semantic systems realized by lexicogrammatical systems

5.1.2 Configuration of Figure

According to Halliday & Matthiessen (2004), a figure is a representation of experience in the form of an organic configuration. In principle it consists of three components with different degree of nuclearity and peripherality: (i) a nuclear process, (ii) the participants of different kinds taking part in the process and (iii) circumstances of different kinds associated with the process.

The reason why a process stands at the center of the configuration is offered by Halliday (1998: 187-188). A language embodies, in its grammar, a theory of human experience. It is normally taken for granted that "the way things are is the way our grammar tells us that they are", and we do not take the effort to ponder over the way the grammar theorizes experience. If things stay unchanged to our perceptions, we do not think that we are experiencing them. In other words, experience does not begin until one becomes conscious of certain change taking place in the outer or inner environment. A process represents some kind of change, with the limiting case of unchanging, so the grammar construes experience around the category of process.

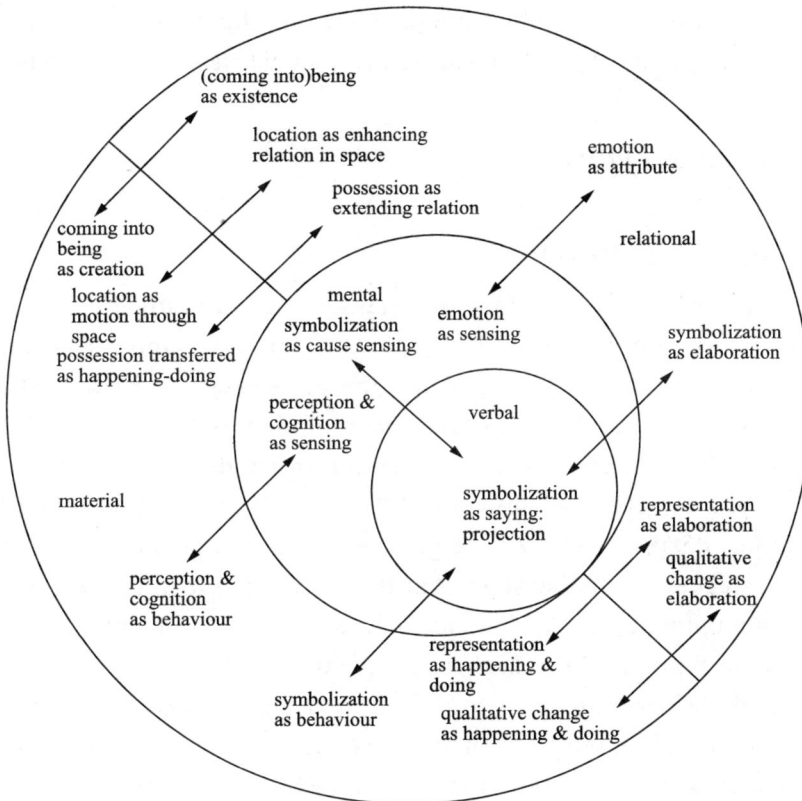

Figure 5-2   The topology of processes (Matthiessen, 1995: 223)

Participants are inherent in the process, and every clause has one to three participants. They are quite close to the center of the configuration because they are directly involved in the process, and the various configurations of participants are the bases for a typology of clauses in terms of process types. The configuration models of "process + participants" constitute the experiential center of the clause. In contrast, circumstantial elements are always optional augmentations of the clause rather than obligatory parts; they are more peripheral in the configuration and are not directly involved in the process. Circumstances specify the spatial or temporal location of the process, its extent in distance or duration, its cause, its manner of occurrence, and so on. The process, its participants, and its circumstances are grammatically represented as constituents in the transitivity structure of a clause.

In the following sections of this chapter, the statistical results of the process types in which metaphorical nominal groups occur and the participant roles that these metaphorical groups play will be presented and discussed respectively.

5.2 Process Types

5.2.1 Statistical Results

As introduced in Chapter 4, all the 900 clauses under investigation are firstly annotated by UAM Corpus Tool 3.3h in terms of process types. The number of clauses with different process types and the percentage each type takes up are presented in Table 5-1. There are 263 material clauses that take up 29.22% of the totality. Relational clauses are dominating in number; more than half of the clauses belong to relational process (490 in number; 54.44%). Among the relational clauses, detailed statistics are given according to the mode and type of the relational category. Statistics show that there are more identifying relational clauses (318 in number; 35.33%) than attributive ones (172 in number; 19.11%), and the intensive type is of the highest frequency (29.22%) among the three subtypes. Mental clauses take up 11.89%, and the cognitive type (72 in number; 8.00%) occurs more frequently than the other three subtypes. There are 18 existential processes and 20 verbal processes, and only 2 instances of behavioral process are found in the data.

Table 5-1   Statistical results for process types

Process type		Number of clause = 900	
		Number	Percent
Material		263	29.22%
Relational		490	54.44%
Mode	attributive	172	19.11%
	identifying	318	35.33%
Type	intensive	263	29.22%
	possessive	58	6.44%
	circumstantial	169	18.78%

(to be continued)

Process type		Number of clause = 900	
		Number	**Percent**
Mental		107	11.89%
Type	perceptive	25	2.78%
	cognitive	72	8.00%
	desiderative	8	0.89%
	emotive	2	0.22%
Existential		18	2.00%
Verbal		20	2.22%
Behavioral		2	0.22%

The comparison between process types in frequency is visualized in Figure 5-3. The statistical results give a general picture of the real environments where the metaphorical nominal groups enter as new participants. The preference for certain type of process is determined by the nature of certain register. The results in this study are basically consistent with discoveries made by Halliday (1988/2007h) that in the language of science, the favored clause types are relational, material and mental. In the following section, specific examples will be given for further illustration.

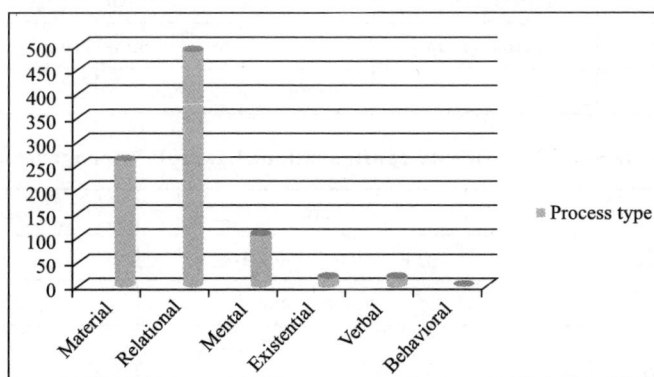

Figure 5-3　Comparison between process types

5.2.2　Analysis

In this section, each process type will be illustrated with one example. The transitivity structure of the clause embodying the metaphorical group and that of its congruent form will be analyzed for comparison.

(1) Material Process

In this example (see Table 5-2 and Table 5-3), the material clause *to increase the complexity of functionalizations* is an embedded Qualifier of the preceding Thing *desire*. Most often such kind of embedded clause is not taken into account in grammatical analysis, but it is included in this study because that is exactly where the metaphorical nominal group works. The nominal group with the quality-thing *complexity* as Thing functions as Goal of the material process. The congruent form of the group is an attributive relational clause where the Qualifier of Thing in the metaphorical form is unpacked into Carrier, and Thing corresponds to Attribute.

(5-1) There has also been a desire <C-4> [[to increase the **complexity** (3*1) of functionalizations]]. (Text 1)

(Congruent: functionalizations *are* **complex**.)

Table 5-2   Transitivity configuration: Example 1—material process (metaphorical)

a	desire	to increase	the	complexity	of functionalizations
Deictic	Thing	Qualifier (embedded)			
		Process: material	Goal		
		verbal group	nominal group		
			Deictic	Thing	Qualifier

Table 5-3   Transitivity configuration: Example 1 (congruent)

functionalizations	are	complex
Carrier	Relational: intensive	Attribute
nominal group	verbal group	nominal: *adj.*

(2) Relational Process

Relational processes are further classified according to the matrix of two modes and three types, so there are 6 subtypes altogether.

(a) Attributive mode & intensive type

In the following example (see Table 5-4 and Table 5-5), the nominal group *the abundance of the tholins [relative to the Cassini-observed species]* with quality-thing *abundance* as Thing serves as Carrier in the relational clause. The Qualifier of Thing is unpacked into two parts in the congruent form: the prepositional phrase led by *of* corresponds to the Carrier, and the embedded Qualifier is agnate to circumstance of the congruent clause.

(5-2) Therefore, we have also included primary nitriles and amines of lengths propyl-hexyl in our study, <C-1> although the **abundance** (1) of the tholins [relative to the Cassini-observed species] is uncertain. (Text 3)

(**Congruent**: the tholins *are* **abundant** relative to the Cassini-observed species.)

Table 5-4   Transitivity configuration: Example 2—attributive & intensive (metaphorical)

the	abundance	of the tholins relative to the Cassini-observed species	is	uncertain
Carrier			Process: intensive	Attribute
nominal group			verbal group	nominal: *adj.*
Deictic	Thing	Qualifier		

Table 5-5   Transitivity configuration: Example 2 (congruent)

the tholins	are	abundant	relative to the Cassini-observed species
Carrier	Process: intensive	Attribute	Circumstance
nominal group	verbal group	nominal: *adj.*	prepositional phrase

(b) Attributive mode & possessive type

The following example (see Table 5-6 and Table 5-7) is a possessive relational clause of the attributive mode: the process is realized by the typical verb *have*, and the metaphorical nominal group is the Possessed. In the congruent clause, the qualitative Attribute *flexible* is in the comparative form introduced by *as*.

(5-3) We believe that it is this structure that allows a cryogenic azotosome <C-6> *to have* the **flexibility** (2*5) of a room temperature lipid bilayer. (Text 3)

(**Congruent**: a cryogenic azotosome *is* **as flexible as** a room temperature lipid bilayer.)

Table 5-6　Transitivity configuration: Example 3—attributive &
possessive (metaphorical)

(a cryogenic azotosome)	have	the	flexibility	of a room temperature lipid bilayer
(Carrier: possessor)	Process: possession	Attribute: possessed		
		nominal group		
		Deictic	Thing	Qualifier

Table 5-7　Transitivity configuration: Example 3 (congruent)

a cryogenic azotosome	is	as flexible as a room temperature lipid bilayer
Carrier	Process: intensive	Attribute
nominal group	verbal group	adverbial group

(c) Attributive mode & circumstantial type

In this example (see Table 5-8 and Table 5-9), the circumstantial element is an attribute ascribed to the Thing *breadth*; the Attribute is realized by a prepositional phrase, and the circumstantial relation is expressed by the preposition *due to*.

(5-4) <C-1>The **breadth** (1) of applications *is largely due to* their highly tunable nature. (Text 1)

(**Congruent**: applications (of MOFs) *are* **broad**.)

Table 5-8　Transitivity configuration: Example 4—attributive & circumstantial
(metaphorical)

The	breadth	of applications	is	largely due to	their highly tunable nature
Carrier			Relational: intensive	Attribute: circumstantial	
nominal group			verbal group	prepositional phrase	
Deictic	Thing	Qualifier			

Table 5-9　Transitivity configuration: Example 4 (congruent)

applications (of MOFs)	are	broad
Carrier	Relational: intensive	Attribute
nominal group	verbal group	nominal: *adj.*

(d) Identifying mode & intensive type

Here the metaphorical entity functions as the Value of the identifying clause with *was* serving as the process (see Table 5-10 and Table 5-11).

(5-5) <C-4> The first property of azotosomes we investigated *was* their flexibility (2*3). (Text 3)

(**Congruent**: how **flexible** they *are*.)

Table 5-10   Transitivity configuration: Example 5—identifying & intensive (metaphorical)

The first property of azotosomes we investigated	was	their	flexibility
Token	Process: intensive	Value	
nominal group	verbal group	nominal group	
		Deictic	Thing

Table 5-11   Transitivity configuration: Example 5 (congruent)

(how) flexible	they	are
Attribute	Carrier	Process: intensive
nominal: *adj.*	nominal group	verbal group

(e) Identifying mode & possessive type

In this kind of relational clause, possession is encoded as a process realized by a possessive verb. The possessive verb is *include* in the following example[①] (see Table 5-12 and Table 5-13); the nominal group *the observation of differences...* functions as the Value (possessed). Here the quality-thing *differences* is not the Thing in the nominal group, but serves as Qualifier of Thing. That is the real case in which a metaphorical group works; a quality-thing does not always serve as Thing in the nominal group.

(5-6) <C-6> Early studies from this field ***include*** the observation of **differences** (6*1) in electrical activity of the human brain in sleep versus wake

---

① There is no consensus as to which mode some possessive verbs belong to. In Halliday & Matthiessen (2004: 246), verbs such as *contain*, *house*, *include*, *exclude* and *involve* are grouped under the category of Attributive, but in Halliday & Matthiessen (2014: 297), they are classified as Identifying. In this study, the second version is adopted.

cycles [[which was first recorded in 1928 via electroencephalographic (EEG) analysis]]. (Text 35)

(**Congruent**: the human brain in sleep cycles and the human brain in wake cycles *are* **different** in electrical activity.)

Table 5-12　Transitivity configuration: Example 6—identifying & possessive (metaphorical)

Early studies from this field	include	the	observation	of	differences	in electrical activity of the human brain in… analysis
Token: possessor	Process: possession	Value: possessed				
		nominal group				
		Deictic	Thing	Qualifier		
				prepositional phrase		
				Prep.	Thing	Qualifier

Table 5-13　Transitivity configuration: Example 6 (congruent)

the human brain in sleep cycles and the human brain in wake cycles	are	different
Carrier	Relational: intensive	Attribute
nominal group	verbal group	nominal: *adj.*

(f) Identifying mode & circumstantial type

In this example (see Table 5-14 and Table 5-15), the Process *affect* expresses the circumstantial feature of Cause. The metaphorical nominal group becomes the Value of the relational clause. This kind of relational clause is taken as the favorite grammatical pattern in modern scientific English: a sequence of two figures is reconstrued as a clause; each figure is construed as a nominal group, and the logical-semantic relation between them is construed as a verbal group (Halliday, 1998).

(5-7) <C-9> The chromosome representation or genome *can strongly affect* the optimization **efficiency** (6). (Text 1)

(**Congruent**: The chromosome representation or genome can strongly affect how **efficient** the optimization *is*.)

Table 5-14　Transitivity configuration: Example 7—identifying & circumstantial (metaphorical)

The chromosome representation or genome	can strongly affect	the	optimization	efficiency
Token	Process: circumstantial (Cause)	Value		
nominal group	verbal group	nominal group		
		Deictic	Classifier	Thing
		determiner	noun	noun

Table 5-15　Transitivity configuration: Example 7 (congruent)

The chromosome representation or genome	can strongly affect	how efficient	the optimization	is
Actor	Process: material	Goal		
nominal group	verbal group	nominalized clause		
		Attribute	Carrier	Relational: intensive
		nominal: *adj.*	nominal group	verbal group

(3) Mental Process

A mental clause construes a quantum of change in the flow of events taking place in a person's consciousness. Senser in the clause is characterized by consciousness. The metaphorical nominal group, most often, functions as the Phenomenon (see Table 5-16); it can be unpacked into the congruent Attribute of an intensive relational process (see Table 5-17). Mental clauses are further divided into perceptive, cognitive, desiderative and emotive types. The following example is an illustration of the perceptive type.

(5-8) <C-9> The high **stability** (7*2) of the subsurface structure against repeated sliding *can also be seen* from the measured grain size profiles along the depth with increasing sliding cycles. (Text 13)

(**Congruent**: the subsurface structure against repeated sliding *is* **highly stable.**)

Table 5-16 Transitivity configuration: Example 8—mental process (metaphorical)

The	high	stability	of the subsurface structure against repeated sliding	can also be seen	from the measured grain size profiles along the depth with increasing sliding cycles
Phenomenon				Process: perceptive	Circumstance
nominal group				verbal group	Prep. phrase
Deictic	Epithet	Thing	Qualifier		

Table 5-17 Transitivity configuration: Example 8 (congruent)

the subsurface structure against repeated sliding	is	highly stable
Carrier	Process: intensive	Attribute
nominal group	verbal group	nominal: *adj.*

(4) Existential Process

The existential clause is characterized by the lexical item *there* which is neither a participant nor a circumstance, because it has no representational function in the transitivity structure. In the following example (see Table 5-18), the metaphorical nominal group becomes the Existent, the only participant in the clause. In the congruent form, the Carrier needs to be recovered from the context (see Table 5-19).

(5-9) As pointed out by the authors, <C-6> *there could be* **difficulties** (4) in the MOFs with the created linkers because there is no guarantee that the SBUs will self-assemble to form a stable crystalline structure with the proposed structure. (Text 1)

(**Congruent**: (It) could be **difficult** (to synthesize) the MOFs with the created linkers.)

Table 5-18 Transitivity configuration: Example 9—existential process (metaphorical)

α there	could be	difficulties	in the MOFs with the created linkers	×β because…
	Process: existential	Existent	Circumstance	
	verbal group	noun	prepositional phrase	

Table 5-19　Transitivity configuration: Example 9 (congruent)

(It)	could be	difficult	(to synthesize) the MOFs with the created linkers
Carrier	Relational: intensive	Attribute	Carrier
nominal-	verbal group	nominal: *adj.*	-group

(5) Verbal Process

The following example (see Table 5-20) is a verbal process realized by the verb *report*; the nominal group *a luminescence based detection of blood bilirubin with... phase* is the Verbiage where the metaphorical quality-thing serves as an embedded Qualifier. While unpacking, the Thing and its post-modifier *a luminescence based detection of blood bilirubin* become the Carrier, and the metaphorically embedded Qualifier *high sensitivity* correspondingly becomes the Attribute *highly sensitive* (see Table 5-21).

(5-10) In addition, <C-5> we report a luminescence based detection of blood bilirubin with <u>high **sensitivity** (1*5) in the liquid phase</u>. (Text 16)

(**Congruent**: a luminescence based detection of blood bilirubin *is* <u>**highly sensitive**</u> in the liquid phase.)

Table 5-20　Transitivity configuration: Example 10—verbal process (metaphorical)

we	report	a luminescence based detection	of blood bilirubin with high sensitivity in the liquid phase
Sayer	Process: verbal	Verbiage	
		nominal group	
		Thing	Qualifier

Table 5-21　Transitivity configuration: Example 10 (congruent)

a luminescence based detection of blood bilirubin	is	highly sensitive	in the liquid phase
Carrier	Process: intensive	Attribute	Circumstance
nominal group	verb	nominal: *adj.*	Prep. phrase

(6) Behavioral Process

The following two examples are the only instances of behavioral processes in the data. Behavioral clauses seldom occur in scientific register.

(5-11a) <C-22> Next we *look* at <u>including viewpoint **invariance**</u> (11*4) in our 3D motion features (i.e. removing the final 3D rotation ambiguity, and making the descriptors completely consistent). (Text 32)

(5-11b) <C-18> The Toraja people *slept* together for <u>**warmth**</u> (15) and for a sense [of <u>**comfort**</u> (16), <u>**safety**</u> (14*2), and <u>**security**</u> (17)]—a practice which Hollan noted began at birth and continued throughout life. (Text 35)

5.3 *Functional Roles of Quality-Thing Nominalizations*

With regard to experiential meaning, the congruent form under investigation is a figure realized by an attributive relational clause, and the meaning it expresses is ascribing certain Attribute to certain Carrier. By means of metaphorization, the whole figure is condensed into an element that is realized by a nominal group with the quality-thing serving as its Thing. And then the metaphorical element gains access to a new figure by taking on a new functional role, and thus expresses new meanings in the new domain of experience. The modes of participant interaction that the semantic system of figures engenders are of particular importance.

5.3.1 Statistical Results: General Features

In order to investigate the way the metaphorical nominal groups play their functional roles in the new environments, three aspects (rank, status and participant type) are taken into consideration. The statistical results are listed in Table 5-22.

Table 5-22　Statistical results of the general features

Feature			Number of group = 996	
			Number	Percent
Rank		group	815	81.83%
	below group (embedded)	one layer	161	16.16%
		two layers	19	1.91%
		three layers	1	0.10%

(to be continued)

Feature				Number of group = 996	
				Number	Percent
Status	single			812	81.53%
	composite (in complex)	taxis	parataxis	175	17.57%
			hypotaxis	9	0.90%
		logico-semantic relation (expansion)	elaborating	9	0.90%
			extending	173	17.37%
			enhancing	2	0.20%
Type	direct participant			826	82.93%
	indirect participant (in circumstance)			170	17.07%

In terms of rank, like ordinary nominal groups, the majority of these metaphorical nominal groups (815 out of 996) remain at the group rank, while the other 181 ones are further rankshifted to be Qualifiers within another nominal group, and some are even embedded more than once. In the following example, the metaphorical nominal group *sound unpleasantness* with quality-thing realized by the noun *unpleasantness* as Thing is embedded as Qualifier of Thing *evaluation* in the nominal group *the stronger evaluation of sound unpleasantness*. Therefore, the original Attribute *unpleasant* in the congruent form *how unpleasant a sound is* is changed into Qualifier of Token in this relational clause of the identifying mode and circumstantial type.

(5-12) <C-35> NS *has been associated with* the stronger **evaluation** of sound **unpleasantness** (18), and self-reported hearing disabilities. (Text 24)

The following example is an existential clause where the Existent is realized by a nominal group with two embedded Qualifiers marked by prepositions *for* and *of*: *Earth's value* serves as Qualifier of *explanation*, and O_2 *atmospheric abundance* is Qualifier of *Earth's value*; therefore, the congruent Attribute *abundant* in O_2 *is atmospherically abundant* is changed to be Qualifier of Qualifier in the nominal group functioning as Existent.

(5-13) <C-13> *There is* no precise explanation [for Earth's value [of O_2 atmospheric **abundance** (7*2)]]. (Text 6)

The next example illustrates how a nominal group with an adjectival nominalization as Thing is embedded three times to be Qualifier of Qualifier of Qualifier. The three Qualifiers are marked by prepositions *of*, *from* and *with* respectively. The metaphorical nominal group functions as Qualifier of Qualifier of Qualifier in Verbiage.

(5-14) <C-24> To our knowledge, sustainable development [of high performance Fe-N-C catalysts and iron oxide/carbon hybrid materials [from economical metal-gelated gelatin bio-molecule [with **controllability** (11) of structure and component]]] *has never been reported.* (Text 5)

A metaphorical nominal group is not different from an ordinary one also in that it can take on a role in a clausal configuration either singly or as part of a group complex by constituting certain degree of interdependency and logico-semantic relation of expansion with some other nominal groups. The statistical results show that 81.53% of the metaphorical nominal groups stand alone in assuming functional roles, while the others occur in complexes. The following two examples are instances of interdependency. In the first example, *reproducibility* and *reliability* are of equal status and thus stand in a paratactic relation; whereas in the second example, *physical activity* and *physical fitness* are linked by *as well as*, indicating a hypotactic relation.

(5-15a) The results of these measurements (Fig. 4, C and D, and figs. S11 and S12) show similar bimodal distributions and temperature dependences to those obtained in Me_2SO, <C-6> [[*demonstrating* the **reproducibility** (2*2) and **reliability** (6*1) of the SMJ platform as well as validating the relationship between the low and high states and SMJ configurations]]. (Text 11)

(5-15b) This putative association is based on evidence <C-2> [[that physical activity as well as physical **fitness** (1*2) *are related to* different types of changes in the brain relevant for cognitive function and learning]]. (Text 22)

The configurational roles that these metaphorical nominal groups take on are what should be investigated thoroughly. Although Process is the central element in a figure, "it is the nature of the participants involved in the process that determines the different process types" (Halliday & Matthiessen, 1999: 467). And in contrast to the single role of process, participants are plurifunctional and they are construed as being experientially more complex; it is characteristic of things that they can take on a variety of roles in figures of all kinds. Therefore, there are "the direct participant roles of Actor, Goal, Senser, Phenomenon, and so on, and also the indirect participant roles within circumstances such as Location and Cause" (Halliday & Matthiessen, 1999: 178). Among the 996 metaphorical nominal groups in this study, 826 (82.93%) of them take on the direct participant roles, while 170 (17.07%) of them occur in circumstances as indirect participants. The following section will focus on the various configurational roles that played by these metaphorical nominal groups.

5.3.2   Statistical Results: Direct Participants

The functional roles of direct participants that these metaphorical elements may assume and the number of each type are summarized in Table 5-23 and will be exemplified in detail.

Table 5-23   Statistics for direct participants

Process type		Functional role	Number of group =996	
			Number	Percent
Material process		Actor	37	3.71%
		Goal	197	19.78%
Relational process	Attributive	Carrier	51	5.12%
		Attribute	85	8.53%
		Attributor	3	0.30%
	Identifying	Token	86	8.63%
		Value	234	23.49%
		Assigner	0	0.00%
Mental process		Senser	1	0.10%
		Phenomenon	96	9.64%
Existential process		Existent	17	1.71%
Verbal process		Sayer	4	0.40%
		Verbiage	15	1.51%
Behavioral process		Behaver	0	0.00%
		Behaviour	0	0.00%

Since participant functions are critical to the distinction between process types, the statistical results are presented according to the types of process where the various participants work. There are only two instances of behavioral clause (see Table 5-1) in this study, and the metaphorical elements do not serve as direct participants (Behaver or Behaviour) in them.

(1) In material process

In material process, the metaphorical nominal groups can take on the roles of Actor and Goal. But statistics show that these two roles are not equally distributed; 197 (19.78%) metaphorical groups realize the functional role of Goal, while only 37 (3.71%) metaphorical groups realize the functional role of Actor. "Material clauses are clauses of doing and happening: a material clause construes a quantum of change in the flow of events as taking place through some input of energy" (Halliday & Matthiessen, 2014: 224). Material clauses convey the notion that some entity "does" something that may be directed at some other entity. The inherent Actor represents the source of the energy that brings about the change; it is the one that fulfills the deed. There are both animate and inanimate Actors. The Goal refers to the goal of impact; it is the participant that is construed as being impacted by the Actor's performance of the process. In the following example (5-16a), the congruent figure realized by the attributive relational clause *these two loops are flexible* is metaphorized into an element realized by the nominal group *the flexibility of these two loops* with the noun *flexibility* as Thing. The metaphorical element then, as the Actor, participates in a new receptive (passive) process *is ... enhanced*, and the Goal *binding of DNA by hUNG* is also a type of nominalization involving a process-thing. Therefore, grammatical metaphor combines the two originally separate clauses *hUNG binds DNA* and *these two loops are flexible* into one process by changing them into participants. In the second example (5-16b), the congruent clause *a coating surface around the mutant phages is present* is metaphorized into the nominal group *the presence of a coating surface around the mutant phages* realizing the Goal in a new material process.

(5-16a) <C-18> Binding of DNA by hUNG *is likely enhanced* by <u>the **flexibility** (10) of these two loops</u> since PC1 represented a motion orthogonal to the principle axis of bound DNA, and it is possible to suggest that PC1 described a motion resembling L272 insertion into bound DNA. (Text 33)

(**Congruent**: these two loops <u>are flexible</u>.)

(5-16b) The wild-type T7 and mutant T7::PhoE phages were inspected by transmission electron microscopy (TEM) in an attempt <C-18> [[*to visualize* the **presence** (7*2) of a coating surface around the mutant phages]]. (Text 20)

(**Congruent**: a coating surface around the mutant phages is present.)

(2) In relational process

Relational clauses are clauses of being, construing a change as unfolding inertly without an input of energy. In relational clauses, there are two parts to constitute the relation of being: something is said to be something else. A relationship of being is set up between two separate entities, so that there are two inherent participants. Relational clauses serve to characterize and to identify, corresponding to the two distinct modes of being: attributive and identifying. These two modes intersect three main types of relation (intensive, possessive and circumstantial) to define six categories of relational clauses. Halliday & Matthiessen (1999, 2004, 2014) and Davidse (1992, 1996) adopt an instantiation-realization approach to intensive relational clauses. "Attributive processes express a type of 'being' which has to be elaborated by an inherently relational expression" (Davidse, 1992: 102). Attributive clauses encode a relation of generalization. The Carrier designates an entity that is always more specific, and the Attribute designates a more general entity. However, identifying clauses construe a relation of realization; the two halves in an identifying clause are on a different level of abstraction: one "is, as it were, the realization of the other" (Halliday, 1967: 228).

As for the attributive mode, the two inherent functional roles are Carrier and Attribute, and there might be an optional participant termed as Attributor. The statistics show that 51(5.12%) metaphorical nominal groups take on the role of Carrier, 85 (8.53%) metaphorical groups play the role of Attribute, and only 3 (0.30%) of such groups take on the configurational role of Attributor. Examples will be given for each type. In the following example (5-17), the congruent figure realized by the relational clause *how relevant PLD is in NAFLD* is metaphorized to be an element realized by the nominal group *the relevance of PLD1 in NAFLD*. The metaphorical element enters an intensive type of relational clause whereby the phase of the process of attribution is marked as durative (*remain*). The metaphorical element becomes Carrier of the new process and is endowed with the new Attribute *unclear*. The Carrier and the Attribute are of the same order in the material rather than semiotic domain of attribution.

(5-17) Although PLD has known roles in cancer and inflammation, <C-8> the **relevance** (6*2) of PLD1 in NAFLD *remains* unclear. We provide the first evidence that PLD1 is a critical determinant of NAFLD. (Text 21)

(**Congruent**: how relevant PLD is in NAFLD.)

There seems to be no consensus as to the status of the Attribute as a participant. Halliday & Matthiessen (1999, 2014) take it as a participant, though not a very typical one. But some scholars hold the idea that the Attribute is not a participant, and Attributive clauses are taken as fully middle one-participant structures. Davidse (1992: 101) states that "the Attribute, whether realized by adjective, prepositional phrase, 'bare' noun or nominal group, is not a participant... In contemporary English, a certain degree of participanthood is a necessary corollary of Subjecthood." Langacker (2004) also argues that the Attribute does not represent a thing, but an inherently relational notion. In this study, it is acknowledged that the Attribute is a participant, because both the Carrier and the Attribute are meanings internal to the semantic system engendered by the figure of being. In the following three examples, the elements realized by the metaphorical nominal groups take on the role of Attribute of different types respectively: entity as Attribute in the intensive clause, circumstance as Attribute in the circumstantial clause and the possessed as Attribute in the possessive clause.

(5-18a) Next, we compared PLD expression levels between the liver of high-fat diet (HFD)-fed mice with hepatic steatosis and mice fed regular chow (RC) without hepatic steatosis <C-7> *to validate* the **relevance** (6*1) of PLD in NAFLD. (Text 21)

(**Congruent**: PLD is relevant in NAFLD.)

(5-18b) <C-14> *Of* particular **importance** (6) *will be* simulations with prognostic dust emissions, allowing inclusion of dust's emission, transport, deposition, and radiative impacts in a self-consistent framework. (Text 10)

(**Congruent**: simulations with prognostic dust emission show abundant will be important.)

(5-18c) We assessed the quality of included RCTs using the criteria shaped by the Cochrane Handbook and found <C-10> [[these studies *had* a very good clinical **homogeneity** (7*2)]]. (Text 15)

(**Congruent**: these studies are very clinically homogeneous.)

The intensive relational clauses have the option of assignment: a third participant that represents the entity assigning the relationship of attribution or identity may get involved in the clausal configuration. In terms of transitive analysis, this additional function is the Attributor in the case of attributive clauses and the Assigner in the case of identifying clauses. But from the ergative point of view, the general term Agent is used to indicate an added feature of agency without distinguishing one mode of relational clause from the other. In this study, the transitive approach is adopted. The following examples are the only three instances whereby the metaphorical element enters a new intensive relational clause as the Attributor, and the process is realized by the causative verb *enable* or *make*.

(5-19a) <C-33> These results also underline [[that the **versatility** (18) of curli fibers enables indiscriminate adhesion to surfaces]], <C-34> which we *attribute here to* the chemical **diversity** (19*1) in the peptide sequence of CsgA subunits. (Text 9)

(**Congruent**: curli fibers are versatile.)

(5-19b) Our findings illustrate <C-22> [[that molecular **mobility** (13*2) *enables* stronger adhesion, specifically through the translation of the subunit across the surface and the local motion of the side chains]]. (Text 9)

(**Congruent**: molecular is mobile.)

(5-19c) <C-14> High **frequency** (6*2) of occurrence of each deviant *makes* it possible to measure discrimination abilities in a short time, as compared to classical oddball paradigms. (Text 24)

(**Congruent**: occurrence of each deviant is highly frequent.)

In the identifying mode of relational clauses, one entity is used to identify the other. The inherent participants are Token and Value, and the meanings construed by them are inherently symbolic ones. Token and Value can identify each other, but they are stratally distinct, with Token being the lower expression and Value the higher content. "The identity either decodes the Token by reference to the Value or it encodes the Value by reference to the Token" (Halliday & Matthiessen, 2014: 280). This directionality determines the voice of the clause (operative or receptive): in the clause of the operative voice, the Subject is also the Token; in the clause of the receptive voice, the Subject is always the Value.

Statistics in this study show that 86 (8.63%) of the metaphorical nominal groups take on the functional role of Token, while 234 (23.49%) of the metaphorical nominal groups assume the role of Value. This obvious numerical advantage of Value over Token is due to the frequent use of receptive voice in the language of science. Another discovery is that in the collected data, no metaphorical nominal groups take on the role of Assigner. In the register of science, what is concerned is to constitute the objective relationship of identity between two entities, so that the entity assigning the relationship is of less or even no importance.

The following examples are instances where metaphorical nominal groups take on the role of Token in various types of identifying clauses. The first example is an intensive identifying clause in which the process is realized by the typical verb *be*. The congruent attributive relational clause *POLD3 depletion and POLD1 depletion are different* is metaphorized to be a nominal group *the difference between them*, and then plays the functional role of Token in the new process. The next three examples are relational clauses of the circumstantial type with the "favorite grammatical pattern" (Halliday, 1998: 193): the metaphorical nominal group realizes the functional role of Token and is connected with Value by the process realized by *caused, were associated with* or *lead to*.

(5-20a) POLD3 depletion induced specifically more anaphase bridges than POLD1 depletion, <C-28> while the **difference** (26*1) between them *was* the opposite for lagging chromosomes, POLD1 depletion being associated with a slightly higher amount of lagging chromosomes. (Text 23)

(**Congruent**: POLD3 depletion and POLD1 depletion are different.)

(5-20b) Malignant pleural effusion (MPE) is one of the common complications of lung cancer, <C-1> which mainly *caused* by the **hyperpermeability** (1) of microvascular tissue or invasion of cancer cells into lymphatic vessels. (Text 15)

(**Congruent**: microvascular tissue is hyperpermeable.)

(5-20c) However, the studies showed <C-3> [[that these particles *were associated with* an **abundance** (3*1) of particles that are not usually associated with firearm discharge]]. (Text 27)

(**Congruent**: particles that are not usually associated with firearm discharge are abundant.)

(5-20d) <C-15> The **correctness** (8*2) of Theorem 1, along with the existence of such a net and the fact that each S-approximation of At (step 2 of Algorithm 1) takes $\Theta(1/\delta 2)$, *lead* directly to the following result [on the **accuracy** (9) and **complexity** (10) of Algorithm 1]. (Text 31)

(**Congruent**: Theorem 1 is correct.)

The following three examples involve identifying clauses of the intensive, circumstantial and possessive types respectively. The metaphorical nominal group in each clause assumes the functional role of Value. In the first example, the process is realized by the verb *show*, and thus the Value *clear similarity... Barbados* is a demonstration of the Token *the data*. In the second example, the process realized by *stems from* indicates a causal relationship between the Token *this phenomenon* and the Value *the mechanical instability of the thin nanostructured layer*. In the third example, the process *lacked* indicates a relationship of possession, with the possessed *specificity* as Value.

(5-21a) The data agree well with previously published data from Bahamas soil sand and <C-16> *show* clear **similarity** (8*1) with the composition of African dust collected in Barbados. (Text 10)

(**Congruent**: Bahamas soil sand is similar to the composition of African dust collected in Barbados.)

(5-21b) <C-6> This phenomenon also *stems from* the mechanical **instability** (6*1) of the thin nanostructured layer and its tendency to form delaminating tribo-layers under dry sliding, which is analogous to that in bulk NG metals. (Text 13)

(**Congruent**: the thin nanostructured layer is mechanically instable.)

(5-21c) <C-5> Despite the **clarity** (4) of the findings in the early studies, the fact [that brake pads can produce some particles that resemble GSR] was on occasion, cited as evidence [[that was unreliable, <C-6> *lacked* **specificity** (5), or was prone to false positives]]. (Text 27)

(**Congruent**: the evidence / the fact [that brake pads can produce some particles that resemble GSR] is not specific.)

(3) In mental process

Mental clauses realize figures of sensing, construing a quantum of change in the flow of events taking place in our consciousness. The process is construed either as flowing in a person's consciousness or as impinging on it. The participants involved in mental process are the Senser and the Phenomenon. The former is construed as a conscious being devoted to inert conscious processing; the latter is what enters into the consciousness of the Senser or is brought into being by the conscious processing of the Senser. Statistics in Table 5-23 show that only one metaphorical nominal group takes on the role of Senser in the new environment, while 96 (9.64%) metaphorical groups enter the new mental process as the Phenomenon. The vast majority of the abstract entities realized by the metaphorical nominal groups are devoid of consciousness, so that they are not in the position of being the Senser.

The following example is a mental clause of desideration. The Senser is *subjects with high NS*, conscious beings who are under study and are highly sensitive to noise. The Senser's wanting is shown by the process *prefer*, and what is preferred is the abstract entity *lower intensities of stimulus presentation* transferred from the congruent relational clause *stimulus presentation is less intense*.

(5-22) If we suppose, however, <C-44> [[that subjects with high NS *could prefer* lower **intensities** (28) of stimulus presentation that would more likely influence the MMN response to the intensity deviant than the MMN in general]]. (Text 24)

(**Congruent**: stimulus presentation is less intense.)

Here comes another example: a mental clause of cognition. Although the Senser *investigations of postmortem anatomy* is not a conscious being, it is in fact a metaphorical form of the congruent clause *we/researchers have investigated postmortem anatomy* and the conscious being is omitted in the metaphorical nominal form. The Phenomenon is realized by the nominal group *the flexibility of the mammalian vocal tract* which is transferred from the congruent clause *the mammalian vocal tract is flexible*.

(5-23) More recent research suggests <C-2> [[that investigations of postmortem anatomy drastically *underestimate* the **flexibility** (2*1) of the mammalian vocal tract]]. (Text 12)

(**Congruent**: the mammalian vocal tract is flexible.)

(4) In existential process

Existential clauses represent that something exists or happens, and they are not very common in the data. Only 18 (2.00%) of all of the 900 clauses involved in this study belong to the existential type (see Table 5-1). This statistical result is consistent with the discovery by Halliday & Matthiessen (2014). Despite the small number of existential clauses, they contribute, textually in particular, to the unfolding of various kinds of texts. *There* has no representational function in the transitivity structure of the clause; it works to indicate the feature of existence. The only participant is the Existent: the entity or event that is being said to exist. In this study, 17 (1.71%) of the metaphorical nominal groups play the role of Existent (see Table 5-23). As indicated by the following example, when the quality construed as Attribute is changed into an entity/thing, the whole configuration where they stay is changed accordingly. For example (5-24), as the Attribute realized by the adjective *different* is turned into the Thing realized by the noun *difference* in a nominal group, the Carrier *Pld1+/+ mice and Pld1-/- mice* in the congruent clause can be either omitted or take on new roles—it can be construed either as a circumstance in the new existential clause or Qualifier of Thing in the metaphorical nominal group.

(5-24) <C-9> *There were* <u>no **differences**</u> (7*1) in food intake and energy expenditure, as measured by CLAMS (Fig. 2b). Additionally, <C-10> *there was* <u>no **difference**</u> (8*1) in (body weight, fat, and muscle) between *Pld1+/+* mice and *Pld1-/-* mice. (Text 21)

(**Congruent**: *Pld1+/+* mice and *Pld1-/-* mice <u>were not different</u> in food intake and energy expenditure / body composition.)

In addition to the most typical expression *there be*, some other verbs can also function as Process in existential clauses. In this study, the verb *exist* is found in four instances. In the following example, the metaphorical entity realized by the noun *heterogeneity* functions as the Existent.

(5-25) We utilized the chi-square test and I2 value to determine <C-23> [whether <u>the **heterogeneity**</u> (7*3) *existed* in included studies]. <C-24> If <u>no **heterogeneity**</u> (7*4) *existed*, the method of fixed effects model was adopted, or using the random effects model. (Text 15)

(**Congruent**: whether the included studies <u>are heterogeneous</u>.)

(5) In verbal process

Verbal clauses are clauses of saying. Saying should be interpreted in a broad sense, covering any kind of symbolic exchange of meaning. Verbal processes play an important role in the creation of narratives, and they seldom occur in the register of science. The most typical participants in verbal clauses are the Sayer and the Verbiage (what is said). Statistics (see Table 5-23) in this study show that only 4 (0.40%) of the metaphorical nominal groups under concern play the role of Sayer, and 15 (1.51%) groups assume the role of Verbiage.

In the following two examples, the processes are realized by verbal groups *are not explained* and *may dictate*; they represent saying in a symbolic sense. The two metaphorical groups *the heterogeneity of the educational system or exercise opportunities* and *social seniority* realize the functional role of Sayer.

(5-26a) Thus, <C-4> the Finnish results *are not explained* by the **heterogeneity** (2*2) of the educational system or exercise opportunities. (Text 22)

(**Congruent**: the educational system or exercise opportunities are heterogeneous.)

(5-26b) <C-20> While social **seniority** (18*1) *may dictate* who sleeps in either position, Musharbash noted <C-21> [[that **seniority** (18*2) *does not equal* age]]. (Text 35)

(**Congruent**: (…who) is socially senior.)

In example (5-27), the metaphorical element realized by the nominal group *heterogeneity with respect to the cellular properties* converted from the congruent figure serves as the Verbiage.

(5-27) <C-9> *To account for* **heterogeneity** (3*1) with respect to the cellular properties, the single particle description is transformed to a structured population balance model. (Text 29)

(**Congruent**: the cellular properties are heterogeneous.)

5.3.3 Statistical Results: Indirect Participants

In terms of the degree of nuclearity or peripherality, circumstances are peripheral in the transitivity structure of a clause, because unlike participants directly involved in the process, circumstances are associated with or attendant on the process. Circumstances are typically expressed by adverbial groups or prepositional groups, but adverbial groups are mostly confined to one type of circumstance (Manner), so prepositional ones are the most typical realizations. A prepositional phrase has a nominal group inside as a constituent, and this nominal group is no different from a nominal group that serves directly as a participant in a clause. In principle, any nominal group can occur in both contexts, and thus the dividing line between participants and circumstances is often blurred. In the contrast we have made between direct and indirect participants, an indirect participant refers to "the status of a nominal group that is inside a prepositional phrase" (Halliday & Matthiessen, 2014: 312). What is concerned here, in this study, is exactly the nominal group inside the prepositional phrase. The metaphorical nominal groups transferred from the congruent attributive relational clauses can also get obliquely involved in a new process, although only 17.07% of the metaphorical nominal groups in the data occur in circumstances.

Circumstances can be interpreted in relation to the process types as a whole, that is, in the context of the overall interpretation of transitivity as the grammar of experience. In this way the semantic space that is constructed by the circumstantial elements can be clarified. A circumstance is itself a process that has become dependent on another process; it works as an augmentation of the process configuration rather than standing on its own. "Circumstances augment the configuration of process plus participants involved in it through the logico-semantic relations of projection and expansion" (Matthiessen et al., 2016: 79), and they are classified into various types: Location, Extent, Cause, Manner, Accompaniment, Role, Angle and Matter. Circumstantial elements can be seen as derivatives from relational or verbal processes as explicated by the following examples of proportionality quoted from Halliday & Matthiessen (2014: 312, 314).

Example (1): *Jack was building a house…*

Extent (duration)—*throughout the year:* relational (circumstantial)—*it was during*::

Location (place)—*near the river:* relational (circumstantial)—*it was at*::

Manner (means)—*out of brick:* relational (circumstantial)—*it was by*::

Cause (purpose)—*for his retirement:* relational (circumstantial)—*it was for*::

Contingency (concession)—*despite his illness:* relational (circumstantial)—*although he was ill*::

Accompaniment (comitation)—*with his daughter:* relational (possessive)—*he had*::

Role (guise)—*as a vacation home:* relational (intensive)—*it was*

129

Example (2): *Jack told his friends…*

Matter—*about the sale:* verbal (Verbiage)—*said…*

Angle (source)—*according to Jack:* verbal (Verbiage)—*… said*

These examples clearly show the relation of horizontal agnation and that of vertical enation. The circumstantial elements are agnate to relational and verbal processes; they realize the same core meaning, but they are not totally synonymous in that the experience has been construed in different ways by the grammar, which has extended the semantic space. In this sense, it can be said that circumstantial elements and the above-mentioned clauses are metaphorical variants to each other.

As far as the present discussion is concerned, circumstance is interpreted as an additional minor process that is parasitic on the major process. Meanwhile it embodies some features of a relational or verbal process, so it introduces an extra entity as an indirect participant in the clause. What is concerned here is the indirect participant that is realized by the metaphorical nominal group.

Table 5-24 and Figure 5-4 show the specific types of circumstances where the metaphorical elements dwell, as well as the number and percentage of each type. The metaphorical elements may occur in almost all of the circumstantial types with the exception of Angle. Cause and Accompaniment are the two with the highest number and percentage: 48 (4.82%) and 35 (3.51%) respectively. Each type will be illustrated with examples.

Table 5-24 Statistics for indirect participants

Circumstance type	Number of group=996	
	Number	Percent
Extent	2	0.20%
Location	20	2.01%
Manner	15	1.51%
Cause	48	4.82%
Contingency	24	2.41%
Accompaniment	35	3.51%
Role	3	0.30%
Matter	23	2.31%
Angle	0	0.00%

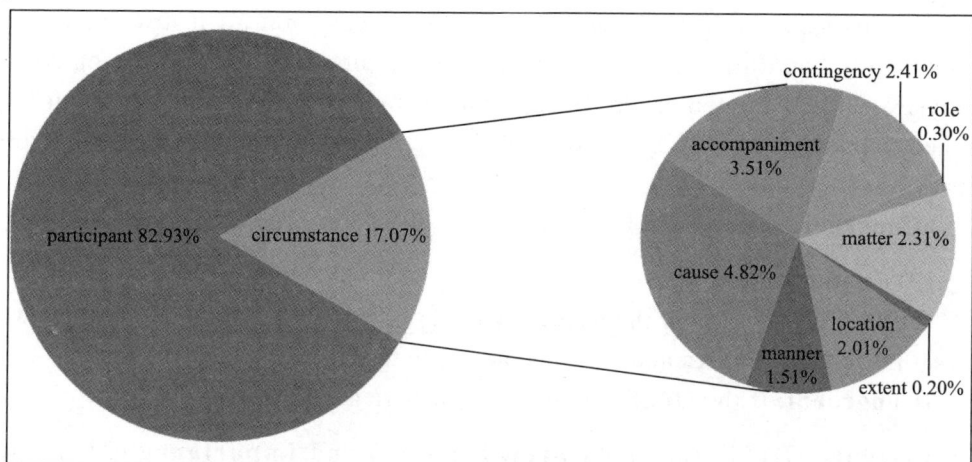

Figure 5-4　Proportions of circumstances

In the following examples, both the metaphorical nominal groups and the prepositions are underlined. These instances can elucidate the complicated environments where grammatical metaphor happens. On the one hand, the metaphorical nominal group transferred from the congruent attributive relational clause is downward rankshifted, and constitutes a prepositional phrase with a preposition. This nominal group is itself an obliquely involved participant. On the other hand, the dependent clause in the congruent clause complex is metaphorized into an element, and consequently the original clause complex is turned into a clause. For instance, in the first example of the circumstantial type of Cause, the prepositional phrase *because of the nonlinearity of the relationship* serves as the circumstance where the metaphorical nominal group is embedded; this phrase is transferred from the original subordinate clause *because the relationship is nonlinear* in a clause complex. Therefore, in this sense, rankshifting occurs twice in these cases, which confirms once again the lowering of grammatical status and the changing of grammatical class in ideational grammatical metaphor.

(1) Cause

(5-28a) Thus, similar outcomes will manifest through therapeutically decreasing AM depletion or decreasing bacterial loads, <C-19> however the therapeutic requirement *may change* because of the **nonlinearity** (8*2) of the relationship. (Text 25)

(**Congruent**: because the relationship is nonlinear.)

(5-28b) <C-4> <u>For purposes of **safety**</u> (4) or cost, not all instruments used in this study *could be used* with radiological samples, and for that reason some analyses were conducted on the Background sample to provide insight about the biogeochemistry that may have occurred in the nearby radionuclide-contaminant area. (Text 26)

(**Congruent**: in order to <u>be safe</u>.)

(2) Contingency

(5-29a) <C-18> <u>Given the **accuracy**</u> (8*1) <u>of the OPLS binding energies</u>, we *expect* these values of Ka and ΔE to be accurate to within 20%. (Text 3)

(**Congruent**: if the OPLS binding energies <u>are accurate</u>.)

(5-29b) <C-1> <u>Despite its **prevalence**</u> (1) and **importance** (2*1), the underlying mechanisms of NAFLD induction *are poorly characterized*. (Text 21)

(**Congruent**: although NAFLD induction <u>is prevalent and important</u>.)

(3) Accompaniment

(5-30) <C-2> <u>Besides **nonuniformity**</u> (1*2) <u>in the process conditions</u>, unsynchronized cell cycles, age distributions (Muller et al., 2010), stochastic effects on the gene expression level and bistable behaviour on the single cell level (Chickarmane et al., 2006; Herberg & Roeder, 2015; Eissing et al., 2004) *play a major role* in the formation of these variances. (Text 29)

(**Congruent**: cells <u>are nonuniform</u>.)

(4) Extent

(5-31) Similarly, viral antigen was detected in small numbers of mononuclear cells in the red pulp of the spleen at 3 days post-infection with HA-MARV, <C-10> and by day 6 post-infection viral antigen *was concentrated* in cells at the marginal zone and <u>throughout the **entirety**</u> (8) <u>of the red pulp</u> (Fig. 3f). (Text 14)

(**Congruent**: viral antigen <u>was all over</u> the red pulp.)

(5) Location

(5-32) <C-2> In addition, Pol 6 *has a role* in DNA double-strand break (DSB) repair via homologous recombination (HR), in DNA repair synthesis as the major gap-filling polymerase, and <u>in common fragile site **instability**</u> (2). (Text 23)

(**Congruent**: fragile site <u>is commonly instable</u>.)

(6) Manner

(5-33) We also explicitly show <C-3> [[how distances in parameter space and distances in image space *are related* through the **smoothness** (3*2) of the template]]. (Text 31)

(**Congruent**: the template is smooth.)

(7) Role

(5-34) However, a clear increase in interorigin distance was observed, <C-15> which *may indicate* a reduction in the overall firing of replication origins, possibly as a consequence of lower **availability** (15) of the Pol 6 subunits and therefore a lower ability to assemble at new RFs. (Text 23)

(**Congruent**: because the Pol 6 subunits are less available.)

(8) Matter

(5-35) In contrast, hamsters inoculated with WT-MARV developed only minimal to mild hepatic necrosis (Fig. 4a, white arrowheads) with neutrophilic infiltration (Fig. 4a, red arrows) by day 6, <C-11> and these lesions *did not* significantly *increase* in **severity** (9*1) at later time points (Supplementary Fig. 4a). (Text 14)

(**Congruent**: these lesions were not more severe.)

5.4　*Summary*

On the basis of the self-designed schemes introduced in Chapter 4, in this chapter, transitivity analyses are conducted as to the process types of the 900 metaphorical clauses and the functional roles that the 996 metaphorical nominal groups take on. When a figure of being realized by an attributive relational clause is metaphorized into an element realized by a nominal group, it may further enter a new figure as either a direct participant or an indirect participant.

Figure 5-5 shows the transference from the congruent mode to the metaphorical mode. In this figure, the minus "-" means that the metaphorical groups do not play certain kind of role, and the plus "+" stand for the presence of the role. In accordance with the results of the previous studies, there are a large number of relational and material processes in the language of science.

Figure 5-6 provides a systemic presentation of the statistics on the functional roles played by the metaphorical groups in this study. Functional analysis is, in effect, an integration of form and meaning; differences in meaning are manifested by different functional elements. Therefore, only if there are discrepancies in functional elements, there are differences in meaning. The analytical results in this chapter will serve as evidence for the discussion on the semantic change in grammatical metaphor in the following chapters.

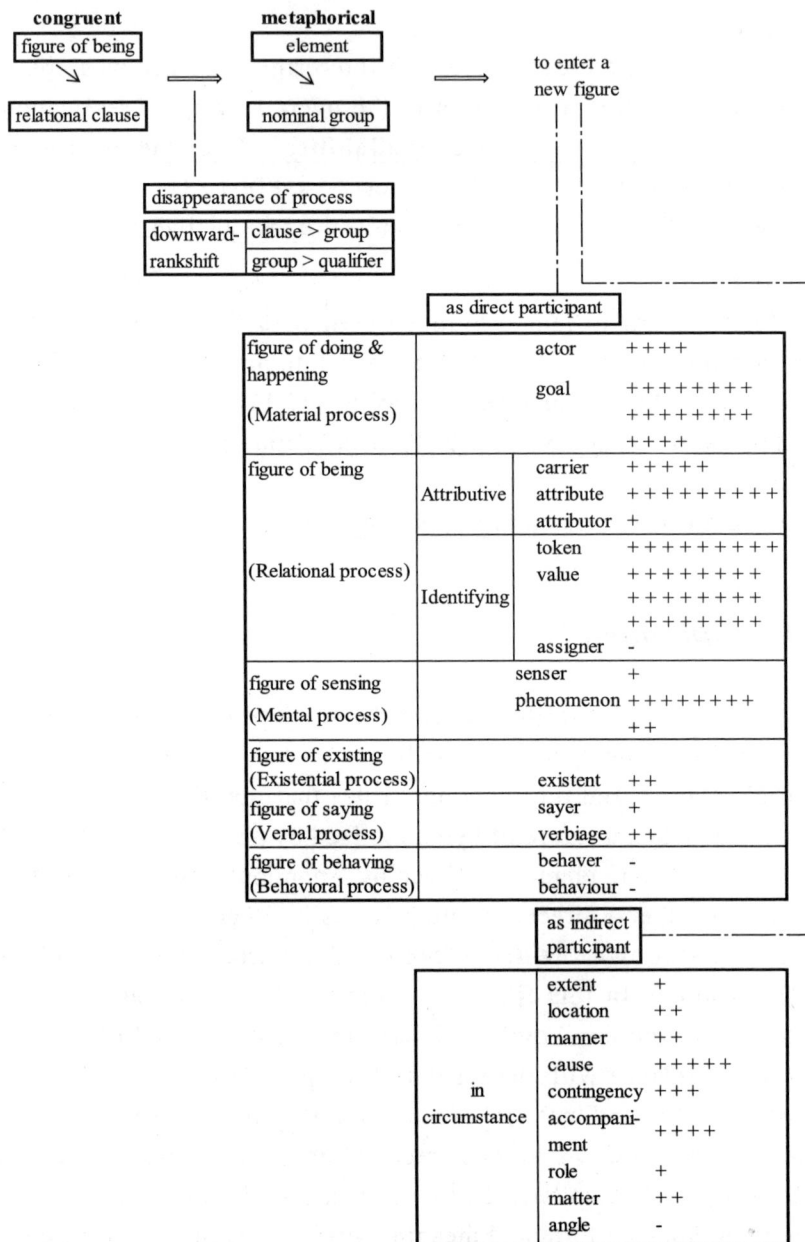

congruent
figure of being → relational clause

metaphorical
element → nominal group

to enter a new figure

disappearance of process

downward-rankshift | clause > group
| group > qualifier

as direct participant

figure of doing & happening (Material process)		actor	+ + +
		goal	+ + + + + + + + + + + + + + + + + +
figure of being (Relational process)	Attributive	carrier	+ + + + +
		attribute	+ + + + + + + + +
		attributor	+
	Identifying	token	+ +
		value	
		assigner	-
figure of sensing (Mental process)		senser	+
		phenomenon	+ + + + + + + + +
figure of existing (Existential process)		existent	+ +
figure of saying (Verbal process)		sayer	+
		verbiage	+ +
figure of behaving (Behavioral process)		behaver	-
		behaviour	-

as indirect participant

in circumstance	extent	+
	location	+ +
	manner	+ +
	cause	+ + + + +
	contingency	+ + +
	accompaniment	+ + + +
	role	+
	matter	+ +
	angle	-

Figure 5-5   From the congruent to the metaphorical

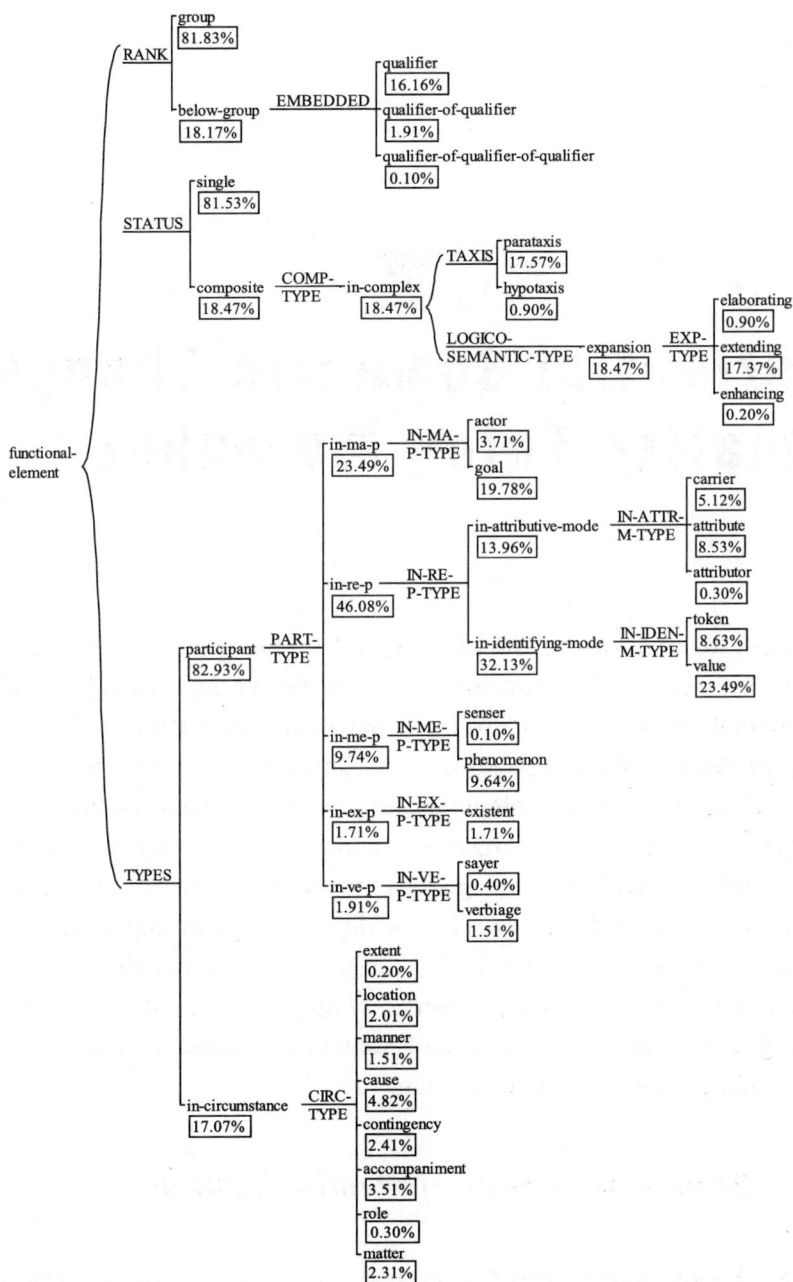

Figure 5-6　Systemic representation of the statistical results of functional elements

Chapter 6

Experiential Semantic Change in Quality-Thing Metaphor①

This chapter focuses on the experiential semantic change in quality-thing metaphor. By means of comparison between the congruent relational clause and the metaphorical nominal group, it has been proved that the transference from the Attribute at the clause rank to the Thing at the group rank may invoke a domino effect on the other elements involved. This chapter further explores the semogenic power of nominalization by analyzing the experiential structures of all the metaphorical nominal groups in the data. Based on the results of lexicogrammatical analyses as well as theoretical foundations, a typology of semantic changes in experiential meaning is proposed, the distribution of different types of experiential semantic change in the data is explored, and the lexicogrammatical realizations and controlling contextual factors of these changes are discussed by exemplification.

6.1 Semogenic Power of Nominalization

6.1.1 Experiential and Logical Structures of Nominal Group

The nominal group is a powerful resource for meaning-making. Its semogenic

---

① Part of this chapter has been accepted for publication by *Foreign Language Research*.

power lies in its potential to be expanded to an indefinite extent. A group can be seen as an expanded word from a historical view. Unlike the verbal group which gets elaborated grammatically on the temporal dimension, the nominal group expands lexically. Since the nominal group is a resource for construing complex things taking off from a single nominal word, its structure should be interpreted complementarily in both experiential and logical ways. "The nominal group is interpreted structurally both univariately as a group of words expanding a nominal Head and multivariately as a configuration of constituent functions. Systemically, this means the group is interpreted in terms of logical systems; structurally, this means there is a logical interdependency structure alongside the multivariate layer" (Matthiessen, 1995: 653). Viewed from an experiential perspective, the nominal group has a multivariate structure: it is organized by one or more of the functional elements that precede the Head noun serving as Thing—"Deictic + Numerative + Epithet + Classifier + Thing". There is also Qualifier which follows the Thing; a Qualifier is typically a rankshifted phrase or clause. Viewed from a logical perspective, the nominal group has a univariate structure which is generated by the device of modification—"Premodifier + Head + Postmodifier".

The semantic principle of this kind of expansion is that "it locates the participating entity along certain parameters ranging from the most instantial to the most systemic" (Halliday, 1998: 197). The Deictic locates the entity instantially because it is tied up with the speech function, while the more lasting attribute is liable to have a classifying function, locating the entity systemically; the other functional elements lie somewhere in between on the cline.

As indicated by Figure 6-1, the Deictic is temporally transitory, discoursally related to time scale, experientially simple, and is determined by the grammatical system of determination; whereas in contrast, the Thing which is experiential rather than discoursal is the most stable in time, and it is closest to the most delicate lexical end of the lexicogrammatical continuum.

The nominal group has in its grammar "the potential for organizing a large quantity of lexical material into functional configurations, in which lexical items operate either directly (as words) or indirectly (through rankshifted phrases or clauses). This potential that nominal groups have for structural expansion is clearly related to their role in the construal of experience" (Halliday, 1998: 197). Nominal groups construe participants which can persist through time, can carry attributes, and can serve as the starting-point of the clause where they occur. Therefore, nominal groups boast two semantic potentials: the potential for referring and the potential for expanding.

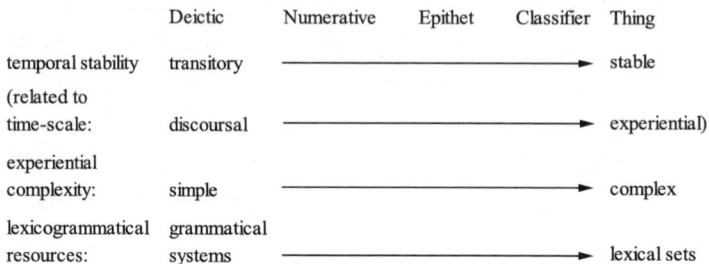

	Deictic	Numerative	Epithet	Classifier	Thing
temporal stability	transitory			→	stable
(related to time-scale:	discoursal			→	experiential)
experiential complexity:	simple			→	complex
lexicogrammatical resources:	grammatical systems			→	lexical sets

Figure 6-1 The semantic movement in the nominal group

(Halliday & Matthiessen, 1999: 210)

As stated in Chapter 3, the three functional components of meaning (ideational, interpersonal and textual) are realized throughout the grammar. A clause, the largest unit of grammar, is composed of three lines of meaning realized by three distinct structures that are combined into one. But below the clause, the grammatical pattern of the group is different. The three components of meaning "are not represented in the form of separate whole structures, but rather as partial contributions to a single structural line" (Halliday & Matthiessen, 2014: 361). That's why the structure of the group is analyzed in one operation instead of three.

6.1.2　Preliminary Statistics on Experiential Structure

In this study, 996 nominal groups embodying quality-thing metaphors have been obtained from the 900 clauses selected; the number of the metaphorical nominal groups is larger than that of the clauses because there might be two or more metaphorical groups in one single clause. Among all these groups under concern, there are two special types.

(1) the "a variety of…" type

In this kind of nominal group, both Head and Thing are present, but they are dissociated from each other rather than being conflated. The premodifying function is assumed by something that is itself a nominal group, so that the Thing is embedded in a prepositional phrase introduced by *of* and then serves as post-Head modifier, as in *a variety of MOFs* (see Table 6-1).

Table 6-1   Nominal group with variety expression (extended Numerative)

	a	variety	of	MOFs
experiential	Numerative: type			Thing
	Deictic	Thing		
logical	Premodifier	Head	Postmodifier	
	β	α		
				Head

Here the headhood of *variety* is mapped onto the thinghood of *MOFs* to construe the total meaning of the group. *Variety* is transferred from a quality realized by an adjective *various*; the nominal group is agnate to *various MOFs* and *MOFs are various*. There are 39 instances of this type in the data, such as *a (wide) variety of, a (completely unexpected) diversity of, the (vast/overwhelming) majority of, an abundance of* and *a (small) minority of.*

(2) the "*of* + metaphorical nominal group" type

In this case, the agnate Attribute in the congruent relational clause is realized by the preposition *of* + a nominal group with a nominalization as Thing/Head. Expressions such as *of (such high) metallicity* and *of (particular / tremendous / growing / great technological) importance / significance* are found in the data. There are altogether 11 instances of this type. For example:

(6-1a) Therefore, as also pointed out by Nepf, <C-3> aquatic vegetation *is of* tremendous **significance** (3) to many ecosystem functions… (Text 18)

(**Congruent**: aquatic vegetation is tremendously significant to many ecosystem functions…)

(6-1b) These **differences** (14*2) in chromosome abnormalities after POLD3 or POLD1 depletion *are of* particular **interest** (18) because they could suggest a specific role of POLD3 over POLD1. (Text 23)

(**Congruent**: These differences in… are particularly interesting because…)

Metaphorical groups of these two special types (50 in number) are excluded, and the other 946 metaphorical groups are analyzed in terms of experiential structure. Thing, of course, is the obligatory element of a nominal group; the other functional elements are optional.

Statistics (see Table 6-2) show that among the 946 groups under investigation,

546 of them (57.71%) possess the element of Deictic by means of which they can enter into the system of determination, and 28 groups (2.96%) have the post-Deictic which identifies a subset of the class of Thing. There are only 6 nominal groups (0.63%) that contain the Numerative; the small number is partially due to the abstract nature of the nominalized quality-thing. There are 166 groups (17.55%) that carry Epithets whereby the quality-things are further endowed with qualities. There are 243 groups (25.69%) that have Classifiers, and 516 groups (54.55%) have Qualifiers.

Table 6-2　Statistical results for the functional elements of metaphorical groups

Element	Deictic	post-Deictic	Numerative	Epithet	Classifier	Qualifier
Number	546	28	6	166	243	516
Percent	57.71%	2.96%	0.63%	17.55%	25.69%	54.55%

These quantitative descriptions can only present a rough picture of the components of nominal groups, but what on earth happens during the process of metaphorization? Are these elements transferred from the agnate clauses directly or are they newly-added? To answer these questions, the way meanings are expanded when an attributive relational clause is metaphorized into a nominal group will be clarified. Exploring semantic expansion through the comparison between the metaphorical group and the congruent clause may naturally go beyond the rank of word and group, extend to the rank of clause, and even go beyond the boundary of clauses. Discussion on the experiential semantic change is also closely related with the functional roles that these metaphorical groups play in the transitivity structure.

6.2　Analytical Framework of Experiential Semantic Change

An analytical framework needs to be constructed to explore the experiential semantic change in grammatical metaphor. To give the framework a solid theoretical foundation, two aspects require consideration: (1) the relationship between the study of meaning in SFL and the classical study of semantics (Lyons, 1977); (2) sources of terminologies in the framework.

In his two-volume *Semantics*, Lyons (1977) states that there are three different kinds of semantic information encodable in language-utterances: descriptive meaning, expressive meaning and social meaning. Descriptive meaning is factual, and it can be asserted, denied or objectively verified; expressive meaning refers to that aspect of meaning which is closely related to the characteristics of particular language user, and social meaning is that aspect which contributes to the establishment and maintenance of social relations. This global tripartite distinction by Lyons can be traced to the ideas of Frege (1892/1960) and Austin (1956/1979,1962). In his influential semantics-founded paper "Sense and Reference", Frege (1892/1960), a pioneer in the study of semantics, discusses the philosophy of language from the perspectives of mathematics and logic. He focuses on the meaning of statements or declarative sentences, and states that thoughts are composed of meanings and a linguistic sign has simultaneously an abstract sense and a concrete reference. Frege's ideas have universal implications for the study of semantics because of their solid mathematical and logical foundations which can transcend the boundaries of various thoughts and languages. The first type of meaning, descriptive meaning in Lyons' terms, coincides with Frege's explanation of the meaning of a statement descriptive of certain state-of-affairs. As to the other two kinds of meaning as well as the relationship between them and descriptive meaning, Lyons (1977: 56) accepts Austin's (1956/1979,1962) view: to make a descriptive statement "is to engage in a particular kind of social activity regulated by conventions similar to, and in part identical with, those which regulate such other acts as making promises, asking questions or issuing commands". To put in another way, descriptive meaning depends on, in a large measure, the social and expressive meanings, "and this is the view taken by perhaps the majority of linguists, anthropologists and social psychologists who have been concerned with semantics" (ibid.). Therefore, although semantics is studied from different perspectives and by means of various approaches, such as behaviorist semantics, logical semantics and structural semantics, there is something in common: the philosophical and logical sources of the study of language meaning.

The study of meaning in SFL is no exception. It inherits the essential and general ideas from the classical study of semantics, and meanwhile distinguishes itself with peculiar features. The accordance between SFL and Lyons' views in meaning can be listed as follows: First of all, both of them start the study of meaning with the study of functions of language. Lyons (1977) distinguishes three functions of language in the first place, and accordingly identifies three kinds of meaning signaled by language. Halliday (1973) views language development of children as the development of the social functions of language, and well explains how the specific functions evolved into the highly generalized realms of meaning which are intrinsic to the language system. Secondly, Lyons' distinction of meaning into the three types (descriptive, expressive and social) corresponds roughly to the two primary meta-meanings (ideational and interpersonal) in SFL, although the ideational meaning in SFL has a broader sense. Lyons (1977) acknowledges Halliday's term interpersonal as the most appropriate one to subsume the social and expressive meanings. Thirdly, both Lyons and Halliday put emphasis on the importance of context in linguistic study. SFL inherits the notion of meaning in context from Firth; Lyons (1977: 607) also asserts that "the Firthian view of meaning has been influential; and it has something of value to contribute to what might ultimately count as a comprehensive and materially, as well as formally, adequate theory of semantics". Fourthly, Lyons (1977: 33) holds that the principle that "meaning, or meaningfulness, implies choice" is one of the most fundamental principles of semantics, which is totally in line with Halliday's notion of system. And finally, in clarifying the relation between semantics and grammar, Lyons (1977) introduces participant-roles and circumstantial roles which bear a resemblance to the elements in clausal transitivity configuration in FG as far as the experiential meaning is concerned.

The study of meaning in SFL is intimately connected with the important notions of stratification and metafunction. In SFL, as the key property of the semiotic system of language, meaning is organized within the semantic stratum (the stratum of meaning) located between context and the stratum of lexicogrammar. "Semantics is 'the way into language' from context—the set of strategies for construing, enacting and presenting non-language as meaning" (Matthiessen et al., 2016: 214), and it is realized by lexicogrammar. Semantics is also metafunctionally diversified. Halliday (1992/2007k: 364) states explicitly that "meaning is a mode of action engendered at the intersection of the material (or phenomenal) and the conscious, as complementary modes of experience", and "by the act of meaning, consciousness imposes order on the phenomena of experience". This statement is to some extent similar to Frege's (1892/1960) ideas of language and thought. With the semiotic dimension of stratification, meaning becomes self-reflexive, so in addition to construing and enacting, there is an intrinsic enabling textual metafunction.

Experiential meaning "is a major component of meaning in the language system that is basic to more or less all uses of language" (Halliday, 1973: 39), so it is a major concern of almost all approaches towards semantics. Terminologies in this framework represent the shared core of studies on semantics from various perspectives and meanwhile accord with characteristics of the authentic data under investigation in this study. The analytical framework of changes in experiential meaning is also built on the convergence between diachronic semantics, structural semantics and SFL. Firstly, semantic change is the concern of diachronic semantics; although this study is by no means designed to trace the semantic change historically, the notion of language evolution applies both to diachronic semantics and to the interpretation of congruence in grammatical metaphor. What is different is that only two historical dimensions (phylogenesis and ontogenesis) are taken into consideration in diachronic semantics, but the concept of congruence is viewed from three evolutionary perspectives with the inclusion of logogenesis, because grammatical metaphor is textually motivated. Secondly, system and structure, the two axial dimensions of language in SFL, are inherited from the Saussurean idea of syntagmatic and paradigmatic relations. The central thesis of structuralism is that "every language is a unique relational structure, or system, and that the units which we identify, or postulate as theoretical constructs, in analyzing the sentence of a particular language (sounds, words, meanings, etc.) derive both their essence and their existence from their relationships with other units in the same language-system" (Lyons, 1977: 232). In the same vein, SFL holds that different kinds of meaning in language are expressed by different kinds of grammatical structure which is interpreted in functional terms (Halliday, 1977/2007o); the meaning of a specific element can only be worked out in the grammatical structure in which it dwells. Thirdly, diachronic semantics summarizes two directions of semantic change: extension (including generalization and abstraction) as well as specialization. It seems that generalization is identified with abstraction in studying semantics diachronically, whereas in this study, abstraction and generalization are taken as two kinds of semantic change, the former being the universal feature of nominalizations and the latter realized by the lexical-grammatical features of nominalized qualities in specific configurations. This analytical framework is diagrammed in Figure 6-2.

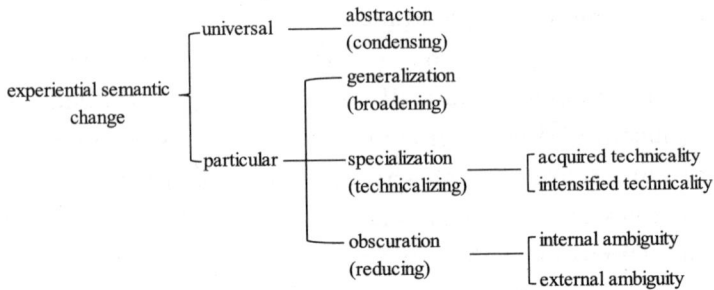

Figure 6-2   Types of change in experiential meaning

The experiential semantic change is broadly classified into universal and particular types. Semantic abstraction which involves meaning condensation is universal for all nominalizations; particular types include semantic generalization, semantic specialization and semantic obscuration. Semantic generalization is in fact a kind of meaning broadening whereby a specific quality is metaphorized into a general thing and thus its original meaning scope is enlarged. Semantic specialization in this context is mainly characterized by technicalizing, which inevitably involves the narrowing down of the meaning scope of a lexical item. Different from the previous discussions on dead metaphor, technicality is taken into account because the focus of attention in this study is what happens in the transference from a quality to a thing. A non-technical quality may acquire technicality when it is turned into a thing, and an inherently technical quality may be more technical in meaning while it is metaphorized into a thing. Therefore, semantic specialization is further divided into acquired technicality and intensified technicality. Another semantic change is termed as semantic obscuration, referring to the ambiguity in meaning that occurs in metaphorization. It is classified into two subtypes with respect to the reasons of meaning ambiguity: internal ambiguity which is caused by the scalar or gradable nature of some qualities and external ambiguity which is caused by some other factors such as the loss of information or the sharing of functional elements in nominal group complexes as a result of metaphorization.

The division of experiential semantic change into these types is also well-based on the analysis of the experiential structure of all the metaphorical nominal groups as well as the transitivity analysis as to the new metaphorical context in which they play different functional roles.

6.3   Statistics on Experiential Semantic Change

The 996 instances of quality-thing nominalization in the data are classified into different types in terms of experiential semantic change according to the proposed framework. It should be noted that one instance may involve more than one type of meaning change simultaneously. The statistical results of the number and percentage of each type are shown in Table 6-3 and Figure 6-3.

Table 6-3   Statistical results for experiential semantic change

Type			Number (Percent)	
universal	abstraction		996 (100%)	
particular	generalization		103 (10.34%)	
	specialization	acquired technicality	446 (44.78%)	358 (35.94%)
		intensified technicality		88 (8.84%)
	obscuration	internal ambiguity	190 (19.08%)	166 (16.67%)
		external ambiguity		24 (2.41%)

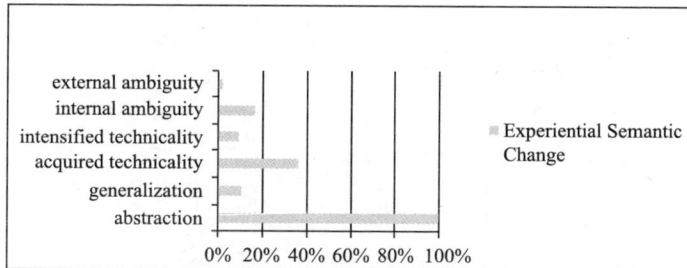

Figure 6-3   Types of experiential semantic change

As a universal feature of nominalization, semantic abstraction is applicable to every quality-thing nominalization. A quality-thing is absolutely more abstract than a quality. Semantic generalization takes place in 10.34% of all the instances under investigation (103 in number). Semantic specialization is quite prominent in that it occurs in 446 (44.78%) instances, among which the vast majority of them (358 in number) belong to the category of acquired technicality, and 88 instances of them are categorized as intensified technicality. Another type of semantic change is obscuration which accounts for 19.08% of all the instances; 166 (16.67%) cases of them are classified as internal ambiguity and 24 (2.41%)

instances are external ambiguity. Each type and subtype of the experiential semantic change will be explained and analyzed in detail in the next section with plentiful illustrative examples.

6.4 Analysis

6.4.1 Semantic Abstraction

This section starts with Thing, the core element in a nominal group, to explore the experiential semantic change in quality-thing nominalization. In this study, 202 adjectival-nouns are obtained from the data. In Figure 6-4, the word cloud presents the lexical items involved in terms of their frequency of occurrence. Detailed information about these items is provided in Appendix II where the token frequency, and both the metaphorical and congruent types of these lexical items are provided.

Figure 6-4　Word cloud composed of lexical items realizing quality-things[①]

One feature that all of these nominalized items share dwells in abstraction: the qualities in real experiential world have been changed into abstract entities. In SFL, these nominalized qualities are treated as entities, which is indicative of Platonic realism. "The postulated extramental entities that were apprehended by the mind in its knowledge and perception of the external world" are called

---

① Calculated by Word Cloud Generator from https://www.jasondavies.com/wordcloud/.

"objective concepts" (Lyons, 1977: 111). By contrast, the medieval nominalist rejected such kind of concepts as unnecessary. They held the idea that there was no such entity as *redness*, but only *red things*; because these individual objects are similar in color, we apply the name *red* to them. Lyons (1977: 207) used the term denotatum to refer to the class of objects or properties to which an expression applies; for example, the denotatum of *red* is a particular property (viz. the color red) and its denotata are red objects.

The term abstraction is hard to define. Traditionally, it is used by philosophers to describe the way in which universal concepts are formed, and by behaviorists to account for how a property is correctly abstracted from the objects that manifest it by virtue of stimulus presence and community's reinforcement of a response (Lyons, 1977). Lyons (1977) makes a hierarchical differentiation between first-order entities, second-order entities and third-order entities. First-order entities such as persons, animals and things are characterized by their constant perceptual properties, their spatiotemporal location and their public observability. Second-order entities refer to events, processes, states-of-affairs and so on, which have temporal location. Although second-order entities realized by the traditionally called abstract nouns are not abstract in the sense that something that has no spatiotemporal location is abstract, they are perceptual and conceptual constructs. Third-order entities refer to such abstract entities as propositions which are nowhere in time and space. Second-order and third-order entities are formed through the process of nominalization, and it is nominalization that renders them the abstract property.

Qualities realized by adjectives are not on their own abstract or concrete; they are engaged in qualifying entities or things. The things or entities on which they are dependent are categorized to be abstract or concrete. In the traditional grammar, Quirk (1972, 1985) differentiates adjectives into three types according to contrasts in meaning: stative/dynamics, gradable/ungradable and inherent/noninherent. Within SFL, Yang (1992) puts forward a distinction between subjective and objective adjectives according to their experiential or interpersonal functions in contexts. Halliday & Matthiessen (1999) classifies qualities according to the fractal types of projection and expansion with the combination of three types of value (binary, scalar and taxonomic). Tucker (1998) designs a system network for quality type and four features are recognized: relative, thing-oriented, situation-oriented and environmental. According to these well-established classifications of qualities or their adjectival realizations, abstraction is obviously none of the criteria for classifying qualities. "Since the 'noun-ness' is being used to construe phenomena that stand out as something else than a noun, metaphors will inevitably be abstract" (Halliday & Matthiessen, 1999: 264). Therefore, semantic abstraction is a universal feature of ideational grammatical metaphor. Semantic junction, the source from which this kind of abstraction arises will be firstly addressed, and then the relation between abstraction and countability will be clarified.

6.4.1.1　Semantic Junction: Bi-junction and Tri-junction

As discussed in Chapter 2, semantic junction is the most prominent and most frequently mentioned semantic feature of grammatical metaphor. According to Halliday (1996/2007b, 1998/2007c, 1999/2007f), Halliday & Matthiessen (1999) and Martin &White (2008), semantic junction has at least given a partial explanation for the synonymy between the congruent and the metaphorical agnates. An ideational metaphor is junctional in the sense that it joins the core meaning of the congruent form with a certain meaning of the metaphorical form. For example, the expression *sufficiently accurate* which realizes an attributive quality is congruent, while *a sufficient accuracy* is the metaphorical construct, which is a junction of "quality + thing". Therefore, quality is the core meaning that the two modes share, and thing is the newly-added meaning. It is this quality meaning that relates the congruent expression with the metaphorical one, and this meaning is never lost regardless of changes in the metaphorical process, because this meaning is not determined by the intrinsic feature of language, but the feature realized by language in certain context. The congruent example realizes an attributive quality of an entity in a real context, and no matter what changes occur in the way of expression, this quality meaning remains the same.

Although the previous researchers have highlighted the importance of semantic junction, all the instances they have offered are characterized by bi-junction, namely, the junction of one category meaning of the congruent mode and one category meaning of the metaphorical mode, such as the frequently quoted "process + thing", "quality + thing" or "circumstance + thing". This general principle also works in quality-thing metaphor, but there are some special cases demonstrating another kind of junction that is provisionally termed as tri-junction.

It has been mentioned that grammatical metaphor is a matter of degree. The congruent and the metaphorical stand at the two opposite poles of the cline of metaphorization, and there are many intermediate forms in between. When the congruent is gradually approaching the metaphorical, all the traces of change are left over there. Some quality-thing metaphors are located somewhere in the middle of the cline. It is not unusual that a process realized by a verb is turned into a quality realized by an adjective, and then turned into a thing realized by a noun. Therefore, correspondingly, the semantic junction involves the semantic features of the three categories: "process + quality + thing". For example, the adjective *productive* realizing a quality derives from the verb *produce* realizing a process, and *productive* is further transformed into the noun *productivity* representing an entity. So this is a special trait of quality-thing metaphor which is distinct from other kinds of metaphor. The accurate construal of a metaphor requires making clear the history of transference from the congruent to the metaphor. Among the 202 lexical realizations of the quality-things, there are 25 items (listed in Table 6-4) involving such kind of transitional phases in metaphorization.

Table 6-4 Lexical realizations of quality-thing involving tri-junction

No.	Grammatical class		
	Verb	Adjective	Noun
1	conduct	conductive	conductivity
2	contract	contractible	contractility
3	select	selective	selectivity
4	detect	detectable	detectability
5	form	formable	formability
6	produce	productive	productivity
7	connect	connective	connectivity
8	reproduce	reproducible	reproducibility
9	resist	resistive	resistivity
10	sustain	sustainable	sustainability
11	repeat	repeatable	repeatability
12	wake	wakeful	wakefulness

(to be continued)

No.	Grammatical class		
	Verb	Adjective	Noun
13	wet	wettable	wettability
14	access	accessible	accessibility
15	apply	applicable	applicability
16	control	controllable	controllability
17	deform	deformable	deformability
18	describe	descriptive	descriptiveness
19	direct	directive	directivity
20	generalize	generalizable	generalizability
21	hyperpermeate	hyperpermeable	hyperpermeability
22	nonpolarize	nonpolarizable	nonpolarizability
23	observe	observable	observability
24	tract	tractable	tractability
25	tune	tunable	tunability

The discovery of the long-been-ignored tri-junction has confirmed, on the one hand, the cline of metaphoricity, and on the other hand, the peculiar status of qualities. Between the most congruent and the most metaphorical, there are intermediate and transitional forms. In some cases, it might be unnecessary to take them into consideration if what is concerned lies in the two poles of the continuum. However, it is undeniable that these intermediate forms contribute a lot to a sound interpretation of the metaphorical process from a historical view. How far shall we unpack a metaphor depends on the immediate needs of the ongoing research. Furthermore, qualities can be process-like or participant-like, because they stand in the middle in terms of temporal stability. As indicated by the lexical items listed in Table 6-4, qualities realized by those adjectives are located somewhere along the cline between processes realized by verbs and things realized by nouns. In order to construe the most metaphorical things in an explicit manner, every stage of transference needs to be taken into account.

6.4.1.2 Abstraction and Countability

There are three vectors along which a lexical item functioning as Thing is located with reference to the grammar: countability, animacy and generality (Halliday & Matthiessen, 2014). Countability, namely, whether a thing is countable or uncountable, is closely related to abstraction. It is usually assumed that abstract entities including nominalized processes and qualities are unbounded. So here comes a question: should number-marked nominalizations be taken as instances of grammatical metaphor? For example, *unstable* can be transferred into the noun *instability* which can function as the Thing in a nominal group, and thus it is an instance of quality-thing grammatical metaphor, but there seems to be no consensus as to the status of its plural form *instabilities* as an instance of grammatical metaphor. Some researchers (e.g. Liu, 2008) exclude those words with a plural inflectional morpheme *-(e)s* or the indefinite article *a(n)* from the category of grammatical metaphor due to their well-established syntactic status. Others (e.g. Martin, 1993b) acknowledge that pluralized nominalizations are instances of grammatical metaphor by giving examples like *inadequacies* and *capabilities*. Therefore, the relation between abstraction and countability should be explicated. There is some connection between the two, but there is no unique mapping. Typically, abstract entities stand at the unbounded end, but "the distinction is made by the grammar, so the same entity may be construed in more than one way" (Halliday & Matthiessen, 2014: 385).

In this study, the notion of cline is adopted once again. Nouns are located along a cline of countability, ranging from those that construe things as absolutely itemized at one end to those that construe things as completely unbounded at the other. An adjectival-noun may be a mass noun, or be countable in number and appear in plural forms. There is also something like a cline of abstraction. Nouns of the mass-kind are abstract entities, whereas those countable ones are lower in the degree of abstraction and thus more approachable to concrete things.

Now that functional grammar is semantically motivated or natural, the grammatically pluralized nominalizations are also meaning-loaded. One of the most important reasons for the general shift in meaning towards thingness by means of grammatical metaphor "has to do with the greater potential for expanding the meaning of things—numbering, describing, classifying and qualifying them" (Martin & Rose, 2007: 110). So the abstract thing can also be numbered. The nominalizations in plural form are not excluded in this study; instead they are included to serve as evidence for the meaning-making power of nominalization, because the grammatical change in number is also indicative of expansion of the meaning potential of language. That is to say, the singular and the plural forms of the same nominalization have different meanings. In the following example, *difference* and *differences* co-exist in one clause; the former carries a general meaning (*A and B are different*), while the latter implies more specific meanings (*A and B are different in certain aspect or in certain manner*). So the first nominal group *the difference between* $\Delta_{T'}$ *(*I_1*,* I_2*) and* Δ_T *(*I_1*,* I_2*)* is agnate to the relational clause $\Delta_{T'}$ *(*I_1*,* I_2*) and* Δ_T *(*I_1*,* I_2*) are different*, whereas the second nominal group *differences between horizontally neighboring pixels in* I_1 is agnate to the relational clause with not only the qualitative attribute (*different*) but a circumstantial element (*in* I_1): *horizontally neighboring pixels are different in* I_1.

(6-2) <C-12> Thus the **difference** (6*4) [between $\Delta_{T'}$ *(*I_1*,* I_2*) and* Δ_T *(*I_1*,* I_2*)*] *is bounded* by the total sum of **differences** (7*1) [between horizontally neighboring pixels in I_1]. (Text 31)

But it needs to be clarified that just as grammatical transcategorization does not guarantee the occurrence of grammatical metaphor, not all the plural forms of nominalizations can be taken as instances of grammatical metaphor. The context where lexical items operate determines their specific meanings. If the lexical item has lost the essential feature of being abstract and the semantic junction disappears, it has become a noun referring to something concrete rather than an abstract entity. In the following example, *impurity* is originally derived from an adjective *impure*, but the plural form *impurities* in this case means *chemical substances inside a confined amount of liquid, gas or solid, which differ from the chemical composition of the material or compound* [①], so it is not an instance of quality-thing metaphor.

(6-3) No oxides or other phases except pure Cu were found, and the composition distributions of Ag and Cu are very homogeneous across the layer without measurable **impurities** including oxygen. (Text 13)

All the pluralized nominalizations under study in the data are presented in Table 6-5. For the first 17 lexical items listed in this table, both their plural and singular forms occur in the data, and the two forms are counted separately

---

① This definition is from https://en.wikipedia.org/wiki/Impurity.

as distinct items. The other 5 items (*abnormalities, disparities, commonalities, insufficiencies* and *novelties*) have no singular counterparts in the data.

Table 6-5   Nominalizations in plural forms

No.	Plural lexical form	Singular lexical form
1	differences	difference
2	instabilities	instability
3	difficulties	difficulty
4	invariances	invariance
5	deficiencies	deficiency
6	responsibilities	responsibility
7	discrepancies	discrepancy
8	latencies	latency
9	sensitivities	sensitivity
10	ambiguities	ambiguity
11	efficiencies	efficiency
12	inconsistencies	inconsistency
13	intensities	intensity
14	similarities	similarity
15	stabilities	stability
16	thicknesses	thickness
17	toxicities	toxity
18	abnormalities	
19	disparities	
20	commonalities	
21	insufficiencies	
22	novelties	

It has been noted earlier that only 6 metaphorical groups in the data are found to carry Numeratives, and all of the Numeratives are indefinite numerals (as shown in the following examples): *a few, more, less* and *little*, with *less* and *little* occurring twice. Due to the inherent abstract feature of the metaphorical entity, it is seldom quantified by specific numerals. Quantification does not have wide application to the quality-thing metaphors.

(6-4a) Here, by comparing analytical and numerical results, we find agreement for $\delta = 0.3a$, so that the resonance frequencies of the planar modes are given by $f_{00n} = nc_0/[2(L + 0.6a)]$. <C-4> Finally, we *find* agreement between our analytical, numerical, and experimental results, with only a few decibel-level **discrepancies** (4*1) [between simulated and experimental curves]. (Text 2)

(**Congruent**: simulated and experimental curves are somewhat discrepant.)

(6-4b) Consistent with the observation that POLD3-depletion induces replication failure and segmental genomic duplication following cyclin E-induced replicative stress in human cell lines, <C-24> POLD3- and POLD1-depleted cells *had* more **difficulties** (21*2) [overcoming replicative stress and DNA damage]. (Text 23)

(**Congruent**: it was more difficult for POLD3- and POLD1-depleted cells to overcome...)

(6-4c) The average rate of growth between 4 h and 24 h inversely correlated to the average clearance rate between 0 h and 4 h such that <C-10> slower clearance *supported* faster growth and less titer **heterogeneity** (6*2). (Text 25)

(**Congruent**: titer is less/ not so heterogeneous.)

(6-4d) For the larger dose (10^3 CFU), <C-13> little **heterogeneity** (6*5) *was observed* in the data and bacterial growth at 4 h pbi was at or above the inoculum. (Text 25)

(**Congruent**: the data are not very heterogeneous.)

(6-4e) Bacterial titers for a coinfection with the PR8-PB1-F2 (1918) virus split into two groups (Figure S3B), which is consistent with an AM: dose ratio closer to the threshold, <C-14> whereas little heterogeneity (6*6) *was observed* for coinfection with the PR8 virus. (Text 25)

(**Congruent**: Bacterial titers for coinfection with the PR8 virus are not very heterogeneous.)

(6-4f) It was also shown that the composition of OM differed greatly between the rhizosphere and non-rhizosphere; <C-3> the rhizosphere OM molecules generally *had* greater overall molecular weights, less **aromaticity** (3) and a greater hydrophilic character. (Text 26)

(**Congruent**: the rhizosphere OM molecules <u>are less aromatic</u>.)

6.4.2   Semantic Generalization

Another kind of semantic change that may occur with the transference from a quality of thing to a junction of "quality + thing" is semantic generalization. Semantic generalization, in this context, refers to the fact that the meaning of the metaphorical thing is generalized to be a theoretical construct and consequently it refers to a category or class of things rather than any specific member in this class. In effect, semantic generalization inevitably involves the broadening of the semantic scope of the thing, because it is not directly pertinent to any specific thing, but a generality of all members of one class.

In terms of lexicogrammar, a thing involving semantic generalization is realized by a noun which serves as the Thing/Head in a nominal group, and it is the sole element in the group without any qualifying or modifying elements. In the following example, the single element realized by the noun *conductivity* constitutes a nominal group; it is not endowed with any other qualities such as Deictic, Epithet or Classifier realized by determiner, adjective or some other nouns. The focus here is not *what is conductive*, nor *what kind of conductivity it is*, but a generalized concept of conductivity. The absence of qualifying elements indicates the generality in meaning of the metaphorical entity: the Thing/Head in the nominal group is not further qualified, and thus the meaning of the thing it realizes is accordingly not confined to the meaning of a specific thing.

(6-5) [[*Introducing* **conductivity** (3*2) in these scaffolds]] resulted in several benefits: enhanced electrical coupling, higher rates of spontaneous beatings of cardiomyocytes cultured on these scaffolds, and improved function of infarcted hearts. (Text 8)

According to the statistics in Table 6-3, 10.34% of the 996 metaphorical nominal groups involve semantic generalization. Regardless of the relatively low percentage, this type of linguistic phenomenon is noteworthy. Apart from the apparent lexicogrammatical features of these instances, the functional roles they take on in the transitivity structure are also worth noting, because semantic generalization in these nominalizations is, to some extent, related to their grammatical functions in transitivity configurations. Based on the grammatical analysis conducted in Chapter 5, the functional roles that those metaphorical nominal groups with semantic generalization may play are summarized in Table 6-6.

Table 6-6   Functional roles of metaphors with semantic generalization

Functional role		Number (Percentage)	
Qualifier (of)	Circumstance	11	28 (27.19%)
	Attribute	3	
	Goal	5	
	Value	4	
	Carrier	2	
	Token	2	
	Verbiage	1	
Circumstance	Matter	15	27 (26.21%)
	Cause	7	
	Location	4	
	Manner	1	
Participant	Goal	17	48 (46.60%)
	Value	13	
	Token	6	
	Attribute	6	
	Carrier	4	
	Phenomenon	2	

It can be seen that more than half of these nominal groups (53.40%) are rankshifted downwards. The rankshifted metaphorical group may serve as the Qualifier of another element or work with a preposition to become the circumstance. The other 46.60% of them can play the roles of Goal, Value, Token, Attribute, Carrier and Phenomenon. Specific examples will be given for further explanation.

In the following example, the prepositional phrase *with partial loss of viability* serves as circumstance of Accompaniment in a possessive relational process. *Loss*, the Thing in the nominal group, is itself a process-thing nominalization transferred from *lose*; the quality-thing nominalization *viability* functions as Qualifier of *loss*. Since configurational function reveals the relation between meaning and grammar, in this case, as a Qualifier of Thing in a nominal group within a prepositional group realizing circumstance, *viability* carries no modifications because its meaning scope is broadened to represent a category of *viability* rather than emphasizing *what is or is not viable*.

(6-6) The protection provided by the lipid coating on the mutant phages appears to be similar or even superior to that observed with microencapsulation approaches, <C-8> where the microencapsulated phages *had* a comparably higher rate of survival than free phages in simulated gastric fluid, but still with partial loss [of **viability** (3*3)]. (Text 20)

In the next example, the nominal group *severity* and the preposition *in* together function as circumstance of Matter in a material process. Once again, the meaning of *severity* is generalized compared with the specific meaning of its congruent form *something is severe*. *Severity* has become an aspect of measurement in which something increases, and the focus is naturally deviated from that in the congruent expression with the missing of Carrier.

(6-7) In contrast, hamsters inoculated with WT-MARV developed only minimal to mild hepatic necrosis with neutrophilic infiltration by day 6, <C-11> and these lesions did not significantly *increase* in **severity** (9*1) at later time points. (Text 14)

Metaphorical groups with generalized meaning can also play participant roles in different processes. The following six examples illustrate the contexts in which they function as participants; the functional roles are Goal, Value, Token, Attribute, Carrier and Phenomenon in sequence.

(6-8a) CsgA modifications may be judiciously used at particular locations <C-20> *to tune* **flexibility** (11*5) (moderate to high-impact regions) or minimize motion propagation (low-impact regions). (Text 9)

(6-8b) As the CsgA subunit undergoes structural changes during the adsorption process, we also study structural events <C-8> [[that *impact* **stability** (7*1)]]. (Text 9)

(6-8c) <C-27> **Stability** (14*1) *is* another important aspect of fuel cell catalysts that needs consideration. (Text 5)

(6-8d) We repeated each experiment at least one time <C-24> *to ensure* **reproducibility** (12). (Text 25)

(6-8e) <C-9> However, **selectivity** (5*2), **specificity** (3*2) and potential device fabrication, which were not addressed in the report, *are essential* for the development of a practicable sensor. (Text 16)

(6-8f) However, <C-23> [[*predicting* **severity** (7*2), outcome, and bacterial titers for infections with reduced doses, where bacterial titers may increase but remain low]], is more challenging. (Text 25)

In terms of comparison between the congruent and the metaphorical forms, the recoverability of the Carrier depends on the role that the metaphorical nominal group plays in the new clausal configuration. When the metaphorical nominal group functions as the Qualifier of a participant or a circumstance, or it functions as circumstance, it is of difficulty to recover the Carrier in its congruent form. When the metaphorical nominal group functions as a kind of participant, the congruent Carrier can be recovered, and in some cases, the thing a quality relies on is omitted in the immediate context but can be recovered in a broader context. However, it is usually of no necessity to work out the Carrier, because the qualifying relationship between the quality and thing is not important any more, and the generalized thing on its own implies certain generalized quality. The status of Carrier is greatly lowered, so that it makes no difference whether the Carrier exists or not.

6.4.3　Semantic Specialization

Another type of semantic change is specialization which involves meaning shrinkage or solidification. The meaning scope of a lexical item is narrowed with more semantic features added. As Lyons (1977: 536) puts it, "a simple lexeme may, by virtue of its use in particular contexts, become more restricted in its sense and denotation than it was in some earlier period." As to the collected data in this study, it is found that semantic specialization is mainly embodied in technicalizing.

The language of science is characterized by grammatical metaphor, and grammatical metaphor can create theoretical abstraction by compacting and changing the nature of everyday language. Grammar, as a theory of experience, construes phenomena into various classes which are realized by lexical items.

Categorizing and taxonomizing involve both the most general grammatical schematization and the most delicate lexicalization (Halliday & Matthiessen, 1999). Technicality has naturally become an important concern in the study of the language of science. Some researchers (Ha & Hyland, 2017) have proposed a method to identify technicality and measure the degree of technicality of a word by using a corpus of financial texts. Almost all technical terms are metaphoric in origin (Halliday & Matthiessen, 1999; Matthiessen et al., 2010); it is stated that they cannot be further unpacked because they have become systemic constructs and their appearances have no instantial textual motivation (Halliday, 1998/2007c, 1999/2007f; Halliday & Matthiessen, 1999). But there is no clear cut between systemic and instantial metaphors; one lexicogrammatical form may realize more than one meaning, and it is in a specified context that the meaning can be figured out. This study is concerned with the semantic change taking place in metaphorization, so what is focalized is where a metaphor stems from. With regard to the fact that, from a historical and dynamic view, technicalized terms start out as grammatical metaphors, they cannot be totally dismissed as some fully-established constructs.

Not all of the qualities in the data are technicalized after they are transferred to be quality-things. According to the statistics in Table 6-3, 44.78% of the metaphors are characterized by technicality, while the other 55.22% are non-technical or at least less technical. There is a long list of non-technical lexical items, for example, *presence, absence, diversity, importance, suitability, complexity, prevalence, difficulty, generality, availability, consistency, completeness, effectiveness, relevance, simplicity, correctness* and *popularity*. Different from technicalized lexical items, these items are more general and not so closely tied to specific fields or scientific disciplines. Both their congruent forms realizing qualities and metaphorical forms realizing things are not technical. Technical taxonomy is not the sole function of grammatical metaphor for the language of science. Textual motivation, in particular, comes into play by changing qualities into things that can carry qualities, can participate in new processes and thus push forward the discursive flow.

Now the focus is shifted onto technicalizing. All the technicalized metaphors are classified into two types: those whose congruent forms are of no technicality but can be used in a technical way in a new context after being grammatically metaphorized, and those whose congruent forms are already technical in meaning and there is an increase in the degree of technicality after being turned into quality-things. The former is termed as acquired technicality, and the latter is named as intensified technicality. Obviously, items with acquired technicality outnumber those with intensified technicality by 358 to 88 (see Table 6-3).

6.4.3.1 Acquired Technicality

A plenty of qualities realized by adjectives are frequently used in casual or daily contexts whereby no technicality is required, but when they are transferred into abstract entities and enter the context of scientific language, they may become technicalized. Lots of such qualities are transcategorized into vectors or units of measurement, for example, *hardness, length, warmth, strength, efficiency, efficacy, breadth, thickness, stiffness, intensity* and *brightness*, to name a few. These words have been taken for granted to function as units of measurement. In Chapter 4, it has been clarified that as one of the criteria for data selection, if such kind of words co-occur with exact numbers, they are excluded from this study; otherwise, in most cases, they are retained because of their contribution to taxonomizing and textual organization. In the following three examples from the same text, *strength* is further categorized respectively by three Classifiers *attachment, adhesive* and *attractive*, so that the pseudo-thing *strength* becomes an umbrella word with various subcategories. Although it is hard and unnecessary to unpack them into congruent forms, they are originally agnate to relational clauses *… be strong in attachment /... be adhesively strong / ... be attractively strong.*

(6-9a) Curli overproduction has been shown to substantially increase adhesion, <C-5> and attachment **strength** (4*3) has been noted *to vary* by surface type: the strongest interactions were seen for hydrophobic plastics, relative to hydrophilic metals or glass. (Text 9)

(6-9b) <C-6> Adhesive **strength** (4*4) *was enhanced* through conjugation with the mussel foot protein, and curli fibers were also interfaced with inorganic nanoparticles and quantum dots. (Text 9)

(6-9c) <C-7> These interactions *can enhance* attractive **strength** (4*5) for compatible residues, namely, positively charged side chains in Arg and Lys and polar side chains in Hsd, Tyr, Thr, and Gln, which have relatively high proportions of attractive energy from electrostatics. (Text 9)

It is worth stressing again that context plays a crucial role in interpreting such metaphors and determining the availability of technicality in them, because the same lexical item may realize different meanings in different contexts. In the following example, *strength* is no longer a technicalized item, because it means *a strong point or advantage*. Actually it is a mixture of both grammatical and lexical metaphor. This non-technical meaning can occur in various less formal contexts, for instance, in this clause *he has his strengths and weaknesses*.

(6-10) <C-21> A key **strength** (13*1) of the present study is the longitudinal study design with four waves, providing an opportunity to assess the mutual relationships between leisure-time physical activity and educational achievement. <C-22> A further **strength** (13*2) of this study is its large sample size, which ensures sufficient statistical power to detect statistically significant associations. (Text 22)

6.4.3.2   Intensified Technicality

Some qualities realized by adjectives are inherently technical due to their intimate relation to specified fields or disciplines. When they are transferred into things, their technicality is retained and further intensified. Lexical items of this type include *toxity, virulence, aromaticity, turbidity, fluorescence, genotoxity, heterozygosity, pathogenicity, hygroscopicity, nonpolarizability, crystallinity, viscoplasticity, inertness, resilience*, and so on. These words are usually marked as discipline-specific in dictionaries; they seldom occur in our everyday experience and they may distinguish laymen from experts with scientific knowledge. In some cases, the metaphorical and congruent forms co-occur (e.g. *viscoplasticity* and *viscoplastic* in the following example). As the Thing in nominal group, a technical thing can also be endowed with attributes: *viscoplasticity* is preceded by Epithet *rigid perfect*, and *hydrophilicity* has Deictic *a* and Epithet *higher* in the given examples.

(6-11a) These viscoplastic equations are expected to capture the features of forming limit curves of sheet metals under various thermo-mechanical conditions. <C-18> By *considering* von-Mises behaviour for rigid perfect **viscoplasticity** (12), a power-law viscoplastic potential function *w* can be defined in the form of [53]. (Text 30)

(6-11b) <C-40> In comparison to other PANI composites, the surface of the patch *exhibits* a higher **hydrophilicity** (13) because of the phosphonic groups in phytic acid. (Text 8)

Technicality of lexical items is closely related to the contextual parameter of field and is a matter of degree. For instance, "heterogeneity" occurs in the following three contexts, but the technicality it possesses is of different degree. In the first example, *heterogeneity* functions as circumstance of Cause in the verbal process. The subject matter of this clause is the limitation of *the included studies*, which is not a matter of science and technology; therefore *heterogeneity* in this context is not technical but quite similar in meaning to the less formal words like *difference* and *variety*. To the contrary, in the next two examples, *heterogeneity* is endowed with technicality, because the subject matters are respectively *chi-squared and I-squared heterogeneity analysis* in mathematics as well as *the canopy-scale parameters and architecturally varying components* in chemistry.

(6-12a) <C-3> Due to the small number and **heterogeneity (2*1) of the included studies**, the magnitudes of effect sizes were not reported. (Text 22)

(6-12b) The heterogeneity analysis showed that the heterogeneity chi-squared was 3.56 (d.f. = 13) and p = 0.995; also I-squared (variation in OR attributable to heterogeneity) was 0.0%; these results suggested <C-9> [[that no **heterogeneity (7*1)** existed in included RCTs]]. (Text 15)

(6-12c) <C-8> Furthermore, spatial **heterogeneity (5*2) in the canopy-scale parameters and architecturally varying components** may originate complex flow patterns, which is difficult to interpret, even if using data collected from real channels with live vegetation. (Text 18)

Another point deserving mentioning in terms of technicality is the fact that process-thing is distinct from quality-thing in that it involves semantic distillation. Halliday (1998) states that the progressive change from a specific process *moves* to the theoretical abstraction *motion* illustrates the gradual distilling effect of nominalization: *moves—is moving—a moving—movement—motion*. This distillation is "the beginning of the evolution of scientific theory in the west", and "this nominalizing metaphor is the principle on which all technical terminology is ultimately based" (Halliday, 1998: 200). But this principle does not work so well for quality-thing metaphors whose process of transference is not so complicated.

6.4.4   Semantic Obscuration

Semantic obscuration means that ambiguity in meaning might occur in metaphorization. Ambiguity in meaning is one of the features of metaphoric code under the condition of uncertainty or the condition where ideational explicitness is sacrificed for textual explicitness (Halliday, 2008). Halliday (1994) points out that some information is lost in nominalization with respect to the congruent mode, so ambiguity in interpreting the metaphorical expression is created. Hita (2003) focuses on the semantic ambiguity in one kind of nominalization (the *alcohol impairment* type) by means of transitive and ergative grammatical analyses. Despite the abundant literature on nominalization, the nature of various ambiguities has not been fully explored. This section will illustrate with examples the different kinds of semantic obscuration in quality-thing metaphors, their causing factors and the neutralization of ambiguity by virtue of context. Here ambiguity is used in a broad sense, referring to implicitness in meaning or misinterpretation.

6.4.4.1   Internal Ambiguity

Internal ambiguity is due to the scalar or gradable nature of qualities. When a scalar quality is metaphorized into a thing, its gradability may be simultaneously transferred or may get lost. As noted in Chapter 3 (see Table 3-11), qualities can be binary, scalar and taxonomic in terms of taxonomic type. The lexical realizations of qualities, that is, the congruent adjectival forms of the nominalizations under investigation in this study, are categorized in Table 6-7.

Table 6-7   Classification of qualities in the data: congruent forms of quality-things

Qualities of				Taxonomic type	Example
Proj.	emotive	attitude			scalar	comfortable, unpleasant, friendly
		usuality			scalar	frequent, prevalent, common, popular

(to be continued)

Qualities of				Taxonomic type	Example
Exp.	elaboration		class	taxonomic	seasonal, musical, viscid, viscoplastic
	enhancement	attribution	status	binary	present, absent, available, linear, abnormal, latent, continuous, integrate, nonlinear, asymmetric, complete, consistent, entire, heterozygous, inconsistent, missing, correct, nonpolarizable, real, reversible, silent, unsuitable
			sense-measure	scalar	stable, accurate, intense, flexible, efficient, efficacious, safe, important, complex, conductive, instable, thick, significant, viable, contractible, ambiguous, detectable, severe, transparent, valid, difficult, formable, productive, reliable, smooth, clear, dense, effective, simple, fluent, noisy, hard, resilient, stiff, suitable, wakeful, broad, acute, brief, bright, dry, comprehensive, easy, durable, elastic, free, functional, general, humid, hydrophilic, hygroscopic, insecure, labile, loud, mature, potent, predominant, rich, salient, secure, short, soluble, supreme, tenable, veracious, vigilant, warm
			propensity (beh. qual.)	scalar [dynamic]	active, sensitive, variable, turbid, robust, strong, selective, pathogenic, fit, hypersensitive, lethal, mobile, reproducible, resistive, responsive, sustainable, crystalline, infective, biostable, inert, malignant, repeatable, responsible, susceptible, toxic, virulent, wettable, abrupt, accessible, applicable, aromatic, benign, conductive, controllable, deformable, descriptive, directive, fatal, fiddly, fluorescent, generalizable, genotoxic, hyperpermeable, immunoreactive, intelligent, novel, observable, phototoxic, porous, reactive, terracentric, tractable, tunable

(to be continued)

Qualities of					Taxonomic type	Example
Exp.	enhance-ment	attribution	quantity	in-exact	scalar	diverse, abundant, scarce, versatile, various, biodiverse, inadequate, deficient, insufficient, sparse
		identity			scalar	different, similar, homogenous, invariant, specific, compatible, connective, relevant, uniform, discrepant, disparate, equal, inhomogeneous, nonuniform, equivalent, indistinct, variant, superior
		locational			taxonomic	prior, senior
		causal			causal	

There are binary qualities such as *present, absent, available, linear* and *abnormal*; lexical items such as *seasonal, musical, viscid, viscoplastic, prior* and *senior* are classified as taxonomic, but the vast majority of qualities are scalar. A quality of scalarity does not imply a matter of yes or no, but a hierarchy of degree—high, medium and low, so that it can be further modified by intensifiers such as *very*, or adjuncts such as *really* and *awfully*.

Now that we are focusing on the quality-thing metaphors, a question is worth considering: when a quality is transferred into an abstract thing, what might happen to its scalarity? Will the feature of scalarity be retained in the thing, partially kept or even get lost? By analyzing the collected data, it has been found that one type of semantic obscuration in interpreting such nominalizations is closely related to this question, and it also affects how such nominalizations should be unpacked.

A nominalization transferred from a quality typically means "the state or quality of being...", but the unpacking of such a nominalization may involve several options. For example, a couple of choices are available in unpacking the nominal group *the electronic stability of the patch in physiological medium* in the following example: *the patch in physiological medium is electronically stable, whether the patch in physiological medium is electronically stable or not* or *how electronically stable the patch in physiological medium is*. Which one is the most appropriate interpretation? The answer lies both in and out of the nominal group.

(6-13) <C-9> To *test* the electronic **stability** (1*8) of the patch in physiological medium, samples fabricated on gold Mylar were assembled in the custom-made chamber filled with PBS and used as the anode. (Text 8)

The maintenance or neutralization of qualitative scalarity in the metaphorical thing depends on the context in which the thing occurs. The influential factors might be within or outside the nominal group: (a) the Epithet in the group, (b) the process in the clause where the nominal group serves as a participant, and (c) some indirect evaluative elements in the clause. Examples will be given to illustrate how to discover the accurate meaning of the nominalized quality by means of the three factors.

(1) According to Epithet

There is almost no uncertainty in determining the congruent agnate clauses of the two nominal groups *far greater dopant stability* and *the enhanced stability [of the protonated species in our patch to the multivalent anionic nature of phytic acid]* because of the presence of affirmative Epithets *far greater* and *enhanced*. They can be unpacked respectively into relational clauses: *dopant is far more stable (in the system)* and *the protonated species [in our patch...acid] is more stable*. Here the congruent intensifiers *far more* and *more* are changed into Epithets *far greater* and *enhanced* in the metaphorical groups, which is evidence of the scalarity of the original qualities.

(6-14a) Ironically crosslinking the dopant phytic acid with both chitosan and PANI has the advantage of <C-3> [[*creating* a system [with far greater dopant **stability** (1*3)]]]. (Text 8)

(6-14b) <C-4> We *attribute* the enhanced **stability** (1*4) [of the protonated species in our patch to the multivalent anionic nature of phytic acid] and its ability to bind strongly to chitosan and PANI. (Text 8)

(2) According to Process

A nominalized quality functions as a participant in a new process, so the nature of the process verb contributes to the construal of the nominal element. For the convenience of description, the verbal items realizing processes are provisionally classified into evaluative type such as *evaluate, test, measure, monitor* and *determine*, and affirmative type such as *confirm, prove, validate, reflect, show, facilitate,* and some commonly used ones in identifying mode and circumstantial type clauses, such as *contribute to, result in, lead to* and *stem from*. In clauses with the evaluative type process, scalarity of quality is retained in the nominalization, which results in the ambiguity in meaning, whereas the second type of process neutralizes the scalarity, so that the degree of scalarity is of less importance.

The underlined nominal groups in the following examples have been unpacked into the congruent forms. It can be seen that, in the first two examples (6-15a and 6-15b), the processes are realized by evaluative verbs *evaluate*, *monitor* and *determine* which presume the fact that the scalarity of certain quality under study is unknown, so that it is of necessity to assess and then to make a judgment as to how effective, how stable or how resistive something is. It is interesting to notice that with such evaluation-loaded processes, the quality meaning may be totally negated; that is to say, the scalarity of the quality may range from zero to one hundred percent. Again in the first example, since we do not know how effective the treatment is, we need to make an evaluation, but the result is uncertain: it may be not effective at all, somewhat effective or extremely effective. In contrast, in the other five examples (from 6-15c to 6-15g), the *effectiveness*, *robustness* or *efficiency* is already acknowledged. What matters is not the degree of *effectiveness, robustness* or *efficiency*, but the fact that something is *effective, robust* or *efficient*.

(6-15a) Indeed, the aim of assessing the impact of disease and treatment on QOL is increasingly stressed as crucial for <C-25> [[*evaluating* the overall treatment **effectiveness** (14) in cancer clinical trials]]. (Text 15)

(**Congruent**: how effective the treatment generally is in cancer clinical trials.)

(6-15b) <C-7> To *monitor* the **stability** (1*7) of the PANI patches during incubation in PBS, <C-8> their surface **resistivity** (2*1) *was determined*. (Text 8)

(**Congruent**: how stable the PANI patches during incubation in PBS are; how resistive they are on the surface at different time points.)

(6-15c) The higher success rate and lower average real power loss significantly <C-17> *confirm* the **effectiveness** (10) of the ABPPO algorithm with an aspect of reaching at the optimum point or best solution. (Text 28)

(**Congruent**: the ABPPO algorithm is effective.)

(6-15d) <C-18> The relatively lower execution time of the ABPPO *confirms* its **robustness** (11). (Text 28)

(**Congruent**: the ABPPO is robust.)

(6-15e) <C-5> More recently, Mura *et al.* in 2015 *reviewed* the **effectiveness** (3) of school-based physical activity interventions on academic achievement. (Text 22)

(**Congruent**: school-based physical activity interventions are effective on academic achievement.)

(6-15f) For interventions that address other health behaviors, including diet and physical activity, culture is increasingly considered to be a variable of interest [[in <C-4> *maximizing* the **effectiveness** (4) of the intervention]]. Therefore, culture may play a role in sleep experience in behavioral sleep research. (Text 35)

(**Congruent**: the intervention is effective.)

(6-15g) <C-2> However, polarization due to the oxygen reduction reaction (ORR) still *contributes* significantly *to* the energy **efficiency** (1*2) of fuel cells and metal-air batteries because of the exceptionally high O=O bond energy and the sluggish nature of ORR. (Text 5)

(**Congruent**: fuel cells and metal-air batteries are efficient in energy.)

In some cases, the process of a clause is on its own nominalized into a thing, but the process meaning is still retained, and the quality-thing serves as its post-modifier. In construing the quality-thing, the nominalized process should be unpacked in the first place. The double-underlined lexical items in the following examples (*studies, test, estimate, prognosis, recovery, restoration* and *assurance*) are all instances of process-thing nominalization that can function as the Thing in a nominal group followed by a quality-thing as its Qualifier. The construal of the quality-thing depends on the process meaning of the nominalized process. The congruent forms of *studies*, *test*, *estimate* and *prognosis* are respectively *study*, *test*, *estimate* and *prognose*; they belong to the category of evaluative type, and their evaluative process meaning implies that what is to be evaluated is a matter of degree rather than polarity. To the contrary, congruent forms of *recovery*, *restoration* and *assurance* are respectively *recover*, *restore* and *assure*, which realize the affirmative type of process meaning and thus presuppose the positive meaning of the ensuing participant.

(6-16a) <C-6> Past and current studies [on food security and environmental

sustainability (3*3) in China] *are* discipline-based, and data describing the issues in space and time are often collected using different methods with little or no coordinated management of data. (Text 4)

(**Congruent**: how sustainable the environment in China was and is.)

(6-16b) <C-21> Modern-day dust deposition measurements *offer* a test [of the **accuracy** (9) of our reconstructed dust fluxes]. (Text 10)

(**Congruent**: how accurate our reconstructed dust fluxes are.)

(6-16c) <C-4> *To gain* a full estimate [of the dynamic **flexibility** (2*2) in the vocal tract], we examined the configuration of the upper respiratory tract not only during vocalization but also during facial displays (such as lip smacking and teeth chattering) and during feeding and swallowing. (Text 12)

(**Congruent**: how dynamically flexible the vocal tract is.)

(6-16d) <C-6> With regard to cancer detection, microRNA based markers *have been employed* for accurate prognosis [of **malignancy** (2)].

(**Congruent**: whether malignant (the cancer) is.)

(6-16e) <C-16> The recovery [of luminescence **intensity** (7*4) of the nanoclusters by bilirubin in the **presence** (4*7) of 4.77 mg/mL Cu^2+ ions] *could be fitted with* single exponential function. The results showed that use of higher concentration of Cu^2+ ions in the medium helped detect higher amounts of bilirubin. (Text 16)

(**Congruent**: the luminescence was intense.)

(6-16f) <C-17> Control experiment, involving addition of water to the copper treated (and Au nanoclusters coated) PVDF membrane *did not show* restoration [of luminescence **intensity** (7*5)], thus clearly indicating the role of bilirubin in the recovery. (Text 16)

(**Congruent**: the luminescence was intense.)

(6-16g) <C-2> The goals of antimicrobial susceptibility testing include the detection of possible drug resistance and assurance [of **susceptibility** (2) to drugs of choice for each particular infection]. (Text 19)

(**Congruent**: ... is susceptible to drugs of choice for each particular infection.)

(3) According to other evaluative elements

In addition to the above-discussed Epithet in the nominal group and the process in the clause, some other elements in the clause, especially some indirect evaluative items can also give clues to the construal of the quality-thing metaphor. Martin & White (2008: 62) state that "the selection of ideational meanings is enough to invoke evaluation, even in the absence of attitudinal lexis that tells us directly how to feel". In the first of the following examples, the "Process + Range" configuration *sets the foundation* and the embedded Qualifiers of the Thing in the circumstance *electronically stable* and *effectively function* all together transmit the signal that *this patch is stable*. The fact that it is stable is stressed, while how stable it is goes to the background. In the second example, the metaphorical nominal group functions in the circumstance of Cause introduced by *because of* indicating that *its electronic stability* is the right reason for its application: *could potentially be applied*. Here once again, the scalarity of *stability* is neutralized; now that the *stability* is presumed, it is of no importance to consider how stable it is. It is the same case in the third example that the circumstance of contingency is introduced by the preposition *given* which guarantees the positive meaning of *sensitivity*.

(6-17a) <C-5> The **stability** (1*5) of this patch in the conductive state under physiological conditions and its demonstrated effect on cardiac electrophysiology *sets* the foundation for the design of electronically stable CP-based scaffolds that could effectively function as electronic interfaces. (Text 8)

(**Congruent**: this patch in the conductive state under physiological conditions is stable.)

(6-17b) <C-6> Significantly, this study *presents* a robust bioelectronic device that, because of its electronic **stability** (1*6), *could potentially be applied* at the biotic-abiotic interface to elucidate the role of conductive materials in electro responsive tissues in both ex vivo and in vivo models. (Text 8)

(**Congruent**: robust bioelectronic device is electronically stable.)

(6-17c) <C-4>These ITCZ changes *are* substantial given the **sensitivity** (2*3) of atmospheric heat transport to ITCZ position and the small magnitude of zonalmean changes in precipitation centroid position estimated for past climates. (Text 10)

(**Congruent**: atmospheric heat transport is sensitive to ITCZ position.)

6.4.4.2   External Ambiguity

Different from the internal ambiguity caused by the inherent scalar nature of qualities, external ambiguity is not caused by factors that are relevant to the quality itself, but rather mainly due to the loss of information in the transference from the congruent to the metaphorical and the entrance of a metaphorical nominal group into a new nominal group complex.

(1) Ambiguity due to information missing

The loss of information is one of the obvious reasons for ambiguous interpretations. As for the quality-thing nominalizations, when a congruent attributive relational clause is turned into an incongruent nominal group, most typically, the Carrier or circumstance in the transitivity structure of the clause may correspond to the Qualifier or Classifier of the Thing in the nominal group (Halliday & Matthiessen, 2014). In the first of the following two examples, the congruent Carrier *functionalizations* is reconstrued in the nominal group as Qualifier realized by the prepositional phrase with *of*. In the second example, the Classifier *actor appearance* may correspond as a whole to the Carrier of the congruent clause, or in another way, *actor* serves as Carrier, but *appearance* occurs in circumstance together with the preposition *in*.

(6-18a) There has also been a desire <C-4> [[*to increase* the **complexity** (3*1) of functionalizations]]. (Text 1)

(**Congruent**: functionalizations are complex.)

(6-18b) Lighting variations are generally not expressed in depth data, <C-13> and actor appearance **differences** (5*1) are eliminated (although differences in body shape remain). (Text 32)

(**Congruent**: actor appearances are different / actors are different in appearance.)

But in some cases, the Qualifier of Thing in the nominal group may not be the exact counterpart of Carrier in the congruent clause, which may cause ambiguity in interpretation. In the next example, although *sleep* functions as Qualifier in the nominal group *the insecurity of sleep*, the group cannot be simply unpacked into *sleep is insecure*. Here some information is missing, but it can be recovered from the context. The source of this example, Text 35, is concerned with the cultural aspects of sleep and their relevance to behavioral sleep research, but not the physiological activity of sleep itself. The embedded Qualifier *with the use of watchmen/guards or sleep in conflict territories* gives further information that those individuals and groups have no sense of security when they are at rest because of the insecure social environment, so the Carrier of the congruent clause should be *the environment of sleep* rather than *sleep*.

(6-19) Sociologists are thus concerned with <C-9> *understanding* not only the social forces governing sleep but also how sleep is institutionalized within social systems; the coordination of sleep; the transition periods before, during, and right after sleep; the phenomenological explorations of falling asleep and being asleep, the obligations of the role of sleep, the **insecurity** (9) of sleep for both individuals and groups [with the use of watchmen/guards or sleep in conflict territories], and the fundamental human rights of sleep. (Text 35)

The mismatch between Qualifier in group and Carrier in clause is also indicated by the following example where ambiguity exists in unpacking the nominal group O_2's *robustness of an exoEarth biosignature gas*: which one, the possessive Deictic or Qualifier, corresponds to the congruent Carrier—O_2 *is robust* or *an exoEarth biosignature gas is robust*? It is difficult to make the judgement in terms of the single clause, so once again context comes into play. In the first clause of this quoted example, it is congruently stated that O_2 *is robust*, and then in the discursive flow, when it is picked up again, it is reconstrued as O_2's *robustness*.

(6-20) Oxygen (O_2) is considered Earth's most robust biosignature gas. O_2 is present in Earth's atmosphere to 20% by volume. O_2 is a reactive gas with a short atmospheric lifetime that without continual replenishment by photosynthesis in plants and bacteria would be present only in trace amounts in Earth's atmosphere, ten orders of magnitude less than present today. Any exoplanetary observer seeing oxygen in Earth's spectrum <C-22> would know that some very exotic, non-geological chemistry *must be producing* it, hence the foundational paradigm of O_2's **robustness** (12) of an exoEarth biosignature gas. (Text 6)

Cases involving Classifier in nominal group seem to be more complicated, and it is usually of difficulty in deciding on its corresponding functional role in the agnate clause. In the following example, there are several possible options as to the agnate clause of the nominal group *embryonic lethality in mice*: (a) *embryos in mice are lethal*, (b) *deletion of REV3L is lethal to embryos in mice* or (c) *deletion of REV3L is embryonically (in an early stage) lethal to mice*. The removal of such ambiguities relies heavily on the context where the metaphorical group occurs. When the clause is metaphorized into a nominal group, it enters into a new process as a participant; the circumstantial verb *cause* indicates that it is an Identifying relational process where the nominalized group functions as Value and the first nominal group *deletion of REV3L* is Token; therefore, the second interpretation is more appropriate, and the congruent circumstance in the process is reconstrued as Classifier of Thing in a nominal group.

(6-21) <C-4> Deletion of REV3L *causes* embryonic **lethality** (4*1) in mice and this subunit seems to own additional functions independent of the accessory subunit REV7, having been reported to be specifically required to prevent common fragile sites expression. (Text 23)

(2) Ambiguity due to complexity of nominal group complex

It is not unusual that two or more nominal groups are logico-semantically combined in one way or another to form a group complex. A nominal group which is transferred from a clause is certainly no exception. A potential problem lies in the ambiguous ownership of certain qualities of the Thing, especially when the groups in the complex stand in an extending (traditionally termed as co-ordination) relation to each other. It may be found that sometimes the qualities of the Thing in the second nominal group in the complex seem to be omitted, so the groups share the same one Deictic or Qualifier or some other functional elements. But it is not certain whether such qualities are attributed to the second Thing or not. In some cases, it is not difficult to make a judgement because of the clear grammatical markers. In the first of the following examples, the two nominals *integrity* and *conductivity* share Deictic *the* and Qualifier *of pure* Fe_3O_4. In the second example, the two nominals *ease* and *difficulty* share Deictic *their*. The determinative Deictic *the* and the possessive Deictic *their* determine grammatically the coverage of the two Things in the two groups.

(6-22a) <C-33> As anode materials for LIBs, Fe_3O_4/carbon hybrids *solve* the structural **integrity** (16) and electrical **conductivity** (17) of pure Fe_3O_4 and greatly improve the rate capability and cycling performance. (Text 5)

(6-22b) <C-1> Adhesive, persistent, and metabolically efficient, bacterial biofilms often *present* significant challenges in healthcare, naval, and industrial settings because of <u>their **ease** (1) of formation and **difficulty** (2) in removal</u>. (Text 9)

While in some other circumstances where Epithet or Classifier are involved, it is not easy to make the decision purely by grammatical realizations without reference to the context, both co-in-text and shared knowledge in communication. For instance:

(6-23a) <C-14> Improvement [in <u>the large-scale **homogeneity** (8) and **smoothness** (9*1) of graphene</u>] *will advance* the use of its thin film [in wafer level integrated electronics]. (Text 7)

(6-23b) These are analyzed in regard to how they propagate throughout <u>the structure</u> in correlated groups of residues. <C-9> Residue clusters are then *assessed* in terms of relative impact [on <u>the structural dynamics and **stability** (7*2)</u>]. (Text 9)

(6-23c) Studies with varying curli production indicate that the fibers are critical for <u>strong</u> adhesion, <C-4> and <u>increased</u> curli expression has been shown *to result* in pellicles [with <u>increased surface **elasticity** (6) and **strength** (4*2)</u>]. (Text 9)

In the first of the above-given examples, although *homogeneity* and *smoothness* share the specific Deictic *the* and the Qualifier *graphene*, the Epithet *large-scale* is exclusively attached to *homogeneity*; the agnate clauses should be *graphene is homogeneous in a large scale* and *graphene is smooth*. In the second example, *structural* should be interpreted as the shared Classifier not only because of the presence of Deictic *the*, but the existence of *the structure* in the previous clause, so the agnate clause should be *residue clusters are structurally stable*. In the last example, things are more complicated because there is no Deictic at all, and Epithet *increased* and Classifier *surface* are different in terms of their relation to the two Things. In view of the context, it can be seen that *increased* is attributed to both of them, while *surface* is not a Classifier of *strength*. And *surface elasticity* has somewhat been technicalized to be kind of taxonomy; it is originally from *pellicles are elastic on the surface*.

This kind of ambiguity originates from the inherent complexity in the structure of a group complex, so it does not have so much to do with the metaphoric process of nominalization, but it may cause difficulty in interpreting and unpacking the metaphorical nominal group, and that is why this phenomenon is put under discussion right here.

6.5　Summary

This chapter deals with the experiential semantic change that occurs in the process of quality-thing nominalization. The research results are basically grounded on the transitivity analysis of the 900 clauses and the analysis of the experiential structure of the 996 metaphorical nominal groups in the data. First of all, the experiential semantic changes are typologically classified into different types: one universal semantic change (abstraction) and three particular semantic changes (generalization, specialization and obscuration). The characteristics and causing factors of each type and subtype are described in detail. Meanwhile, it should be noted that there is no clear cut between these types. As presented in Figure 6-5, topologically these different types shade into one another.

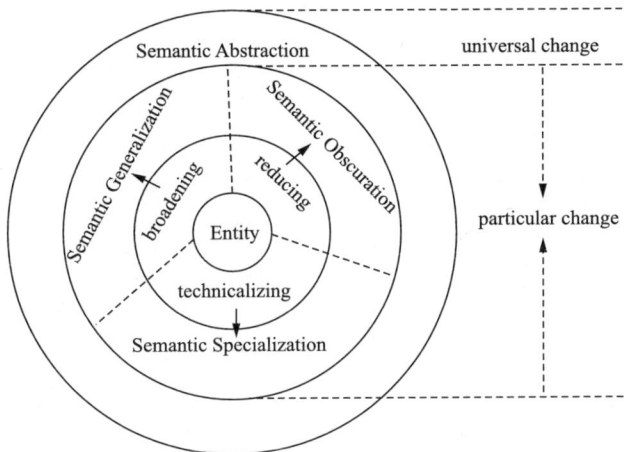

Figure 6-5　Topological presentation of experiential semantic change

For example, semantic generalization and semantic specialization are not contradictory to each other; they are viewed from different perspectives. The more general a lexicogrammatical realization is, the broader its semantic scope is, and consequently the fewer semantic features it has; however, the more technical a lexical item is, the narrower its semantic scope is, and the more semantic features it has. Another discovery in this chapter lies in the layering relation of various semantic changes. Apart from the distinction between universal and particular types, there is a hidden distinction between primary and secondary types. Semantic abstraction implies meaning condensation which involves a junction of different category meanings; semantic generalization involves the broadening of meaning scope; semantic specialization implies technicalizing as a result of the narrowing of meaning scope, and semantic obscuration involves loss of information. The secondary meanings trigger the primary meanings. It has also been found out that these particular types of semantic change are quantitatively different: acquired technicality of semantic specialization, internal ambiguity of semantic obscuration and semantic generalization are of the highest frequency, while intensified technicality and external ambiguity are less frequently presented in the data.

Chapter 7

Implications for the Study of Interpersonal and Textual Semantic Changes in Quality-Thing Metaphor

It has been stated in Chapter 3 that the three modes of meaning are stranded in one clause; now that there are changes in the experiential meaning in the transference from the congruent form to the metaphorical form, there should be changes in the other two strands of meaning. It has been confirmed by Halliday & Matthiessen (2004: 642) that "the significance of grammatical metaphor of the ideational kind extends beyond the ideational metafunction to both the textual and interpersonal ones", because "there is a realignment of the textual and interpersonal environments in which ideational systems operate". This chapter provides some tentative perspectives from which to approach changes in interpersonal and textual meanings as far as the data under study is concerned. The interpersonal semantic change can be viewed from the perspective of the evaluative power of language, and the textual semantic change can be connected to the reference system that a metaphor may enter, which is also applicable to the cases of other kinds of ideational metaphors. Some preliminary results have been presented to evidence such changes, but no further step is taken to go into details because of the limited space of this book.

7.1 Approaching Interpersonal Semantic Change

"Science is also interpersonal; it is not only about construing our experience of some realm of phenomena according to a theoretical model, it is also about exchanging meanings in the community, thereby enacting the roles and relations within the institution of science" (Matthiessen et al., 2016: 9). The most abstruse scientific theory is actualized only when it takes the form of a social act (Lemke, 1990, 1995; Halliday, 1998), so the interpersonal resources of language are important contributors to the negotiation of scientific knowledge as well as to building and maintaining scholarly communities. Exploration of the interpersonal semantic change in quality-thing metaphors may start with an important aspect of the interpersonal resources—evaluation. In this section, a distinction will firstly be made between evaluative qualities and non-evaluative qualities involved in the data. Those of no evaluative power will be excluded from further analysis, while those evaluative ones will be further investigated. The purpose is to discover what would happen to the evaluative nature in qualities when they are metaphorized into quality-things.

7.1.1 A Tentative Classification of Interpersonal Semantic Change

"Interpersonal meanings are certainly lexicalized" (Matthiessen et al., 2016: 12), and this could happen in several ways: lexicalized interpersonal meanings are an important part of the resources of modal assessment in the clause (Halliday & Matthiessen, 2004) and of attitudinal epithesis in the nominal group (ibid.), and of appraisal system (Martin & White, 2008). What is studied here is the transference from a quality to a quality-thing, and most of the adjectives that realize qualities are evaluation-loaded. The modal assessment is not discussed in this study; instead the major concern is what might happen to the evaluative meaning that a quality realizes when it is metaphorized into a thing. The following question awaits an answer: will the evaluative meaning that a quality boasts be carried over to the corresponding quality-thing after metaphorization?

Qualities realized by adjectives tend to be sources of appraisal, but in the register of scientific writing, a certain amount of them are not obviously evaluative in nature, and when they are nominalized into things, they naturally carry no sense of evaluation. All the 996 metaphorical instances and their corresponding congruent expressions are analyzed to check for the presence or absence of evaluative meanings in them. It has been found that 527 out of 996 (52.91%) of the instances under investigation are not evaluative, because they function either as objective descriptions of physical phenomena or as technicalized items without any personal evaluations made by the writers. In the case of objective statement, as indicated by the following examples, qualities as well as their nominalizations are merely descriptions of physical properties of some substances or chemicals. In the first example, *molecules [with an ability to form cell membranes] are available* is a factual proposition, which amounts to an existential clause *there are molecules [with an ability to form cell membranes]*. In the second example, *highly soluble* is the feature of a certain chemical, and in the third example, *genome duplications are more frequent* is also an objective statement that the nominalized process *genome duplication* occurs time and again. In the same vein, *availability, solubility* and *frequency* are not used for personal evaluation.

(7-1a) <C-22> The **availability** (9) [of molecules [with an ability to form cell membranes]] *does not* by itself *demonstrate* that life is possible. (Text 3)

(**Congruent**: molecules [with an ability to form cell membranes] are available.)

(7-1b) <C-22> It is highly economical because it *is* a naturally abundant and sustainable resource [with a high **solubility** (10) in polar solvents], and thus could be a promising precursor for nitrogen-dopedcarbons. (Text 5)

(**Congruent**: it is highly soluble.)

(7-1c) Indeed, Pol32 is required for Break Induced Replication (BIR), the HR pathway repairing one-ended DSBs22. A similar role has been proposed recently for human POLD3, <C-6> whose depletion *results in* a high **frequency** (6*1) of genome duplications. (Text 23)

(**Congruent**: genome duplications are more frequent.)

When a quality is metaphorized to be an abstract entity, in some cases it becomes a theoretical construction or taxonomy that is not value-laden as it used to be, so that the original evaluative feature gets lost or at least weakened to some degree. It is easily understandable that the technicalized items carry no evaluative meaning although they contribute to the construction of a scholarly community due to the special tenor of scientific context. As discussed in the previous chapter, most technical items are field-dependent, so they are more experiential than interpersonal in meaning. Words such as *pathogenicity, vigilance* and *toxicity*, provide good examples. There are still some words which appear to be common attitude-loaded words but are technicalized in specific contexts and thus lose the evaluative meaning. For instance, the adjectives realizing qualities *safe* and *accurate* may be evaluative in some contexts, but in the following examples, their nominalizations *safety* and *accuracy* do not work for evaluation; instead they have been conceptualized to be two experiential categories that are not different from some other categories such as *toxicity, specificity,* and *sensitivity.*

(7-2a) <C-18> We searched the relevant studies [on <u>the clinical benefits</u> <u>and **toxicities** (13) of rAd-p53</u>] in treating MPE <C-19> to *disclose* <u>the clinical</u> <u>benefits and **safety**</u> (4*5). (Text 15)

(7-2b) <C-19> Table 1 *shows* the mean and standard deviation [for <u>well</u> <u>turbidity detection **accuracy** (9*1)</u>], <u>well turbidity detection **sensitivity** (10),</u> <u>well turbidity detection **specificity** (11)</u>, <u>MIC determination **accuracy** (9*2)</u>, and <u>drug susceptibility interpretation **accuracy** (9*3) of our AST reader</u> when using only the best performing single exposure image (i.e., bright exposure) and when combining the dim, moderate, and bright exposure images to digitally increase the dynamic range. (Text 19)

But "technical terms may of course be interpersonalized, in a sense slipping from an experiential taxonomy into the interpersonal realm of assessment" if they are criticized from the perspective of competing approaches or commentators, and are endowed with pejorative evaluation (Matthiessen et al., 2016: 13). The data under investigation are all from original scientific research articles, and there isn't anything like differing theories or competing remarks; therefore, instances of interpersonalized technical terms are hardly found in this study.

With the exclusion of the above-discussed non-evaluative instances, the 469 evaluation-loaded ones are analyzed. By comparing their congruent and metaphorical modes, it has been found that in some cases, the original evaluative meaning tends to disappear in the metaphorical form, while in some other cases, the evaluative meaning in the congruent quality is taken over by the metaphorical quality-thing. In this tentative study, the ways in which the evaluative meaning may be changed are provisionally and roughly classified into two modes (see Figure 7-1): neutralization and transference.

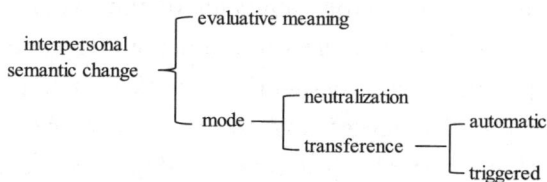

Figure 7-1   A tentative approach to interpersonal semantic change:
from the perspective of evaluation[1]

In the neutralization mode, the congruent evaluative power in the qualities is neutralized in their metaphorical counterparts, whereas in the transference mode, the initial evaluation carried by the congruent qualities is taken over by the metaphorical quality-things. Transference is further divided into automatic and triggered subtypes. The automatic type means the transference of evaluation is mostly peculiar to some kind of lexical items or configurations without too much influence of the contextual factors; triggered transference refers to the case where the maintenance of the evaluative meaning in a quality-thing needs to be motivated by the context.

This preliminary study only focuses on how the evaluative meaning might be changed; what type of evaluative meaning to be changed is not a concern for present discussion. The various categories of evaluation, for example, engagement, attitude and graduation in the appraisal system proposed by Martin & White (2008), require investigation in specific contexts, which will be explored in future study.

Halliday (1979/2007p: 206) puts that "interpersonal meanings cannot easily be expressed as configurations of discrete elements" and "even when the meaning is realized in a single word or a phrase, this can be interpolated at more or less any point in the clause." Therefore, the cooperation between the evaluative items and the context in which they are located contributes to the evaluative power. This study of semantic change is based on the comparison between the congruent and the metaphorical expressions. The three strands of meaning co-work in

---

① Here evaluation is used in a general sense without going further to discuss the specific types of evaluative meaning. The changes in different types of evaluation will be investigated in future research.

one clause, and it is particularly impossible to separate the ideational meaning from the interpersonal meaning. The discussion on the interpersonal semantic change is also based on the previous analyses of the experiential structures of metaphorical nominal groups and the transitivity configurations they work in. Evaluative meaning is produced in specific contexts; it is meaningless to talk about evaluation in the absence of any context. Even the same metaphorical expression may display different evaluative meanings when it occurs in different contexts. Comparison between the next two examples can illustrate this point. The nominal group *their stability* exists in both instances but carries different senses of evaluation. *Stability* in the first case embodies the positive evaluative meaning transferred from the congruent expression (a*crylonitrile azotosomes are stable over long time scales*), because the attributive intensive relational process realized by the verb *ensure* indicates that what is ensured is positive; in the second case, the positive meaning is neutralized in the identifying intensive relational clause, because the verb *assess* implies a sense of uncertainty: *they may or may not be stable.*

(7-3a) Acrylonitrile azotosomes show high barriers to decomposition that are sufficient <C-9> *to ensure* their **stability** (4*1) over long time scales]]. (Text 3)

(**Congruent**: they (acrylonitrile azotosomes) are stable over long time scales.)

(7-3b) <C-10> The second criterion that we used to assess azotosomes *was* their **stability** (4*2). (Text 3)

(**Congruent**: how stable they (azotosomes) are.)

7.1.2 Preliminary Statistics on Interpersonal Semantic Change

The 469 instances under investigation are analyzed according to the proposed types of interpersonal semantic change. Each type is counted, and statistics are presented in Table 7-1.

Table 7-1　Preliminary statistics on interpersonal semantic change

Type	Neutralization	Transference	
		Automatic	Triggered
Number (Percent)	271 (57.78%)	107 (22.81%)	91 (19.41%)

There are 271 (57.78%) instances that belong to the type of neutralization, which means that most of the qualities lose their original evaluative power when they are metaphorized into things. The other 42.22% of all the instances are classified to be the type of transference, among which 107 of them are instances of automatic transference, and 91 are instances of triggered transference. Each type will be explicated and exemplified in detail in the following sections, and reasons for neutralization and transference of evaluation will also be discussed.

7.1.3　Neutralized Evaluative Meaning

The first type of the interpersonal semantic change is neutralization. The general principle for this type is that the nominalized item represents an adjustable degree or extent that can be up-scaled or down-scaled, but not a specified state. There are some cases to be explained.

As discussed in the section of Semantic Obscuration in Chapter 6, the evaluative power of some lexical items will be neutralized if they co-occur with some evaluative verbs. For example, the adjectives *efficient* and *accurate* that realize qualities belong to Appreciation, the subsystem of Attitude in the bigger system of appraisal, and they have a positive connotation of appreciation. But when they are nominalized to be *efficiency* and *accuracy*, and become participants of the process *probe* in this context, their evaluative value is somewhat neutralized, because the verb *probe* implies a sense of uncertainty: *sensory processing* may or may not be efficient, and *automatic sound feature discrimination* may or may not be accurate, so that we have to discover how efficient or how accurate they are by probing. Verbs such as *confirm* and *prove* are classified into the invocation type which can indirectly express certain attitude (Martin & White, 2008), while verbs such as *probe* or *test* are not inherently attitudinal.

(7-4) By using the multifeature paradigm in our study, <C-16> we *probed* the **efficiency** (10*1) of sensory processing in the auditory cortex as reflected by the P1 component of an event-related potential (ERP), and the **accuracy** (11) of automatic sound feature discrimination as reflected by MMN. (Text 24)

The evaluative process can also be nominalized, and the nominal group realizing the quality-thing serves as its postmodifier. In the following example, the process *evaluate* is metaphorized into *evaluation* qualified by the Deictic and Epithet *the stronger* and postmodified by a prepositional phrase introduced by *of*. The original negative meaning conveyed by the congruent *unpleasant* is neutralized in the metaphorical *unpleasantness*, because it has become a target to be evaluated, but not the quality or state of being pleasant.

(7-5) <C-36> NS *has been associated with* the stronger evaluation [of sound **unpleasantness** (18)], and self-reported hearing disabilities. (Text 24)

(**Congruen**t: how unpleasant a sound is.)

Clauses with processes realized by evaluative verbs are not the only situations where evaluative meanings can be neutralized. The following example is a material process realized by the verb *increase* which is not in itself evaluative, but it implies that what can be increased or decreased is something referring to an extent that is neutral rather than a state which is either positive or negative. The Thing of the Goal realized by the metaphorical nominal group, *severity*, does not necessarily mean the quality or state of being severe, and in this context, the degree of it can be up-scaled. Therefore, process type is an important factor influencing the meaning choice of its participants, but is not the unique determinant of meaning neutralization.

(7-6) <C-16> Secondary bacterial infections *increase* the **severity** (7*1) of influenza-associated illnesses and the mortality rates during influenza pandemics. (Text 25)

(**Congruent**: influenza-associated illnesses are severe.)

When a nominalized quality-thing is neutralized in evaluative meaning, new epithets may be added to it to realize certain evaluative meaning. For example, *accuracy* in this case is neutralized in the interpersonal meaning, while the Epithet *good* sheds new light on the positive evaluation.

(7-7) Similar to the approximation of the overall virus release integral, <C-29> good **accuracy** (11*6) *is obtained* for all approaches except the ME formula (highlighted with a blue curve) for the approximation of the first moments. (Text 29)

(**Congruent**: all approaches except the ME formula are very accurate.)

Apart from epithets realized by adjectives, a past or present participle may also function as Epithet in a nominal group. Typical items that have been found in the data are: *increasing, declining, enhanced, increased, heightened* and *improved*. These epithets are usually taken as adjectives, so that some of them are listed as independent entries in the dictionary, and even have their own inflectional forms such as *increasing/increasingly* and *increased/increasedly*. But viewed from the perspective of grammatical metaphor, they are originally transferred from processes in clauses, so they are taken as condensed forms of clauses. In fact what is happening is that "some part of the experiential structure of a clause is being downgraded to function as Epithet" (Halliday & Matthiessen, 2014: 380). Epithet of this kind can be taken as a reduced form of a non-finite clause and hence is agnate to a Qualifier. In the following example, *the enhanced stability* is systematically related to *stability which has been enhanced*.

(7-8) <C-4> We *attribute* the enhanced **stability** (1*4) of the protonated species in our patch to the multivalent anionic nature of phytic acid and its ability to bind strongly to chitosan and PANI. (Text 8)

(**Congruent**: the protonated species in our patch is more stable.)

Interpersonal meanings tend to be scattered prosodically throughout a whole grammatical unit or even a text. As to the unit of nominal group, interpersonal meanings can be embodied in the person system, the attitudinal type of Epithet, connotative meanings of lexical items, and in prosodic features (Halliday & Matthiessen, 2014). Although epithets realized by the participles are not as strong in evaluative meaning as those realized by attitude-laden adjectives, they contribute indirectly to appraisal in one way or another in combination with other elements in various contexts. "The degree of play between discourse semantics and lexicogrammar which Halliday's concept of grammatical metaphor affords is an important aspect of appraisal theory" (Martin & White, 2008: 11). Since such items are agnate to the down-ranked non-finite clauses, problems arise while unpacking them into the congruent form. It is very hard to find a corresponding item functioning as the Submodifier of Attribute in the congruent relational clause, because they are new additions as a result of grammatical metaphor rather than items that are directly transferred from the congruent mode. A relatively proper solution is to replace them with the more grammaticalized item *more* or *less* according to their connotative orientation (positive or negative). For example:

(7-9a) Pt or its alloys are the best known ORR catalysts, <C-4> but their applications *are limited* by <u>the high cost and **declining activity**</u> (3*1). (Text 5)

(**Congruent**: (Pt or its alloys) are <u>less active</u>.)

(7-9b) <C-27> Clusters near the edge of the b sheet *show* **increased responsiveness** (15*1), particularly to the more mobile terminal regions. (Text 9)

(**Congruent**: Clusters near the edge of the b sheet <u>are more responsive</u>.)

(7-9c) <C-31> Clusters 7 to 12, excluding 8, *show* **a heightened sensitivity** (16) <u>to</u> perturbations, most strongly in clusters 7 and 12. (Text 9)

(**Congruent**: Clusters 7 to 12, excluding 8, <u>are more sensitive</u> to perturbations.)

(7-9d) <C-1> <u>The **increasing prevalence** (1) of antimicrobial resistance</u> *represents* a severe threat to global health and is becoming more common to bacterial pathogens in high mortality diseases including pneumonia, diarrheal disease, and sepsis. (Text 19)

(**Congruent**: antimicrobial resistance is <u>more / increasingly prevalent</u>.)

(7-9e) <C-37> Increasing the number of comparisons *N leads to* **improved descriptiveness** (17), however the resulting histograms also become more sparse. (Text 32)

(**Congruent**: (the result) is <u>more descriptive</u>.)

7.1.4 Transferred Evaluative Meaning

7.1.4.1 Automatic Transference

The evaluative nature of the congruent quality can be automatically transferred to the nominalized quality-thing. The most obvious cases are the two special types of quality-thing nominalization: (a) the "*be of* + metaphorical nominal group" type, and (b) the "a variety of ..." type. Martin & White (2008) point out that it is possible to nominalize certain attitude so that it comes out grammatically as a thing. They give an example: *the contrast in styles is of considerable interest*—"a semantic process whereby something attracts our attention is rendered as a grammatical entity nominating a type of attraction" (Martin & White, 2008: 10). Similar examples that most frequently occur in the data in this study are ...*be of tremendous significance* or ...*be of particular importance*. In this sense, the attitudinal meaning can not only be realized by attitude-loaded lexical items, but also be expressed in an indirect way by some lexical items realizing experiential meaning. As to the second type, apart from the most commonly used *a variety of*, there are some other similar expressions in the data: *the majority of*, *the versatility of*, *an abundance of* and *a diversity of*. These items do not carry the interpersonal meaning of attitude, but they belong to the subsystem of graduation, and they are instances of quantification which can add force to the expressions they modify.

Automatic transference also involves some evaluative qualities of the binary type. Binary qualities have nothing to do with degree; they are matters of yes or no. When they are nominalized, their evaluative meanings are retained in the nouns realizing quality-things. Lexical items such as *correct/correctness, consistent/consistency, complete/completeness* and *real/realism*, are typical examples in the data. In the following examples, *correctness* refers to a definite state of being correct rather than a changeable degree, because *the scheme* or *Theorem 1* is either correct or incorrect, and there is no middle point.

(7-10a) In the remainder of this section <C-14> we *formalize* the **correctness** (8*1) of the scheme. (Text 31)

(**Congruent**: the scheme is correct.)

(7-10b) <C-15> The **correctness** (8*2) of Theorem 1, along with the existence of such a net and the fact that each S-approximation of Aτ (step 2 of Algorithm 1) takes Θ (1/δ2), *lead directly* to the following result [on the **accuracy** (9) and **complexity** (10) of Algorithm 1]. (Text 31)

(**Congruent**: Theorem 1 is correct.)

It is interesting to note that even the evaluative meanings of some scalar qualities can be naturally carried over onto the metaphorical things. When such qualities are nominalized, scalarity in them is greatly weakened or disappears, and what matters is confined to their connotative meanings. Lexical items such as *free/freedom, novel/novelty, simple/simplicity, brief/brevity, friendly/friendliness, benign/benignity* and *strong/strength*[1] belong to this type. In the following examples, both *simplicity* and *freedom* have definite positive meaning.

(7-11a) <C-12> For **simplicity** (8*2), and to ensure that the results are not detector specific, the overlaps *have been computed* using a flat PSD. (Text 34)

---

① In this case, strength means advantage or strong point.

(**Congruent**: for (the research) to be simple.)

(7-11b) <C-26> The anisotropic barostat *allows* the membrane the **freedom** (13) [to change or lose its structure], <C-27> *increasing* the **realism** (14) of the simulation. (Text 3)

(**Congruent**: the membrane is free to change or lose its structure.)

In the data, there is one instance of the taxonomic quality whose evaluative meaning is automatically transferred to its nominalization; this unique instance is *prior/priority*.

(7-12) <C-1> The necessity of significantly increasing domestic agricultural production *is* a **priority** (1) if food security is to be achieved. (Text 4)

(**Congruent**: the necessity of significantly increasing domestic agricultural production is prior.)

7.1.4.2 Triggered Transference

Context plays an even more important role for the triggered transference, because it is difficult to make a judgement as to the evaluative meaning of a quality-thing without reference to context, and it is a certain context that triggers evaluation which is otherwise neutralized. This situation is quite similar to domination, a type of prosodic realization proposed by Martin & White (2008: 20): "the prosody associates itself with meanings that have other meanings under their scope." In this study, there are a couple of triggers which can dominate or help to drag out the evaluative meaning of the quality-things: verbs realizing processes in clauses, prepositions introducing prepositional phrases, epithets in nominal groups and some other co-configurational elements.

The typical types of evaluation-triggers and the number of instances in the data are summarized in Table 7-2. The total number (84) is inconsistent with the results (91) shown in Table 7-1, because some metaphorical groups share the same process, preposition or epithet. Each type will be illustrated with examples from the data.

Table 7-2　Typical types of evaluation-trigger

Type of trigger				Number	Typical example
Process	Material			15	increase, dwarf, provide, safeguard, add, address, resolve, aid, enhance, promote
	Relational	intensive	identifying	18	demonstrate, show, reflect, exhibit, indicate, set, underscore, suggest, re-emphasize
			attributive	11	ensure, confirm, keep, complicate, validate
		circumstanti-al	identifying	8	contribute to, lead to, support, suffer from, be based on, result in
			attributive	3	be because of, be due to, rely on
		possessive	identifying	1	provide
			attributive	3	have
Preposition				17	with, given, because of, due to, despite, for
Epithet				2	the *faint* planet, the *proven* clinical efficacy
Others				6	the *possibility* of, leave many *opportunities* to, in the *absence* of, new *problems* of, set the *foundation* for, is *discouraging*

(1) Process-triggered evaluation

It has been found that if the metaphorical nominal groups assume independent functional roles in clausal configurations, both material and relational processes may trigger the otherwise neutralized evaluation in the quality-things. Relational processes of this kind outnumber material processes; there are only 15 instances with material process as evaluation-trigger. The typical verbs realizing material processes listed in Table 7-2 can be roughly classified into three types according to the meanings they imply: positive contribution (e.g. *increase, aid, enhance, provide, add, safeguard*), negative contribution (e.g. *dwarf*) and problem-solving (e.g. *address, resolve*). For example, the negative evaluation transferred from *ambiguous* to *ambiguity* is triggered by the verb *resolve*, because what is to be resolved should be something problematic and imperfect.

(7-13) By normalizing these local descriptors, <C-32> we *are able to resolve* the scale **ambiguity** (14*2) which remained in our auto-calibration of Sect. 5. (Text 32)

(**Congruent**: the scale is ambiguous.)

In some cases, the process verb is not the sole factor which can induce evaluation. It is the cooperation between process verb and other elements that contributes to evaluation. In this example, *is dwarfed* is a receptive material process, the metaphorical nominal group *the brightness of the adjacent host star* is the Actor, and the Goal is *the faint planet*. The verb *dwarf* implies that the Actor is superior to the Goal, and the double-underlined Epithet *faint* forms an obvious contrast to *brightness*, so that *brightness* embodies a positive evaluation in this context. *The adjacent host star* is definitely bright, and *how bright is it* is a question to be dismissed. This clause is quiet similar in meaning to this one: *the faint planet is overshadowed by the bright adjacent host star.*

(7-14) Here, our understanding has advanced greatly in the last 20 years, but we are severely limited as to the underlying raw data we can collect from something as small as a shell of gas a few hundred kilometers thick around a faint planet tens of trillions or more kilometers away, <C-8> where the faint planet *is dwarfed* by the **brightness** (4) of the adjacent host star. (Text 6)

(**Congruent**: the adjacent host star is bright.)

In the case of relational processes as triggers, things are more complicated. According to statistics in Table 7-2, there are 29 instances of the intensive type, 11 instances of the circumstantial type, and 4 instances of the possessive type; each type has both identifying and attributive modes. Most of the intensive verbs embody the meaning of *display* or *guarantee*. As illustrated by the following examples, *demonstrate* and *ensure* trigger the positive evaluation in *importance* and *stability*.

(7-15a) <C-13> Our work *demonstrates* the **importance** (5*2) of constraining dust's effects on regional SSTs in both past and modern climates. (Text 10)

(**Congruent**: constraining dust's effects on regional SSTs in both past and modern climates is important.)

(7-15b) Acrylonitrile azotosomes show high barriers to decomposition (17 kcal/mol) that are sufficient <C-9> *to ensure* their **stability** (4*1) over long time scales]]. (Text 3)

(**Congruent**: they (acrylonitrile azotosomes) are stable over long time scales.)

The next two examples are demonstrations of circumstantial verbs as triggers. These verbs imply a definite cause-and-effect relationship between the two participants involved. In the first instance, *difficulty* means what is difficult instead of the degree of being difficult, and thus it has kind of negative evaluation. Similarly, in the second instance, *the validity of the assumptions* is the basis on which *such an approach* relies, so that it has to be something positive; without this circumstantial process, its evaluative power might be neutralized in some other contexts.

(7-16a) <C-6> The gradient and Newton methods, for instance, *suffer from* **difficulty** (3) in handling inequality constraints. (Text 28)

(**Congruent**: it is difficult for the gradient and Newton methods to handle inequality constraints.)

(7-16b) Such an approach, however, would be of indirect nature <C-3> and crucially *relies on* the **validity** (3) of the assumptions in the numerical modeling process. (Text 34)

(**Congruent**: the assumptions in the numerical modeling process are valid.)

The third type of relational verbs is possessive. There are only two instances of this kind in the data. What is possessed should be something definite rather than an uncertain degree, so *stiffness* in the first instance embodies a positive evaluation, while *ambiguity* in the second instance indicates a negative evaluation.

(7-17a) Experiments mapping biofilm mechanics have shown <C-3> [[that curli *provide* **stiffness** (3*2) and mechanical **homogeneity** (5) within their biofilms and serve to reinforce the biofilm structure, making up most of the insoluble biofilm matrix]]. (Text 9)

(**Congruent**: their biofilms are stiff and mechanically homogeneous.)

(7-17b)... <C-11> because the planet's physical properties lay hidden beneath too few measurements or *have* an **ambiguity** (6*2) in their interpretation. (Text 6)

(**Congruen**t: their interpretation is ambiguous.)

(2) Preposition-triggered evaluation

Metaphorical nominal groups can also be embedded within prepositional phrases, and the prepositions may be triggers of evaluation in the metaphorical groups. As is shown by the following example, the metaphorical expression can be construed as *despite the fact that NAFLD induction is prevalent and important*. The preposition *despite* is followed by a fact, which renders the two nominalizations a positive sense of evaluation.

(7-18) <C-1> Despite its **prevalence** (1) and **importance** (2*1), the underlying mechanisms of NAFLD induction *are poorly characterized*. (Text 21)

(3) Epithet-triggered evaluation

As is discussed earlier, lexicalized interpersonal meaning is also realized by the attitudinal epithets in the nominal group. Most of such epithets can be transferred from their congruent forms, and the evaluative nature can be simultaneously taken over. As the example shows (see Figure 7-2), Epithet *extraordinary* corresponds to the Submodifier of Attribute *extraordinarily*; they play different roles in terms of experiential meaning, but they are not so different in attitudinal meaning.

Metaphorical	nominal group	the	extraordinary	complexity	of host-pathogen and pathogen-pathogen interplay
		Deictic	Epithet	Thing	Qualifier

Congruent	relational clause	host-pathogen and pathogen-pathogen interplay	is	extraordinarily	complex
		Carrier	Process: intensive		Attribute
				Submodifier	Head

Figure 7-2　Example of transferred appraisal

(7-19) Although well-characterized animal models have allowed for the study of various factors <C-3> that *affect* bacterial acquisition and **pathogenicity** (1*2) after influenza, <C-4> the extraordinary **complexity** (3) of host-pathogen and pathogen-pathogen interplay complicates investigating every possible interaction simultaneously. (Text 25)

(**Congruent**: host-pathogen and pathogen-pathogen interplay is extraordinarily complex.)

In the above example, the Epithet *extraordinary* does not influence the negative evaluative meaning of the Thing realized by the noun *complexity*. But not all of the epithets in the metaphorical nominal groups are naturally transferred from the congruent clauses in the same way. As discussed in Section 7.1.3, in addition to the most popular epithets realized by adjectives, present and past participles of verbs can also serve as epithets. In the data under investigation, one special instance of participle-as-epithet which can trigger evaluation is discovered. In the following example, Epithet *proven* in the nominal group is agnate to a projecting clause *it has been proved that...*; and *proven* implies a positive proclamation, indicating the fact that *each antibiotic for various bacterial species* is *efficacious*. Different from the universally accepted "lower rank syndromes" whereby figures are reconstrued as elements and "higher rank syndromes" whereby sequences are reconstrued as figures (Halliday, 1998: 216-217), what happens here is that a sequence congruently realized by a clause complex is reconstrued directly as an element realized by a nominal group, with the rank of clause being skipped over (see Figure 7-3). This combination of rankshift and rankskip is exactly an illustration of the semogenic power of nominalization.

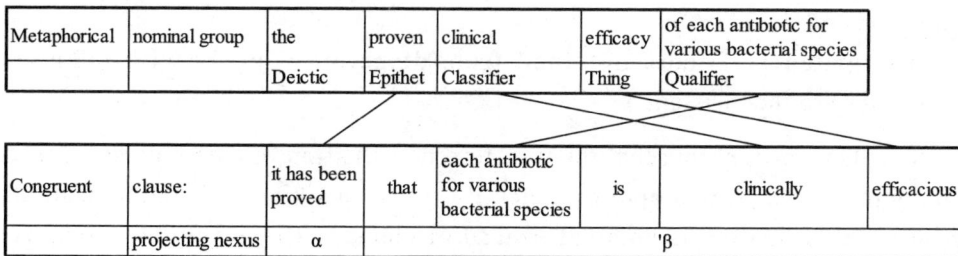

Metaphorical	nominal group	the	proven	clinical	efficacy	of each antibiotic for various bacterial species
		Deictic	Epithet	Classifier	Thing	Qualifier

Congruent	clause:	it has been proved	that	each antibiotic for various bacterial species	is	clinically	efficacious
	projecting nexus	α	'β				

Figure 7-3   Example of epithet-triggered evaluation

(7-20) The MIC value must be interpreted using a table of values <C-15> [[that *relate to* the proven clinical **efficacy** (4) of each antibiotic for various bacterial species]]. (Text 19)

(**Congruent**: it has been proved that each antibiotic for various bacterial species is clinically efficacious.)

(4) Other co-configurational elements-triggered evaluation

Evaluation is prosodically distributed; it is not brought about by merely one evaluative element, but produced by the coordination of various elements in a context. Apart from the above-mentioned evaluation triggers, there are some less obvious ones which may be some attitude-loaded lexical items. In the first example, *of efficacy* is the postmodifier of the Head noun *possibility* which is a nominalized modality, and *possibility* triggers the positive evaluation in *efficacy* together with the other two lexical items of positive meaning (*benefits* and *effectively*). In the second example, the word *problems* implies a negative meaning, and *such as* indicates that *the inconsistency of 3D data* forms an elaboration of *problems*, so that *problems* dominates the negative evaluation of *inconsistency*.

(7-21a) Although the fever caused by rAd-p53 is viewed as an obvious adverse effect in clinical treatment, <C-17> sometimes it also *indicates* the possibility [of **efficacy** (3*4)] and benefits of rAd-p53 therapy, suggesting that rAd-p53 can effectively mobilize the immune systems of human body to kill the tumor **cells**. (Text 15)

(**Congruent**: it is possible for rAd-p53 therapy to be efficacious in clinical treatment.)

(7-21b) However, <C-14> this also *introduces* new problems such as the **inconsistency** (6) of 3D data obtained from disparate sources with unknown calibrations. (Text 32)

(**Congruent**: 3D data obtained from disparate sources with unknown calibrations are inconsistent.)

It is also worth noting that the transferred evaluation in nominalization tends to be objectivized, which applies generally to various kinds of nominalizations. Because the evaluation is nominal instead of clausal, it is not propositionalized and thus cannot be challenged or argued about. That is to say, the evaluation is down-ranked grammatically and consequently it is hard to be argued about but can only be accepted. For example, as to the congruent clause *each annotated metabolite is significant*, we can argue about it: *Is it? / Yes, it is / No, it isn't; It may be; No, it can't be*, but it is almost impossible to argue about its metaphorical expression *the significance of each annotated metabolite*, because what is expressed in the nominalization has to be taken for granted.

(7-22) <C-9> The volcano plot *shows* the fold change and <u>the **significance** (8)</u> <u>of each annotated metabolite</u>. (Text 17)

(**Congruent**: each annotated metabolite <u>is significant</u>.)

7.2   *Approaching Expansion in Textual Meaning*

There is "a gain in textual meaning in the shift from the congruent mode of realization to the metaphoric mode" (Halliday & Matthiessen, 2004: 643). Textual meaning is intrinsic to language itself, and it is a prerequisite to the effective operation of both experiential and interpersonal metafunctions; it appears in an enabling role (Halliday, 1973; Halliday & Matthiessen, 1999). Therefore, in this sense, what will be discussed here about the textual effects of ideational metaphor is not merely confined to the quality-thing type. Although this study focuses on the quality-thing metaphors with data analysis, the findings have universal implications in this respect.

When a quality is metaphorized into a quality-thing, it may take on a textual role by entering the system of reference or securing a thematic position. The analysis of the data under study indicates that there is some relation between the functions in a nominal group (Deictic, post-Deictic and Epithet) and the textual meanings they realize. As is shown by Table 7-3, co-reference, generic reference and metaphorical Theme[①] are closely related to the Deictic, while comparative reference is realized by post-Deictic and Epithet. In this section, different types of expansion in the textual meaning will be analyzed, counted and explicated in detail.

Table 7-3   Functions in nominal group and corresponding textual meanings

Grammar	Deictic		post-Deictic	Epithet
Textual meaning	co-reference	Metaphorical Theme	comparative reference	
	generic reference			

---

① Metaphorical Theme is proposed by Martin (1992), but it is not different from the idea of "textual accommodation" mentioned by Halliday & Matthiessen (2004: 642-643) in considering the textual effects of ideational metaphor. When a sequence is realized metaphorically by a clause, the figures making up the sequence are correspondingly realized metaphorically by nominal groups serving as elements of the clause, and these nominal groups can be given textual status such as Theme or New.

7.2.1 Entering the System of Reference

If a figure is realized metaphorically by a nominal group rather than congruently by a clause, it then gains access to the textual systems of the nominal group, most importantly, the system of determination, so that it can be taken textually as a discourse referent. A quality assigned to a thing or an Attribute in a relational clause cannot appear as a referent or be tracked down in a discourse, but when it is nominalized to be a quality-thing as the Thing/Head of a nominal group, it can be referred to again in the discursive flow. The original clause is condensed into a nominal group, and thus it can occur as Theme/Rheme or part of Theme/Rheme in a new clause. In this sense, the ideational metaphor accommodates the textual meaning. Therefore, Deictic is of particular importance in anchoring the quality-thing in textual development, and it is through nominalization that the congruent attributive relational clause gains additional textual meaning which is represented by textual reference and meaning packaging.

In this study, with the exception of the 50 instances of the special types (the *a variety of* type and the *of + nominalization* type), among the 946 nominal groups under observation, 544 of them carry Deictic of different types (including elliptical ones), and the other 402 ones have no Deictic. Table 7-4 summarizes the number and percentage of each type of Deictic that occurs in the data.

Table 7-4   Items functioning as Deictic

Type			Item	Number		Percent	
Deictic	specific	demonstrative	the	413	429	78.86%	88.79%
			(elliptical the)	16			
			this	11		2.02%	
			these	7		1.29%	
		possessive	their	14	15	2.76%	
			(elliptical their)	1			
			its	14	15	2.76%	
			(elliptical its)	1			
			embedded nominal group	6		1.1%	

(to be continued)

Type			Item	Number	Percent	
Deictic	non-specific	total	no	14	2.57%	11.21%
		partial	a(n)	42	7.72%	
			one	3	0.55%	
			any	2	0.37%	
				total: 544	100%	

In order to make a clear explanation, the distinction between specific and non-specific reference, and the distinction between particular and general/generic reference should be clarified. "The textual status at issue in the system of reference is that of identifiability" (Halliday & Matthiessen, 2014: 623). If the given element is identifiable, the listener or audience will have to recover its identity from somewhere else in the text; if it is not identifiable, it will be established as a new element of meaning while interpreting the text. Grammatically, if the Deictic of the referent is specific, its identity is recoverable. From Table 7-4, it can be seen that the specific type of Deictic takes up a large proportion (88.79%), including the demonstrative type (*the, this* and *these*) and the possessive type (*their, its* and some embedded nominal groups). The specific reference can be anaphoric or cataphoric. Anaphoric reference points backwards to an antecedent that has already been part of the text's system of meaning; alternatively, cataphoric reference points forwards to a referent that is to be introduced into the unfolding text. Cataphoric reference is rare, but structural cataphora is common where the reference is located within the same nominal group (Halliday & Hasan, 1976), and usually a Deictic *the* or *that/those* is present to indicate that the Qualifier of the nominal group is what is defining. The following are examples of specific references (both cataphoric and anaphoric): Examples 7-23a and 7-23b involve cataphoric (structural) references; Example 7-24 presents an instance of anaphoric reference.

(7-23a) <C-13> Histopathologic scores further *highlighted* the **severity** (9*2) of lesions in livers and spleens of HA-MARV-infected hamsters compared to those of WT-MARV-infected hamsters. (Text 14)

(7-23b) <C-23> To *test* the mechanical **reliability** (15) of our as-grown glassy graphene thin film, we sonicated the film on a quartz substrate in an ultrasonic cell crusher (80 W and 40 kHz). (Text 7)

(7-24) The functionalizable sites that are <u>equivalent</u> are first identified and numerically labeled, as shown in Fig.1A for the organic SBUs of ZBP Zn2(1,4-benzenedicarboxylate)2(pyrazine). Here, <u>equivalent</u> functionalization sites are determined from symmetry and refer to those that will enable the SBUs to be reversed (or rotated) to give a structure with the same connectivity. <C-11> This **equivalence** (8) *is used to limit* the search space to structures that are considered more synthetically feasible. (Text 1)

Among the specific type of Deictic, *the* accounts for 78.86%. *The* is a particular kind of determinative Deictic which means that "the subset in question is identifiable; but this will not tell you how to identify it—the information is somewhere around, where you can recover it" (Halliday & Matthiessen, 2014: 367). *This*, *these* and *such* are mainly used for anaphoric reference, and may involve textual condensation, which will be discussed in a later section. Lexical items realizing possessive Deictic include personal pronouns such as *their* and *its*; some embedded nominal groups such as *China's, O_2's, the smartphone's, the mutant's, Algorithm 1's* and *the point's* also function as devices of reference, especially of co-reference. The pronoun Deictic has to be recovered from the context when the metaphorical nominal group is unpacked into the congruent form. In the first of the following examples, *its* is recovered from the previous clause, so the nominal group *its popularity* is unpacked to be the relational clause *Monte Carlo integration is popular*. The same principle also works for the second example where *their* co-refers to the two kinds of *repair* that have been mentioned in the previous clause.

(7-25a) When applying random based rules, abscissas are determined by random sampling of the integration region. <u>The corresponding numerical integration method</u> is also known as <u>Monte Carlo integration</u> (Davis and Rabinowitz, 1994). <C-17> Its **popularity** (5) *is based* on the straightforward generation of abscissas and it is commonly used to generate reference solutions. (Text 29)

(**Congruent**: <u>the corresponding numerical integration method</u> /Monte Carlo <u>integration</u> is popular.)

(7-25b) <u>Proper repair</u> involving POLD3 and REV3L may be required for replication or <u>repair</u> to bypass the hybrids as well as other DNA damages, <C-9> so that in <u>their</u> **absence** (8*3) DNA breaks *would accumulate* without generating *de novo* hybrids. (Text 23)

(**Congruent**: when <u>repairs</u> are absent.)

Deictic realized by an embedded nominal group is in most cases agnate to the Carrier of the congruent relational clause, but can also be unpacked as the circumstance of the congruent clause. As illustrated by the following instances, *Algorithm 1* in the first example becomes the Carrier of the congruent clause, while *China* in the second example appears in the circumstance of the relational clause.

(7-26a) Interestingly, the fact <C-18> [[that <u>Algorithm 1's</u> **complexity** (10*2) *depends on* the total variation of the template I_1]] is not an artifact of the analysis of the algorithm. (Text 31)

(**Congruent**: how complex <u>Algorithm 1</u> is.)

(7-26b) <C-7> Although the recent rise of farmers' markets and community-supported agriculture represents only a small segment of the food system, it may provide a new avenue *to improve* <u>China's food</u> **safety** (4*1) in the future. (Text 4)

(**Congruent**: how safe food <u>in China</u> is.)

As to the non-specific reference, there are also some total or partial determiners realizing the non-specific type of Deictic in the data: *no, a(n), one* and *any*; they convey the meaning of none or some unspecified sub-set. But they only take up a small proportion (11.21%) among all the Deictic-marked nominal groups. Examples are provided here:

(7-27a) Besides being active in alkaline medium, IAG-C catalyst is also found <C-28> to be an effective ORR catalyst in acidic media with 4e **selectivity** (12*2) and, at the same time, <C-29> *shows* **a** much better **stability** (14*2) than the Pt/C electrode. (Text 5)

(7-27b) Although this effect is audible <C-5> and *sounds* like **a** slight **indistinctness** (4) or foreign accent, the monkey version of such phrases is still clearly understandable (audio file S2). (Text 12)

(7-27c) <C-19> **One** obvious **difference** (13) is that the I2D/IG ratio of glassy grapheme is much higher than that of glassy carbon, increasing from 0.2 to

0.8. Even so, the relative high D band still indicates disorder in glassy graphene. (Text 7)

(7-27d) Thereby, <C-12> **any** observed cellular **heterogeneity** (3*4) *would be* an effect of initial cell-to-cell **variability** (2*7) <C-13> while **heterogeneity** (3*5) [resulting from the delayed infection process] *is* negligible. (Text 29)

(7-27e) The heterogeneity analysis showed that the heterogeneity chi-squared was 3.56 (*d.f.* = 13) and *p* = 0.995; also I-squared (variation in OR attributable to heterogeneity) was 0.0%; these results suggested <C-9> that **no heterogeneity** (7*1) *existed* in included RCTs. (Text 15)

Martin (1992) proposes the notion of discourse semantics and Martin & Rose (2007) have further modified the idea. In the framework of discourse semantics, reference is discussed in the textual system of Identification for tracking participants in discourse. Presenting reference used to introduce an element indefinitely and presuming reference used to track down what has been mentioned in the system of Identification correspond exactly to the non-specific and specific types of reference that have been discussed above. Although a distinctive set of terms are employed to describe the system of Identification, there is no basic difference between Martin's ideas and those put forward by Halliday & Hasan (1976, 1985/1989). Martin's study of text "functions for the most part to recontextualize Halliday and Hasan's conception of cohesion from the perspective of discourse semantics" (Martin, 1992: 26).

It is worth noting that there are 402 out of 946 nominal groups (42.49%) that have no Deictic. But the absence of the Deictic element is not of no value; on the contrary, it is also systemically meaningful within the system of non-specific determination, and the value selected is realized by a form that has no Deictic in the expression. It is one of the frequently used ways to introduce plural participants. As is shown in the following example, *responsibilities* is introduced in an indefinite way by the plural form and the lack of determiner. Most importantly, *responsibilities* here does not refer to specific abstract entities, but generalizes the types of responsibilities, and two kinds of responsibilities (individual and collective) are presented in the example. Reference of this kind is called generic reference (Martin & Rose, 2007: 179).

(7-28) It would be prudent, therefore, to revise how the governance of environmental protection in China is delivered and <C-23> to better *identify* individual and collective **responsibilities** (13*3). (Text 4)

There is also a contrast between references to particular members of a class and reference to the class itself. The former is defined as particular reference, and the latter is called generic reference. When a nominal group refers to a particular thing or a set of things, all of the specific and non-specific determiners can function as Deictic, but their values within the number systems are different. When a nominal group refers to a class of things, the use of determiners as Deictic is relatively constrained. Generic reference has been studied under the title of "generics" not only in linguistics but also in philosophy and logic (Lyons, 1977). It has been found that there is some connection between the types of texts and the two kinds of reference. Particular references are more likely to occur in recreating and reporting texts, while generic references are more likely to be found in expounding texts (Halliday & Matthiessen, 2014: 373). All of the data in this study are chosen from expounding scientific texts. The high frequency of the absence of Deictic in the data has proved Martin's statement that texts with high levels of nominalization "typically involve generic rather than specific (particular) reference and so few of the nominalized participants play a role in long reference chains" (Martin, 1992: 138). In most cases, nominal groups without any Deictic are used to refer to classes of things instead of referring to things that are presumed. In the following example, the sole element in the nominalized group is the Thing *missingness*; the absence of Deictic implies that the quality-thing has been taken as an abstract entity representing a general type of phenomenon.

(7-29) <u>Data are assumed to be missing</u> at random with respect to the outcome variables, <C-29> but **missingness** (16) *was allowed to be dependent* on the covariates. Without any covariates, the model is similar to a pairwise analysis in which all available data are used to estimate pairwise associations. (Text 22)

7.2.2   Metaphorical Theme—Textual Status in the Metaphoric Mode

As mentioned earlier, determiners like *this* and *these* may indicate anaphoric reference. There is a special case where the quality-thing in the nominal group refs backwards to a cluster of information rather than an individual antecedent; that is to say, the nominalization packages or condenses a large chunk of previous information, and then what is condensed becomes the point of departure (Theme) or the new information of the next clause. This phenomenon is termed as metaphorical Theme and metaphorical New by Martin (1992). It can be grouped under the umbrella of texture metaphor, because on the one hand, it is a nominalization within a clause, and on the other hand, it exerts its influence beyond the single clause by connecting in meaning the Theme or the New of successive yet distinct clauses in the text, and thus plays an important role in textual cohesion (Dong & Zhang, 2017). The following examples illustrate this point. In the first example, the nominal group *this similarity* packages the information ranging from clause <a> to clause <c>; the congruent form *similar* appears earlier in the two relational processes *look qualitatively similar* and *looks similar*. In the second example, the nominal group *these differences* is a meaning condensation of the previous clause which is marked by lexical items *larger* and *smaller*. The third example is an illustration of the metaphorical New whereby what is expressed in the process *...does not necessarily provide an adequate indication* is condensed into the nominal group *this inadequacy*, and it in turn becomes the new information of the following clause.

(7-30a) <a> Overall, precipitation changes in the coupled and slab ocean simulations <u>look qualitatively similar</u>, <b> reflecting both local and more remote responses to the warming over the TNA region where the dust forcing was applied. <c> In both experiments, the spatial structure of the precipitation response to dust reduction <u>looks similar</u> to a correlation map between local precipitation and summer TNA surface temperature in the unperturbed slab ocean simulation (fig. S11). <C-20> This **similarity** (8*5) *suggests* that the observed precipitation responses in the reduced dust experiments are primarily due to the TNA SST warming in response to reduced dust loading. (Text 10)

(7-30b) The negative values obtained for both $\Delta H°$ and $\Delta S°$ from the ^{1}H NMR titration data indicate that the complexation of BPP34C10 with MV^{2+} in solution is enthalpically driven in both CD_3SOCD_3 and D_2O. Note that Table 1 shows the <u>relatively larger</u> values of K_a and $\Delta G°$, as well as the <u>smaller</u> values of $\Delta H°$ and $\Delta S°$ in the SMJ system.<C-7> **These differences** (5*2) can be attributed to <u>the **presence** (7) of graphene electrodes</u>, <C-8> which might *improve* <u>the</u>

efficiency (8) of host-guest interactions. (Text 11)

(7-30c) However, a computer model based on a plaster cast of the vocal tract of a monkey cadaver <u>does not necessarily provide an adequate indication</u> of the range of vocal tract shapes produced in living animals. <C-3> To *remedy* **this inadequacy** (3), we first examined the vocal anatomy of behaving macaques using x-ray videos. (Text 12)

This phenomenon well demonstrates the power of expansion, one of the mighty semogenic powers of nominalization. The discoursal argument or statement is carried forward by packaging some semantic construct from the preceding discourse, and what is packaged becomes the point of departure for a further step in the discursive flow. As far as the quality-thing nominalization is concerned in this study, there are only 10 instances of metaphorical Theme that have been found in the data, but this inferiority in number should not degrade its value. It has been proved that, similar to process-thing nominalizations, quality-thing nominalizations can also exert their power in textual semantic expansion.

7.2.3   Comparative Reference: post-Deictic and Epithet

Apart from the above-mentioned relation of co-reference and generic reference set up by Deictic items, there is another kind of reference: comparative reference which defines a relation of contrast. Different from co-reference whereby the same entity is referred to again, the reference item in comparative reference signals what is referred to by a frame of reference. The comparative reference items functioning in nominal groups mainly include post-Deictic, Numerative and Epithet, because "the comparison is made with reference either to general features of identity, similarity and difference or to particular features of quality and quantity" (Halliday & Matthiessen, 2014: 633). Few Numeratives have been found in the data in this study, so post-Deictics and Epithets will be taken as major concerns.

This subsection is aimed at discovering how the post-Deictic and Epithet in a nominal group with nominalization as the Thing contribute to the realization of textual cohesion. Among the 946 nominal groups under investigation, 28 of them have post-Deictics, and 166 of them are found to possess Epithets (see Table

6-2). Those post-Deictics and Epithets that can function as comparative reference items are listed in Table 7-5.

Table 7-5 Comparative reference items

		post-Deictic	Epithet
general	identity	same	
	similarity	similar	comparative adjective: such
	difference	other, different	
particular			comparative adjective: higher, greater, lower, better, further, smaller, larger, superior, (much) better, (far) greater
			Submodifier + Subhead: adjective: more average, (more) predictable

There are two broad types of comparative reference items: general and particular. Among the general type, three subtypes (identity, similarity and difference) are distinguished. No particular post-Deictics are found. In order to explore the changes in meaning taking place in nominalization, comparison between the metaphorical and the congruent modes has to be conducted. Specific examples with each type of the reference items will be given to illustrate how the reference meaning is expressed in both metaphorical and congruent ways.

(1) post-Deictic: *same*

The post-Deictic *same* is used to indicate the general feature of identity; it presumes the comparison between two items. In this example, the nominal group *the same abruptness* is agnate to the relational clause *A is as abrupt as B*. As the Thing *abruptness* is unpacked into the Attribute *abrupt*, the post-Deictic *same* is simultaneously changed into the Submodifier (*as...as*) of the Attribute.

(7-31) It is difficult to test <C-27> [[whether the end-AHP rise in dust flux *occurred* with the same timing and **abruptness** (12) in the Bahamas as on the African margin because the transport time of sediments from bank tops to channel sediments is approximately 400 to 600 years, imparting a lag and smoothing the record in the Bahamas cores]]. (Text 10)

(**Congruent**: the end-AHP rise in dust flux in the Bahamas was as abrupt as that on the African margin.)

(2) post-Deictic: *similar* and *different*

Epithet (Submodifier + Subhead: adjective): *more average*

These two categories are grouped together because they share the same mode of variation in unpacking the metaphors. As is shown by the following examples, the post-Deictic or Epithet realized by an adjective in the nominal group is agnate to the Submodifier (realized by an adverb) of the Attribute in the congruent clause. *Similar, different* and *more average* are agnate to *similarly, differently* and *more averagely* respectively.

(7-32a) At such temperatures, it *might seem* almost impossible for a flexible organic membrane <C-2> to form, let alone one [with similar **flexibility** (2*1) to that of a lipid bilayer]. (Text 3)

(**Congruent**: one (organic membrane) and a lipid bilayer are similarly flexible.)

(7-32b) In consequence, <C-23> different **efficiencies** (10) of the genetic modifications can be mapped to broadening parameter distributions. (Text 29)

(**Congruent**: the genetic modifications are differently efficient.)

(7-32c) This typical behavior allowed us to take an "average-case" approach regarding the total-variation, in which we model it as a linear function of n_1. This allows the net sizes to depend only on the template dimension n_2 and precision δ, <C-19> resulting in more average, predictable, memory and runtime **complexity** (10*3). (Text 31)

(**Congruent**: the "average-case" approach is more averagely and predictably complex in memory and runtime.)

(3) post-Deictic: *other*

The post-Deictic *other* presumes the existence of something else with which what is being talked about is compared. Its functional role usually remains unchanged in the congruent clause. In the following example, when the Thing *sensitivity* is unpacked to be the Attribute *sensitive*, its classifier *environmental* goes naturally to the position of circumstance, and *other* becomes post-Deictic of the Thing *environment* in a new nominal group.

(7-33) A recent epidemiological study reports <C-4> [[that up to 88% of individuals with high noise **sensitivity** (2*3) *self-declare* at least one other environmental **sensitivity** (2*4)]]. (Text 24)

(**Congruent**: 88% of individuals [[who are highly sensitive to noise]] are sensitive at least to one other environment.)

(4) Epithet: general comparative adjective: *such*

The Epithet *such* is quite special in that the Thing it is attributed to is usually a condensation of the materials in the preceding clause or clauses. As discussed in the previous section, the Thing serves as the metaphorical Theme. But meanwhile, *such* presumes the existence of some other kind of Thing. In the following example, *such deficiencies* refers backwards to the underlined information in the preceding clause, but it implies that there might be some other kinds of *deficiencies* determined by other factors.

(7-34) To better understand the role of human Pol 6 in the control of genome stability we evaluated the impact of depleting POLD1 and POLD3 on DNA replication and DDR. We found a general increase in genome instability <C-11> as determined by DNA breaks accumulation, activation of the DNA damage checkpoint, impaired S-phase progression under replication stress and accumulation of chromosome **abnormalities** (10) in POLD1- and POLD3-depleted cells. <C-12> Such **deficiencies** (11) were accompanied by a decrease in the **density** (12) of active replication origins, which suggests a key role of POLD1 and POLD3 in this process. (Text 23)

(5) Epithet: particular comparative adjective

This type of comparative reference is the one that most frequently occurs in the data. The lexical items are some particular adjectives in the comparative form with or without Submodifiers such as *higher, greater, lower, better, smaller* and *larger*. But problems occur when the metaphorical nominal groups are unpacked; the comparative meaning realized by such lexical items can only be realized by either *more* or *less*. The metaphorical forms of these Epithets cannot be retained in the congruent clauses, but can only be substituted by two more grammaticalized adverbs according to whether their meanings are positive or negative. As to the unpacking of these items, there seems to be a shift from particular lexical items which are unbounded to more generalized and bounded grammatical items. And thus there is a kind of transference from grammaticalization to lexicalization in turning the congruent form to the metaphorical form, which once again verifies that the nominalized Thing can be further modified and consequently its meaning is expanded. For example:

(7-35a) <C-2> On the other hand, nanoscale particles such as metal nanoparticles, quantum dots, carbon dots, graphene quantum dots and atomic clusters usually *provide* higher **sensitivity** (1*2) to detection using either surface plasmon resonance based optical changes or changes in the emission characteristics of the nanoparticle based sensor. (Text 16)

(**Congruent**: graphene quantum dots and atomic clusters are usually more sensitive to detection...)

(7-35b) Ironically crosslinking the dopant phytic acid with both chitosan and PANI has the advantage of <C-3> [[*creating* a system [with far greater dopant stability (1*3)]]]. (Text 8)

(**Congruent**: dopant is far more stable in the system.)

(7-35c) The non-independence of observations due to cluster sampling was taken into account. <C-28> Chi-square tests values closer to zero indicate a better fit, i.e. a smaller **difference** (15*5) between expected and observed covariance matrices. (Text 22)

(**Congruent**: observed and expected covariance matrices are less different.)

The above-mentioned five modes of variation in unpacking the metaphorical groups into congruent clauses are summarized in Figure 7-4.

	Mode 1	Mode 2
metaphorical (in group)	post-Deictic + Thing	post-Deictic / Epithet (*adj.*)+ Thing
congruent (in clause)	as + Attribute +as	Submodifier (*adv.*) + Attribute
	Mode 3	Mode 4
metaphorical (in group)	post-Deictic + Classifier + Thing	Epithet (such)+ Thing
congruent (in clause)	Attribute + Circumstance: post-Deictic + Thing	Carrier (recovered) + Attribute
	Mode 5	
metaphorical (in group)	Epithet (comp *adj.*)+ Thing	(lexicalization)
congruent (in clause)	Submodifier (more/less) + Attribute	(grammaticalization)

Figure 7-4   Variation modes of comparative reference

By comparing the metaphorical and congruent modes, it can be found that the transformation from the Attribute in the clause to the Thing in the group is central, because it has an inevitable knock-on effect on the realignment of all the other elements, and that is an illustration of the grammatical metaphor syndrome. In Mode 1, the metaphorical comparative post-Deictic of Thing is agnate to the congruent Submodifier (*as...as*). In Mode 2, the metaphorical post-Deictic of Thing also corresponds to the congruent Submodifier of Attribute but is realized by an adverb. In Mode 3, the post-Deictic and Classifier of the Thing in the metaphorical nominal group are moved to the place of circumstance in the congruent clause. In Mode 4, the metaphorical *such* is agnate to the Carrier in the congruent clause, and this Carrier needs to be recovered from the previous clause or clauses. Mode 5 of unpacking is characterized by a transference from specification to generalization as well as a transference from lexicalization to grammaticalization, whereby the Epithet realized by a particular comparative adjective in the metaphorical nominal group is agnate to a generalized Submodifier of Attribute in the congruent clause, and the Submodifier can only be realized by either *more* or *less* according to the positivity or negativity of the transferred meaning.

When we are talking about reference, the cohesive device, we are transcending the boundary of clauses and entering the realm of text. Different from groups and clauses which are grammatical units, text is a unit of meaning. The textual accommodation of ideational grammatical metaphor is elaborated and the increase in textual meaning due to grammatical metaphor is further validated in this study. First of all, when an attributive intensive relational clause is metaphorized into a nominal group, it enters the system of Deictic of the nominal group and consequently the system of Reference in the text, which is a direct result of metaphorization. Since Deictic is an exclusive element in a nominal group, it is a new addition that does not exist in the congruent clause, and Deictic plays a major role in co-reference. Secondly, the combination of Deictic (*this* or *these* in particular) and quality-thing nominalization is also found to serve as metaphorical Theme that refers backwards to a package of information in the preceding clauses. Thirdly, some post-Deictics and Epithets are resources of comparative reference; it cannot be denied that their congruent agnates are also items of the same kind of reference. But the functions of the metaphorical and congruent elements are quite different, so that the meanings they realize are not synonymous, and the generalized expressions for comparative reference in the congruent clause tend to be particularized in the metaphorical mode.

Because the purpose of this study is to discover the semantic changes that occur in metaphorization by means of comparison between the congruent and metaphorical expressions, what has been discussed about reference in this section is well based on the grammatical analysis of the experiential structure of nominal groups. Other kinds of textual effects of grammatical metaphor are not included here, although they are of great importance in interpreting grammatical metaphor. For example, lexical organization, one of the ways by which cohesion is created, is also a commonplace occurrence in the data. The following are instances of lexical cohesion. In the first example, *breadth* is related in meaning to *a wide range* in the previous clause; similarly, in the second example, *directivity* relates to *direction*. As to the third example, the co-occurrence of the metaphorical form *accuracy* and the congruent form *accurate* creates lexical cohesion.

(7-36a) MOFs have garnered significant attention for <u>a wide range</u> of applications, such as gas separation and storage, catalysis, and proton-conducting membranes. <C-1> <u>The **breadth** (1) of applications</u> *is largely due to* their highly tunable nature. (Text 1)

(7-36b) In this configuration, the tubes are acoustically coupled, and we expect the radiation by the structure to take place <u>in all three directions</u>, <C-2> *covering* the entire surrounding space without <u>a specific **directivity**</u> (2). (Text 2)

(7-36c) <C-18> Given <u>the **accuracy** (8*1) of the OPLS binding energies</u>, we *expect* these values of Ka and ΔE to <u>be accurate</u> to within 20%. (Text 3)

7.3　Summary

This chapter discusses, in a tentative manner, the interpersonal and textual semantic changes in the shift from the congruent to the metaphorical. The primary principle is followed that semantics is realized by lexicogrammar and controlled by context, and it is further proved that the three brands of meaning are interwoven, so that what is discussed in this chapter is still grounded on the lexicogrammatical analyses of the metaphorical clauses and nominal groups in the previous chapters.

In approaching the interpersonal semantic change, the evaluative power of language may be taken into consideration, which is seldom touched upon by the previous studies. The data for investigation in this study involve quality-thing metaphors, and qualities which work as Epithets in nominal groups or Attributes in relational clauses are usually important sources of evaluation; therefore, it is of both interest and significance to study whether the congruent evaluation is retained in the metaphorical mode. Meanwhile, because the data are from scientific research articles, a lot of qualities do not work for evaluation but are rather simple descriptions of physical or chemical phenomena due to the special characteristics of this register. Those non-evaluative qualities are excluded from investigation, and only those that are evaluative are taken into account. By analyzing the authentic data, some possible types of change in evaluative meaning are discovered and counted. It has been found that the original evaluative power in more than half of the instances of qualities under study is neutralized after being metaphorized; for others, the congruent evaluation can be taken over by the metaphorical quality-things, but apart from the naturally transferred ones, an equal amount of them need to be triggered by other elements in the clausal configurations. It is also worth noting that the instances of evaluation in this study are mostly indirect evaluation, and thus are not so obviously evaluative.

As to the textual semantic expansion, which is universal to all types of ideational metaphor, the study is mainly based on the analyses of the functions in nominal group (Deictic, post-Deictic and Epithet) and their relation to the system of reference and the thematic prominence. The different types of Deictic and the corresponding types of reference are clarified and exemplified. In addition, it has been found that there are a small number of metaphorical Themes, and five modes of change in comparative reference are summarized. In this preliminary study, all the data are clauses taken from texts, and the discursive presentation of references throughout a text is not conducted, which is one of the limitations of this study.

Chapter 8

Conclusion

In the previous chapters, the semantic change in grammatical metaphor has been investigated by focusing on the quality-thing ideational metaphor with detailed data analysis. This chapter will conclude this study by summarizing the major findings and contributions and making suggestions for future research with reference to the limitations of this study.

8.1 Major Findings

Focusing on the quality-thing ideational grammatical metaphor, this study explores the various types of semantic change that occur when a congruent form is turned into a metaphorical one. It is a data-based empirical study that is guided by the theories of SFL; it seeks evidence of semantic changes from the changes in the stratum of lexicogrammar in combination with contextual analysis. The major findings of this study can be summarized into the following four aspects.

(1) Classification of experiential semantic change in quality-thing metaphor

There are primarily four types of experiential semantic change in the quality-thing ideational metaphor: semantic abstraction, semantic generalization, semantic specialization and semantic obscuration. There are also some subtypes: semantic generalization includes acquired technicality and intensified technicality, and semantic obscuration is further divided into internal ambiguity and external ambiguity.

Semantic abstraction means that qualities describing experiential things are turned into abstract entities after being metaphorized. Semantic generalization refers to the fact that the meaning of the metaphorical thing is generalized to be a theoretical construct and consequently the thing refers to a category or class of things rather than any specific member in this class. Semantic generalization inevitably involves broadening of the semantic scope of the thing, because it is not directly pertinent to any specific thing, but a generality of all members of one class. Semantic specialization involves meaning shrinkage or solidification; the meaning scope of a lexical item is narrowed with more semantic features added. In this study, semantic specialization is mainly embodied in technicalizing. In the case of acquired technicality, those qualities whose congruent forms are of no technicality can be used in a technical way in a new context after being grammatically metaphorized into quality-things; in the case of intensified technicality, those qualities whose congruent forms are already technical in meaning have an increase in the degree of technicality after being grammatically metaphorized. Semantic obscuration means that ambiguity in meaning might occur in the process of grammatical metaphor. Internal ambiguity is due to the scalar or gradable nature of qualities; external ambiguity is caused by the loss of information in the transference from the congruent to the metaphorical and the entrance of a metaphorical nominal group into a new nominal group complex.

(2) Distribution of different types of experiential semantic change in the data

These different types of experiential semantic change demonstrate certain regularity of distribution in the data under investigation. Semantic abstraction is a general change, while the other three are particular changes. Statistics show that semantic generalization takes place in 10.34% of all the instances (103 in number) under investigation. Semantic specialization is the most prominent in number with an occurrence of 446 (44.78%) instances, among which the majority of them (358 in number) belong to the category of acquired technicality, and 88 instances thereof are categorized as intensified technicality. Semantic obscuration accounts for 19.08% of all the instances with 166 (16.67%) cases classified as internal ambiguity and 24 (2.41%) instances falling under the subtype of external ambiguity.

(3) Lexicogrammatical realizations and controlling contextual factors of these experiential semantic changes

Experiential semantic changes have specific lexicogrammatical realizations and are controlled by contextual factors. There are 202 lexical realizations of quality-things in this study, and all of them are characterized by semantic abstraction. It has been accepted that this kind of abstraction derives from semantic junction, but apart from the frequently mentioned "quality + thing" junction, this study discovers that some processes realized by verbs may be changed into qualities realized by adjectives and then turned into things realized by nouns, so that these quality-thing metaphors involve the tri-junction of three semantic categories of "process + quality + thing". Although instances of tri-junction have no priority in number, it serves as evidence of metaphoricity and further confirms the special status of quality. The notion of cline is also adopted to treat the relation between abstraction and countability in this study by taking the pluralized nominalizations into account. Abstract things can also be quantified, and nominalizations with plural markers are illustrations of the semogenic power of grammatical metaphor; the singular and plural forms of a nominalization realize different meanings.

The thing which is characterized by semantic generalization is lexicogrammatically realized by the Thing without any qualities in a nominal group. It has been discovered that this semantic change is related to the functional roles these metaphorical nominal groups play in clausal transitivity configurations. Statistics show that 53.4% of these groups rankshift downwards; a rankshifted metaphorical group may serve as the Qualifier of another element or work with a preposition to become the circumstance. In this case, the Carrier in the congruent relational clause is unrecoverable. The other 46.6% of these metaphorical nominal groups may play functional roles such as Goal, Value, Token, Attribute, Carrier or Phenomenon in clauses; in this case, the congruent Carrier can be recovered, but it is of no necessity to be recovered due to its weakened status.

Data involving semantic specialization in this study mainly refer to those technicalized items. A plenty of qualities realized by adjectives may acquire technicality when they are transferred into abstract entities and enter the context of scientific language; mostly they are transcategorized into vectors or units of measurement, and they contribute to taxonomizing and textual organization. Lexical items realizing quality-things with intensified technicality are usually marked as discipline-specific in dictionaries. Technicality of lexical items is closely related to the contextual parameter of field and is a matter of degree.

Additionally, in terms of technicality, the transference from a quality to a thing is relatively simple and void of the semantic distillation that is typical of technicalized process-thing.

In terms of semantic obscuration, it has been found in this study that one type of semantic obscuration in interpreting such quality-thing metaphors is closely related to the scalar nature of qualities. The maintenance or neutralization of qualitative scalarity in the quality-thing depends on the context in which the quality-thing occurs. Three factors that may help to eliminate such kind of ambiguity have been discovered: (a) the Epithet in the group, (b) the process in the clause where the nominal group serves as a participant, and (c) some indirect evaluative elements in the clause. Semantic obscuration can also be caused by the loss of information in metaphorization or the entrance of a metaphorical nominal group into a new nominal group complex. By comparing the congruent and the metaphorical forms, it has been found that when the Qualifier or Classifier of Thing in the metaphorical nominal group does not correspond exactly to the Carrier in its congruent clause, ambiguity in meaning arises. It has also been discovered that semantic obscuration may lie in the ambiguous ownership of certain qualities of the Thing in a nominal group complex, especially when the groups in the group complex form an extending relation.

In addition, this study complements the typological analysis of the semantic change, indicating that there is no clear cut between different types. It is also pointed out that there exists a kind of layering relation between certain types in addition to the distinction between the general type and particular types.

(4) Tentative approaches to interpersonal and textual semantic changes in quality-thing metaphor

Interpersonal semantic change can be preliminarily explored from the perspective of evaluation in view of the inherent features of the authentic data. This study proposes a tentative classification of interpersonal semantic change: neutralization and transference, with transference being further divided into automatic and triggered types. Statistics show that the evaluative meanings are neutralized in up to 57.78% of all the instances when qualities are metaphorized into things, and the other 42.22% retain their original evaluative meanings. It has been found that if the nominal realizing the metaphorical thing co-occurs with an evaluative process verb, its evaluative meaning tends to be neutralized, and in some cases, the evaluative process is in itself nominalized, and thus the nominal group realizing the quality-thing becomes its post-modifier. Typical cases of automatic transference have been discovered: the two special structures of quality-thing nominalization (*"be of +* metaphorical nominal group" and *"a variety of..."*), some binary qualities and some scalar qualities whose scalarity is greatly weakened or even vanishes when they are metaphorized. In triggered transference, four types of triggers have been discovered: (a) verbs realizing processes in clauses, (b) prepositions introducing prepositional phrases, (c) epithets in nominal groups, and (d) some other co-configurational elements.

Textual semantic change can be preliminarily explored from the more generally-applied perspective of Reference. After analyzing the Deictic, post-Deictic and comparative Epithet in 946 metaphorical nominal groups, this study has discovered the relation between the textual meanings they realize and their congruent forms. The Deictic is related to co-reference, generic reference and metaphorical Theme, while the post-Deictic and comparative Epithet have something to do with comparative reference. It has been found that in the system of co-reference, instances of specific reference take up 88.79%, while instances of non-specific reference account for merely 11.21%. Additionally, 42.49% of the instances in the data have no Deictic; the absence of Deictic carries value in the system of non-specific reference. There are ten metaphorical nominal groups with the Deictic *this* or *these* which refers backwards to the large patch of information rather than a single precedent. This kind of condensation of information which may serve as the point of departure of a clause is termed as metaphorical Theme. In addition, five modes of change in textual meaning realized by comparative reference have been worked out by comparing the congruent with metaphorical forms.

8.2   *Contributions of This Study*

This study has made some contributions in theoretical, methodological and practical aspects.

Firstly, this study gets to the core of the theory of grammatical metaphor by exploring, in a systematic way, the various types of semantic change (changes in experiential meaning in particular) that occur in the transference from a congruent mode to a metaphoric mode. The discoveries of this study, to a certain extent, fill the gap in the previous studies, provide evidence for a meaning-based new classification of grammatical metaphor, and further contribute to the enrichment of the theory of grammatical metaphor.

Secondly, different from most of the previous related studies, this study adopts both qualitative and quantitative research methods by focusing on the quality-thing ideational metaphor. To investigate the changes in meaning with the consideration of contextual factors, a relatively large quantity of authentic data (900 clauses from scientific research articles) are analyzed at different ranks in terms of both clausal transitivity configurations and experiential structures of nominal groups; all the quality-thing metaphors in the data are unpacked into their congruent forms for comparison.

Thirdly, this study is a grammatical investigation of language itself, so it is of some value for both critical and positive discourse analyses. Meanwhile, the findings can be applied to help cultivate the consciousness of metaphor in language learners and help them take in the determinant contextual factors in choosing a congruent or metaphorical expression; therefore, this study has some implications for classroom language teaching and construction of language-based learning theory.

8.3 Limitations and Suggestions for Future Research

This study has managed to answer the research questions, but it has the following limitations.

First of all, there exists some limitation regarding data collection. In this study, all the data are chosen from texts of natural science, a very typical register that is characterized by ideational grammatical metaphor, while texts from other registers are not involved. The quantity of data needs to be increased and more text types should be included in future studies. Additionally, this study is mainly confined to the grammatical unit of clause; it would be much better if a further step is taken to go beyond clauses and extend to texts. Investigation into the textual semogenic power of grammatical metaphor, reference-tracking in particular, requires study of discursive flow rather than mere clauses.

Secondly, this study is mainly concerned with the experiential semantic change and has conducted detailed lexicogrammatical analyses in terms of clausal transitivity configurations and the experiential structures of nominal groups, but it only provides tentative approaches as to the interpersonal and textual semantic changes due to the limited space of this book. Future studies should go further in interpersonal and textual aspects.

Thirdly, this study focuses on the quality-thing ideational metaphor; although the research findings give insights into the essential question of meaning in the theory of grammatical metaphor, they cannot cover all the modes of semantic change in every type of grammatical metaphor. In the future study, different types of grammatical metaphor, especially the interpersonal metaphor, need to be given more consideration.

Bibliography

[1] Allerton, D. J. *Stretched Verb Constructions in English*[M]. London & New York: Routledge, 2002.

[2] Astiga, K. Happening Things: Grammatical metaphor in ancient Greek[P]. Paper presented at ASCS (Australian Society for Classical Studies) 24th Conference and General Meeting, 2002.

[3] Austin, J. L. *How to Do Things with Words*[M]. Oxford: Clarendon Press, 1962.

[4] Austin, J. L. Performative Utterances[C]// J. O. Urmson & G. J. Warnock. *Philosophical Papers*. Oxford: Oxford University Press, 1979: 233-252.

[5] Banks, D. The evolution of grammatical metaphor in scientific writing[C]// A. M. Simon-Vandenbergen, M. Taverniers & L. Ravelli. *Grammatical Metaphor: Views from Systemic Functional Linguistics*. Amsterdam: Benjamins, 2003: 127-147.

[6] Banks, D. *The Development of Scientific Writing: Linguistic Features and Historical Context* [M]. London & Oakville: Equinox Publishing Ltd., 2008.

[7] Bernstein, B. *Class, Codes and Control. Vol.1: Theoretical Studies Towards a Sociology of Language*[M]. London: Routledge & Kegan Paul, 1971.

[8] Bhat, D. N. S. *The Adjectival Category: Criteria for Differentiation and Identification*[M]. Amsterdam: John Benjamins, 1994.

[9] Bouchard, D. *The Semantic of Syntax: A Nominalist Approach to Grammar*[M]. Chicago: The University of Chicago Press, 1995.

[10] Bussmann, H. *Routledge Dictionary of Language and Linguistics*[M]// G. P. Trauth & K. Kazzazi. Beijing: Foreign Language Teaching and Research Press, 2000.

[11] Butt, D. Theories, maps and description: an introduction[C]// R. Hasan, C. Cloran & D. G. Butt. *Functional Descriptions: Theory in Practice*. Amsterdam: John Benjamins Publishing Company, 1996: xv-xxxv.

[12] Byrnes, H. Emergent L2 German writing ability in a curricular context: a longitudinal study of grammatical metaphor[J]. *Linguistics and Education*, 2009(20): 50-66.

[13] Chomsky, N. Remarks on nominalization[C]// R. A. Jacobs & P. S. Rosenbaum. *Readings in English Transformational Grammar*. Waltham: Ginnand Company, 1970:184-221.

[14] Chomsky, N. *The Minimalist Program*[M]. Cambridge: The MIT Press, 1995.

[15] Chomsky, N. *Language and Mind*[M]. New York: Harcourt Brace Jovanovich, 2006.

[16] Christie, F. & J. R. Martin. *Knowledge Structure: Functional Linguistic and Sociological Perspectives*[M]. London: Continuum, 2007.

[17] Coffin, C. *Historical Discourse: The Language of Time, Cause and Evaluation*[M]. London: Continuum, 2006.

[18] Colombi, M. C. Grammatical metaphor: academic language development in Latino students in Spanish[C]// H. Byrnes. *Advanced Language Learning: The Contribution of Halliday and Vygotsky*. London & New York: Continuum, 2006:147-163.

[19] Davidse, K. A semiotic approach to relational clauses[J]. *Occasional Papers in Systemic Linguistics*, 1992(6): 99-137.

[20] Davidse, K. Turning grammar on itself: identifying clauses in linguistic discourse[C]// C. Butler, M. Berry, R. Fawcett & G. Huang. *Meaning and Form: Systemic Functional Interpretations*. Norwood: Ablex, 1996: 367-393.

[21] De Beaugrande, R. *Linguistic Theory: The Discourse of Fundamental Works*[M]. London: Longman Group UK Limited, 1991.

[22] Derewianka, B. *Language Development in the Transition from Childhood to Adolescence: the Role of Grammatical Metaphor* [D]. Sydney: Macquarie University, 1995.

[23] Derewianka, B. Grammatical metaphor in the transition to adolescence[C]// A. Simon-Vandenbergen, M. Taverniers & L. Ravelli. *Grammatical*

Metaphor: Views from Systemic Functional Linguistics. Amsterdam: Benjamins, 2003:185-219.

[24] Devrim, D. Y. Grammatical metaphor: What do we mean? What exactly are we researching? [J/OL]. *Functional Linguistics*, 2015 (2):50-56 [2016-08-28]. https://functionallinguistics.springeropen.com/articles/10.1186/s40554-015-0016-7.

[25] Dik, S. C. *The Theory of Functional Grammar (Part I): The Structure of the Clause* [M]. Holland: Foris Publications, 1989.

[26] Eggins, S. *An Introduction to Systemic Functional Linguistics*[M]. 2nd edition. New York & London: Continuum, 2004.

[27] Fan, W. F. *A Systemic-Functional Approach to Grammatical Metaphor*[M]. Beijing: Foreign Language Teaching and Research Press, 2001.

[28] Fawcett, R.P. *Cognitive Linguistics and Social Interaction: Towards an Integrated Model of a Systemic Functional Grammar and the Other Components of a Communicating Mind*[M]. Heidelberg: Groos, 1980.

[29] Fawcett, R. P. Grammatical Metaphor Questioned[P]. Lecture at Beijing University, 2006.

[30] Fawcett, R. P. *Invitation to Systemic Functional Linguistics through the Cardiff Grammar*[M]. London: Equinox, 2008.

[31] Fontaine, L. *Analyzing English Grammar: A Systemic Functional Introduction*[M]. New York: Cambridge University Press, 2013.

[32] Fowler, R. *Linguistic Criticism*[M]. New York: Oxford University Press, 1996.

[33] Frawley, W. *Linguistic Semantics*[M]. Hillsdale: Erlbaum, 1992.

[34] Frege, G. On sense and reference[C]// P. T. Geach & M. Black. *Translations from the Philosophical Writings of Gottlob Frege*. Oxford: Blackwell, 1960: 36-56.

[35] Galve, I. G. The textual interplay of grammatical metaphor on the nominalizations occurring in written medical English[J]. *Journal of Pragmatics*, 1998(30): 363-385.

[36] Ghadessy, M. *Register Analysis: Theory and Practice*[M]. London & New York: Pinter, 1993.

[37] Gleason, H. A. *Linguistics and English Grammar*. New York: Holt, Rinehart & Winston, 1965.

[38] Goatly, A. *The Language of Metaphors*[M]. London: Routledge, 1997.

[39] Gregory, M. Meta-functions: aspects of their development, status and use in systemic linguistics[C]// M. A. Halliday & R. P. Fawcett. *New Developments in Systemic Linguistics*. London & New York: Frances Pinter, 1987: 94-106.

[40] Ha, A. Y. H. & K. Hyland. What is technicality? A technicality analysis model for EAP vocabulary[J]. *Journal of English for Academic Purposes*, 2017(28): 35-49.

[41] Halliday, M. A. K. Categories of the theory of grammar[J]. *Word*, 1961(17): 241-292.

[42] Halliday, M. A. K. Notes on Transitivity and Theme in English [J]. *Journal of Linguistics*, 1967, *3*(2): 199-244.

[43] Halliday, M. A. K. Options and functions in the English clause[J]. *Brno Studies in English*, 1969(8): 81-88.

[44] Halliday, M. A. K. Functional diversity in language, as seen from a consideration of modality and mood in English[J]. *Foundations of Language*, 1970, *6* (3): 322-361.

[45] Halliday, M. A. K. *Explorations in the Functions of Language*[M]. London: Edward Arnold, 1973.

[46] Halliday, M. A. K. Functions and universals of language[C]// G. R. Kress. *System and Function in Language*. London: Oxford University Press, 1976a: 26-31.

[47] Halliday, M. A. K. The form of a functional grammar[C]// G. R. Kress. *System and Function in Language*. London: Oxford University Press, 1976b: 7-25.

[48] Halliday, M. A. K. Grammatical categories in modern Chinese: an early sketch of the theory[C]// G. R. Kress. *Halliday: System and Function in Language*. London: Oxford University Press, 1976c: 36-51.

[49] Halliday, M. A. K. Sociolinguistic aspects of mathematical education[C]// M. A. K. Halliday. *Language as Social Semiotic: The Social Interpretation of Language and Meaning*. London: Edward Arnold, 1978a: 194-204.

[50] Halliday, M. A. K. Antilanguages[M]// M. A. K. Halliday. *Language as Social Semiotic: The Social Interpretation of Language and Meaning*. London: Edward Arnold, 1978b: 164-182.

[51] Halliday, M. A. K. Language in urban society[M]// M. A. K. Halliday. *Language as Social Semiotic: The Social Interpretation of Language and Meaning*. London: Edward Arnold, 1978c: 154-163.

[52] Halliday, M. A. K. Language as code and language as behavior: a systemic-functional interpretation of the nature and ontogenesis of dialogue[C]// R.P. Fawcett, M. A. K. Halliday, S. M. Lamb and A. Makkai. *The Semiotics of Culture and Language. Vol. 1: Language as Social Semiotic*. London: Frances Pinter, 1984: 3-35.

[53] Halliday, M.A.K. *An Introduction to Functional Grammar*[M]. London: Edward Arnold, 1985a.

[54] Halliday, M. A. K. Systemic background[C]// W. S. Greaves & J. D. Benson. *Systemic Perspectives on Discourse*. Northwood: Ablex, 1985b.

[55] Halliday, M. A. K. *An Introduction to Functional Grammar*[M]. London: Edward Arnold, 1994.

[56] Halliday, M. A. K. Things and relations: regrammaticalizing experience as technical knowledge[C]// J. R. Martin and R. Veel. *Reading Science: Critical and Functional Perspectives on Discourses of Science*. London: Routledge, 1998:185-235.

[57] Halliday, M. A. K. Learning how to mean[C]// J. J. Webster. *Collected Works of M.A.K. Halliday. Vol. 4: The Language of Early Childhood*. London: Continuum, 2004a: 28-59.

[58] Halliday, M. A. K. Grammar and the construction of educational knowledge[C]// J. J. Webster. *Collected Works of M. A. K. Halliday. Vol. 4: The Language of Early Childhood*. London: Continuum, 2004b: 353-372.

[59] Halliday, M. A. K. Grammatical metaphor in English and Chinese[C]// J. J. Webster. *Collected Works of M. A. K. Halliday. Vol. 8: Studies in Chinese Language*. London: Continuum, 2005a: 325-333.

[60] Halliday, M. A. K. Introduction: towards an appliable description of the grammar of a language[C]// J. J. Webster. *Collected Works of M. A. K. Halliday. Vol. 7: Studies in English Language*. London: Continuum, 2005b: xii-xxx.

[61] Halliday, M. A. K. Computational and quantitative studies[M]// J. J. Webster. *Vol. 6 of the Collected Works of M. A. K. Halliday*. London: Continuum, 2005c.

[62] Halliday, M. A. K. Language and the reshaping of human experience[C]// J. J. Webster. *Collected Works of M. A. K. Halliday. Vol. 5: The Language of Science*. Beijing: Peking University Press, 2007a: 7-23.

[63] Halliday, M. A. K. On grammar and grammatics[C]// J. J. Webster. *Collected*

Works of M. A. K. Halliday. Vol. 1: On Grammar. Beijing: Peking University Press, 2007b: 384-417.

[64] Halliday, M. A. K. Language and knowledge: the "unpacking" of text[C]// J. J. Webster. *Collected Works of M.A.K. Halliday. Vol. 5: The Language of Science*. Beijing: Peking University Press, 2007c: 24-48.

[65] Halliday, M. A. K. Language structure and language function[C]// J. J. Webster. *Collected Works of M.A.K. Halliday. Vol. 1: On Grammar*. Beijing: Peking University Press, 2007d: 173-195.

[66] Halliday, M. A. K. Introduction: on the "architecture" of human language[C]// J. J. Webster. *Collected Works of M. A. K. Halliday. Vol. 3: On Language and Linguistics*. Beijing: Peking University Press, 2007e:1-29.

[67] Halliday, M. A. K. The grammatical construction of scientific knowledge: the framing of the English clause[C]// J. J. Webster. *Collected Works of M. A. K. Halliday. Vol. 5: The Language of Science*. Beijing: Peking University Press, 2007f: 102-134.

[68] Halliday, M. A. K. Spoken and written modes of meaning[C]// J. J. Webster. *Collected Works of M. A. K. Halliday. Vol. 1: On Grammar*. Beijing: Peking University Press, 2007g: 323-351.

[69] Halliday, M. A. K. On the language of Physical Science[C]// J. J. Webster. *Collected Works of M. A. K. Halliday. Vol. 5: The Language of Science*. Beijing: Peking University Press, 2007h: 140-158.

[70] Halliday, M. A. K. Introduction: how big is a language? On the power of language[C]// J. J. Webster. *Collected Works of M. A. K. Halliday. Vol. 5: The Language of Science*. Beijing: Peking University Press, 2007i: xix-xxxii.

[71] Halliday, M. A. K. Some notes on "deep" grammar[C]// J. J. Webster. *Collected Works of M. A. K. Halliday. Vol. 1: On Grammar*. Beijing: Peking University Press, 2007j: 106-117.

[72] Halliday, M. A. K. How do you mean?[C]// J. J. Webster. *Collected Works of M. A. K. Halliday. Vol. 1: On Grammar*. Beijing: Peking University Press, 2007k: 352-368.

[73] Halliday, M. A. K. On the grammar of scientific English[C]// J. J. Webster. *Collected Works of M.A.K. Halliday. Vol. 5: The Language of Science*. Beijing: Peking University Press, 2007l: 181-198.

[74] Halliday, M. A. K. On the ineffability of grammatical categories[C]// J.J. Webster. *Collected Works of M. A. K. Halliday. Vol. 1: On Grammar*.

Beijing: Peking University Press, 2007m: 291-322.

[75] Halliday, M. A. K. Language and the order of nature[C]// J. J. Webster. *Collected Works of M. A. K. Halliday. Vol. 3: On Language and Linguistics*. Beijing: Peking University Press, 2007n: 116-138.

[76] Halliday, M. A. K. Ideas about language[C]// J. J. Webster. *Collected Works of M.A.K. Halliday. Vol. 3: On Language and Linguistics*. Beijing: Peking University Press, 2007o: 92-115.

[77] Halliday, M. A. K. Modes of meaning and modes of expression: types of grammatical structure, and their determination by different semantic functions[C]// J. J. Webster. *Collected Works of M. A. K. Halliday. Vol. 1: On Grammar*. Beijing: Peking University Press, 2007p: 196-218.

[78] Halliday, M. A. K. *Complementarities in Language*[M]. Beijing: The Commercial Press, 2008.

[79] Halliday, M. A. K. *Selected Works of M. A. K. Halliday on Applied Linguistics*[M]. Beijing: Foreign Language Teaching and Research Press, 2015.

[80] Halliday, M. A. K., A. McIntosh & P. Strevens. *The Linguistic Sciences and Language Teaching* [M]. London: Longman, 1964.

[81] Halliday, M. A. K. & C. I. M. M. Matthiessen. *Construing Experience through Meaning: A Language-based Approach to Cognition* [M]. London: Cassell, 1999.

[82] Halliday, M. A. K. & C. I. M. M. Matthiessen. *An Introduction to Functional Grammar* [M]. Beijing: Foreign Language Teaching and Research Press, 2004.

[83] Halliday, M. A. K. & C. I. M. M. Matthiessen. *Halliday's Introduction to Functional Grammar* [M]. Oxon: Routledge, 2014.

[84] Halliday, M. A. K. & J. J. Webster. *Continuum Companion to Systemic Functional Linguistics* [M]. New York: Continuum, 2009.

[85] Halliday, M. A. K. & J. R. Martin. *Writing Science: Literacy and Discourse Power* [M]. Pittsburgh: University of Pittsburgh Press, 1993.

[86] Halliday, M. A. K. & R. Hasan. *Cohesion in English* [M]. London: Longman, 1976.

[87] Halliday, M. A. K. & R. Hasan. *Language, Context, and Text: Aspects of Language in a Social-Semiotic Perspective* [M]. Oxford: Oxford University Press, 1989.

[88] Hasan, R. Code, register and social dialect[C]// B. Bernstein. *Class, Codes and Control. Vol. 2: Applied Studies Towards a Sociology of Language.* London: Routledge & Kegan Paul, 1973: 253-292.

[89] Hasan, R. The grammarian's dream: lexis as most delicate grammar[C]// M. A. K. Halliday & R. P. Fawcett. *New Developments in Systemic Linguistics. Vol.1: Theory and Description.* London & New York: Frances Pinter Publishers, 1987: 184-211.

[90] Hasan, R. Semantic variation and sociolinguistics[J]. *Australian Journal of Linguistics,* 1989, *9*(2): 221-275.

[91] Hasan, R. Meaning in sociolinguistic theory[C]// J. J. Webster. *Collected Works of Ruqaiya Hasan. Vol. 2: Semantic Variation: Meaning in Society and in Sociolinguistics.* London & Oakville: Equinox Publishing Ltd., 2009: 271-308.

[92] He, Q. S., B. J. Yang & B. L. Wen. Textual metaphor from the perspective of relator[J]. *Australian Journal of Linguistics,* 2015, *35*(4): 334-350.

[93] Heyvaert, L. A *Cognitive-Functional Approach to Nominalization in English*[M]. Berlin: Mount de Gruyter, 2003.

[94] Hita, J. A. Ambiguity in grammatical metaphor: one more reason why the distinction transitive/ergative pays off[C]// A. Simon-Vandenbergen, M. Taverniers & L. Ravelli. *Grammatical Metaphor: Views from Systemic Functional Linguistics.* Amsterdam: Benjamins, 2003: 101-126.

[95] Iedema, R. *Literacy of Administration (Write it Right Literacy in Industry Research Project—Stage 3)* [Z]. Sydney: Metropolitan East Disadvantaged Schools Program, 1995.

[96] Jespersen, O. *The Philosophy of Grammar*[M]. London: George Allen & Unwin Ltd., 1924.

[97] Johansen, J. D. Sign structure and sign event in Saussure, Hjelmslev, and Peirce[C]// V. M. Colapietro & T. M. Olshewsky. *Peirce's Doctrine of Signs: Theory, Applications, and Connections.* Berlin: Mouton de Gruyter, 1996: 329-338.

[98] Jones, A. Why are logical connectives sometimes detrimental to coherence?[C]// A. Manboob & N. Knight. *Appliable Linguistics.* London: Continuum, 2010: 200-220.

[99] Koptjevskaja-Tarmn, M. *Nominalizations*[M]. London: Routledge, 1993.

[100] Labov, W. Contraction, deletion, and inherent variation of the English

copula[J]. *Language*, 1969(45): 715-762.

[101] Lamb, S. M. The sememic approach to structural semantics[J]. *American Anthropologist*, 1964, *66* (3): 57-78.

[102] Lamb, S. M. Epilegomena to a theory of language[C]// S. M. Lamb & J. J. Webster. *Language and Reality*. London: Continuum, 2004: 71-117.

[103] Langacker, R. W. *Foundations of Cognitive Grammar. Volume II*: *Descriptive Application*[M]. Beijing: Peking University Press, 2004.

[104] Lees, R. B. *The Grammar of English Nominalization*[M]. Hague: Mouton, 1960.

[105] Lemke, J. L. *Semiotics and Education*[M]. Toronto: Victoria University, 1984.

[106] Lemke, J. L. *Talking Science: Language, Learning, and Values*[M]. Westport: Ablex Publishing, 1990.

[107] Lemke, J. L. *Textual Politics: Discourse and Social Dynamics*[M]. London: Taylor & Francis, 1995.

[108] Liu, C. Y. *Functional-Cognitive Stylistic Approach to Grammatical Metaphor: A Case Study of English Metalinguistic Texts* [M]. Xiamen: Xiamen University Press, 2008.

[109] Lukin, A., A. R. Moore, M. Herke, R. Wegener & C. Wu. Halliday's model of register revisited and explored[J]. *Linguistics and the Human Sciences*, 2008, *4*(2): 187-213.

[110] Lyons, J. *Semantics (2 volumes)* [M]. Cambridge: Cambridge University Press, 1977.

[111] Martin, J. R. Intrinsic functionality: implications for contextual theory[J]. *Social Semiotics*, 1991, *1*(1): 99-162.

[112] Martin, J. R. *English Text*: *System and Structure* [M]. Amsterdam: Benjamins, 1992.

[113] Martin, J. R. Technology, bureaucracy and schooling: discursive resources and control[J]. *Cultural Dynamics*, 1993a, *6*(1): 84-130.

[114] Martin, J. R. Life as a noun: arresting the universe in science and humanities[C]// M. A. K. Halliday & J. R. Martin. *Writing Science: Literacy and Discourse Power*. Pittsburgh: University of Pittsburgh Press, 1993b: 221-267.

[115] Martin, J. R. Genre and literacy—modeling context in educational linguistics[J]. *Annual Review of Applied Linguistics*, 1993c (13): 141-172.

[116] Martin, J. R. Construing knowledge: a functional linguistic perspective[C]// F. Christie & J. R. Martin. *Knowledge Structure: Functional Linguistic and Sociological Perspectives.* London: Continuum, 2007: 34-64.

[117] Martin, J. R. *Systemic Functional Grammar: a Next Step into the Theory— Axial Relations*[M]. Translated by P. Wang & Y. S. Zhu. Beijing: Higher Education Press, 2013.

[118] Martin, J. R. & C. I. M. M. Matthiessen. Systemic typology and topology[C]// Z. H. Wang. *SFL Theory.* Shanghai: Shanghai Jiao Tong University Press, 2010.

[119] Martin, J. R., C. I. M. M. Matthiessen & C. Painter. *Deploying Functional Grammar*[M]. Beijing: The Commercial Press, 2010.

[120] Martin, J. R. & D. Rose. *Working with Discourse: Meaning Beyond the Clause*[M]. Beijing: Peking University Press, 2007.

[121] Martin, J. R. & P. R. R. White. *The Language of Evaluation: Appraisal in English*[M]. London: Palgrave Macmillan, 2008.

[122] Martin, J. R. & R. Veel. *Reading Science: Critical and Functional Perspectives on Discourses of Science*[M]. London: Routledge, 1998.

[123] Martin, J. R. & R. Wodak. *Re/reading the Past: Critical and Functional Perspectives on Discourse of History*[M]. Amsterdam: Benjamins, 2003.

[124] Mathesius, V. *A Functional Analysis of Present Day English on a General Linguistic Basis*[M]. Beijing: World Publishing Company, 2008.

[125] Maton, K. Theories and things: the semantics of disciplinarity[M]. F. Christie & K. Maton. *Disciplinarity: Functional Linguistic and Sociological Perspectives.* London: Continuum, 2011: 62-86.

[126] Maton, K. Making semantic waves: a key to cumulative knowledge-building[J]. *Linguistics and Education*, 2013(1): 8-22.

[127] Maton, K. *Knowledge and Knower Structure: Towards a Realist Sociology of Education*[M]. New York: Routledge, 2014.

[128] Matthiessen, C. I. M. M. Systemic grammar in computation: the Nigel case[P]. Paper presented at The First Annual Conference of the European Chapter of the Association for Computational Linguistics, University of Pisa, 1983.

[129] Matthiessen, C. I. M. M. Semantics for a systemic grammar: the chooser and inquiry framework[C]// J. D. Benson, M. J. Cummings & W. S. Greaves. *Linguistics in a Systemic Perspective.* Amsterdam: Benjamins,

1988: 221-242.

[130] Matthiessen, C. I. M. M. Register in the round: diversity in a unified theory of register analysis[C]// M. Ghadessy. *Register Analysis: Theory and Practice*. London: Pinter, 1993: 221-292.

[131] Matthiessen, C. I. M. M. *Lexicogrammatical Cartography: English Systems*[M]. Tokyo: International Language Sciences Publishers, 1995.

[132] Matthiessen, C. I. M. M., K. Teruya & M. Lam. *Key Terms in Systemic Functional Linguistics*[M]. London: Continuum, 2010.

[133] Matthiessen, C. I. M. M., K. Teruya & W. J. Lin. *Key Terms in Systemic Functional Linguistics*[M]. London: Continuum, 2016.

[134] Matthiessen, C. I. M. M. & M. A. K. Halliday. *Systemic Functional Grammar*: *A First Step into the Theory*[M]. Beijing: Higher Education Press, 2009.

[135] Painter, C. *Learning Through Language: A Case Study in the Development of Language as a Resource for Learning from 2.5 to 5 Years*[D]. Sydney: University of Sydney, 1993.

[136] Painter, C. The use of a metaphorical mode of meaning in early language development[C]//A. M. Simon-Vandenbergen, M. Taverniers & L. Ravelli. *Grammatical Metaphor: Views from Systemic Functional Linguistics*. Amsterdam: Benjamins, 2003: 151-167.

[137] Pankova, M. R. Toward mastering the discourses of reasoning: use of grammatical metaphor at advanced levels of foreign language acquisition[J]. *The Modern Language Journal*, 2010, *94* (2): 181-197.

[138] Plemenitaš, K. Aspects of nominalization from a cognitive perspective[C]// S. Starc, C. Jones & A. Maiorani. *Meaning Making in Text: Multimodal and Multilingual Functional Perspectives*. Hampshire: Palgrave Macmillan, 2015: 72-91.

[139] Quirk, R. et al. *A Grammar of Contemporary English*[M]. London: Longman, 1972.

[140] Quirk, R. et al. *A Comprehensive Grammar of the English Language*[M]. London: Longman, 1985.

[141] Ravelli, L. J. *Metaphor, Mode and Complexity: An Exploration of Co-varying Patterns*[D]. Sydney: Department of Linguistics, University of Sydney, 1985.

[142] Ravelli, L. J. Grammatical metaphor: an initial analysis[C]// E. Steiner &

R. Veltman. *Pragmatics, Discourse and Text: Some Systemically-Oriented Approaches*. London: Pinter, 1988: 133-147.

[143] Ravelli, L. J. The consequences of choice: discursive positioning in an art institution[C]// A. Sanchez-Macarro & R. Carter. *Linguistic Choice across Genres: Variation in Spoken and Written English*. Amsterdam: Benjamins, 1998: 137-153.

[144] Roeper, T. Chomsky's Remarks and the Transformationalist Hypothesis[C]// P. Štekauer & R. Lieber. *Handbook of Word-Formation*. Netherlands: Springer, 2005: 125-146.

[145] Schleppegrell, M. J. *The Language of Schooling: A Functional Linguistics Perspective*[M]. Mahwah: Lawrence Erlbaum Associates, Inc., 2008.

[146] Steiner, E. Ideational grammatical metaphor: exploring some implications for the overall model[J]. *Languages in Contrast*, 2002, *4*(1): 137-164.

[147] Taverniers, M. Grammatical metaphor in SFL: a historiography of the introduction and initial study of the concept[C]// Simon-vandenbergen, A. M. , M. Taverniers & L. Ravelli. *Grammatical Metaphor: Views from Systemic Functional Linguistics*. Amsterdam: John Benjamins Publishing Company, 2003: 5-33.

[148] Teich, E. *Systemic Functional Grammar in Natural Language Generation: Linguistic Description and Computational Representation*[M]. London: Cassell, 1999.

[149] Thompson, G. *Introducing Functional Grammar*[M]. London: Arnold, 1996.

[150] Thompson, G. Seeing double: complementarities of perspectives on interpersonal grammatical metaphor[P]. Paper presented at The 40th International Systemic Functional Congress, Guangzhou, Sun Yat-sen University, 2013.

[151] Thompson, G. *Introducing Functional Grammar*[M]. 3rd edition. London, New York: Routledge, 2014.

[152] Tucker, G. H. *The Lexicogrammar of Adjectives: A Systemic Functional Approach to Lexis*[M]. London: Cassell, 1998.

[153] Vendler, Z. *Linguistics in Philosophy* [M]. New York: Cornell University Press, 1967.

[154] Whorf, B. L. *Language Thought and Reality: Selected Writing of Benjamin Lee Whorf* [M]. Cambridge: The MIT Press, 1956.

[155] Wignell, P. *On the Discourse of Social Science*[M]. Darwin: Charles Darwin University Press, 2007.

[156] Yang, Y. N. Grammatical Metaphor in Chinese [D]. Singapore: National University of Singapore, 2007.

[157] Young, R. F. & H. T. Nguyen. Modes of meaning in high school science[J]. *Applied Linguistics*, 2002, *23*(3): 348-372.

[158] 陈新仁. 语法隐喻旳认知语用解读 [J]. 外国语, 2014, 37(2):33-41.

[159] 丛迎旭. 概念语法隐喻研究的限制与扩展 [J]. 外国语, 2011, 34(5):46-53.

[160] 丛迎旭. 基于语义变化的概念语法隐喻模式与类型 [J]. 现代外语, 2013, 36(1):33-39.

[161] 董娟, 张德禄. 语法隐喻理论再思考——语篇隐喻概念探源 [J]. 现代外语, 2017, 40(3):293-303.

[162] 范文芳. 名词化隐喻的语篇衔接功能 [J]. 外语研究, 1999(1):9-12.

[163] 范文芳. 试论语法隐喻的综合模式 [J]. 外语教学, 2007, 28(4):12-15.

[164] 何伟. 语法隐喻:形式变体和意义变体 [J]. 解放军外国语学院学报, 2008(3):1-6.

[165] 胡壮麟. 评语法隐喻的韩礼德模式 [J]. 外语教学与研究, 2000(2):88-94.

[166] 胡壮麟. 认知隐喻学 [M]. 北京:北京大学出版社, 2004.

[167] 黄国文. Cleft sentences as grammatical metaphor [M]// 黄国文, 王宗炎. 语篇与语言的功能. 北京:外语教学与研究出版社, 2002:34-41.

[168] 孔亚明. 歧义之系统功能语言学研究 [J]. 天津外国语学院学报, 2007, 14(1):45-52.

[169] 林正军, 杨忠. 语法隐喻的语义关系与转级向度研究 [J]. 外语教学与研究, 2010, 42(6):403-410.

[170] 刘国辉, 汪兴富. 名化、级差转移、原型范畴化研究框架体系的思考——诠释 Heyvaert 的 *A Cognitive-Functional Approach to Nominalization in English* (2003)[J]. 外国语, 2005(4):37-43.

[171] 刘婷婷, 张奕. 概念语法隐喻的认知解读 [J]. 现代外语, 2014, 37(5):628-637.

[172] 罗载兵, 蒋宇红. 语法隐喻的语义波建构模式 [J]. 外语研究, 2015 (3):24-29.

[173] 汤斌. Maton 的合理化语码理论与系统功能语言学的合作 [J]. 现代外语,

2014，37(1):52-61.

[174] 田永弘．论语法隐喻的客观性语义功能 [J]．现代外语，2017，37(5)：179-188.

[175] 王馥芳．语法隐喻理论可能"消解"论 [J]．外语教学理论与实践，2013(1):22-29.

[176] 魏在江．英汉语篇隐喻对比研究 [P]．中国英汉语比较研究会第八次全国学术研讨会．南昌:江西财经大学，2008.

[177] 谢金荣，彭水香．语法隐喻的语义分析 [J]．重庆交通学院学报:社科版，2004，4(1):112-115.

[178] 严世清．隐喻论 [M]．苏州:苏州大学出版社，2000.

[179] 严世清．语法隐喻理论的发展及其理论意义 [J]．外国语，2003(3):51-57.

[180] 杨炳钧．语法隐喻理论及有关质疑 [P]．第16届中国系统功能语言学学术周．成都:成都理工大学，2016.

[181] 杨信彰．英语形容词的语义意义 [J]．厦门大学学报:哲社版，1992(3):118-121.

[182] 杨忠. Transcategorization in grammatical metaphor and lexical metaphor [M]//张克定,王振华,杨朝军．系统・功能・评价．北京:高等教育出版社，2007:42-50.

[183] 张德禄．系统功能语言学的句法研究 [J]．同济大学学报:社会科学版，2012，23(1):89-98.

[184] 张德禄，董娟．语法隐喻理论的发展模式研究 [J]．外语教学与研究，2014(1):56-68.

[185] 张高远,王克非．名词化研究的新路径 [J]．外国语，2004(6)：45-50.

[186] 赵静,张德禄．对转类动名化意义整合的初步探讨 [J]．现代外语，2009，32(4):369-377.

[187] 赵艳芳．认知语言学概论 [M]．上海:上海外语教育出版社，2001.

[188] 朱永生．名词化、动词化与语法隐喻 [J]．外语教学与研究，2006，38(2):83-90.

[189] 朱永生,严世清,苗兴伟．功能语言学导论 [M]．上海:上海外语教育出版社，2004.

Appendix I

Data Resources

No.	Article	Journal	Download Information	Word	Discipline
1	Materials design by evolutionary optimization of functional groups in metal-organic frameworks	*Science*	http://advances. sciencemag.org/ on December 20, 2016	4,107	Chemistry
2	Reconfigurable origami-inspired acoustic waveguides	*Science*	http://advances. sciencemag.org/ on December 20, 2016	2,734	Applied Sciences and Engineering
3	Membrane alternatives in worlds without oxygen of an azotosome	*Science*	http://advances. sciencemag.org/on December 20, 2016	4,340	Astrobiology
4	Addressing China's grand challenge of achieving food security while ensuring environmental sustainability	*Science*	http://advances. sciencemag.org/on December 20, 2016	2,442	Environmental Sciences
5	Gelatin-derived sustainable carbon-based functional materials for energy conversion and storage with controllability of structure and component	*Science*	http://advances. sciencemag.org/on December 20, 2016	3,726	Functional Carbons

(to be continued)

No.	Article	Journal	Download Information	Word	Discipline
6	The search for signs of life on exoplanets at the interface of chemistry and planetary science	*Science*	http://advances. sciencemag.org/on December 20, 2016	7,578	Space Sciences
7	Ultra-smooth glassy graphene thin films for flexible transparent circuits	*Science*	http://advances. sciencemag.org/on December 20, 2016	2,535	Applied Sciences and Engineering
8	A conducting polymer with enhanced electronic stability applied in cardiac models	*Science*	http://advances. sciencemag.org/on December 20, 2016	7,545	Polymers
9	Adhesion mechanisms of curli subunit CsgA to abiotic surfaces	*Science*	http://advances. sciencemag.org/on December 20, 2016	5,083	Applied Sciences and Engineering
10	Glacial to Holocene changes in trans-Atlantic Saharan dust transport and dust-climate feedbacks	*Science*	http://advances. sciencemag.org/on December 20, 2016	5,823	Paleoclimate
11	Complex formation dynamics in a single-molecule electronic device	*Science*	http://advances. sciencemag.org/on December 20, 2016	3,842	Molecular Physics
12	Monkey vocal tracts are speech-ready	*Science*	http://advances. sciencemag.org/on December 20, 2016	4,465	Human Evolution
13	Lowering coefficient of friction in Cu alloys with stable gradient nanostructures	*Science*	http://advances. sciencemag.org/on December 20, 2016	3,859	Metals
14	A hamster model for Marburg virus infection accurately recapitulates Marburg hemorrhagic fever	*Nature*	www.nature.com/ scientificreports/on December 16, 2016	4,497	Infectious Diseases
15	Evaluation of efficacy and safety for recombinant human adenovirus-p53 in the control of the malignant pleural effusions via thoracic perfusion	*Nature*	www.nature.com/ scientificreports/on December 16, 2016	3,580	Respiratory Medicine

(to be continued)

233

No.	Article	Journal	Download Information	Word	Discipline
16	Thumb imprint based detection of hyperbilirubinemia using luminescent gold nanoclusters	*Nature*	www.nature.com/ scientificreports/ on December 16, 2016	3,370	Chemistry
17	Interstitial cystitis-associated urinary metabolites identified by mass-spectrometry based metabolomics analysis	*Nature*	www.nature.com/ scientificreports/ on December 16, 2016	2,836	Meta-bolomics
18	Rethinking the process of detrainment: jets in obstructed natural flows	*Nature*	www.nature.com/ scientificreports/ on December 16, 2016	4,100	Mechanical Engineering
19	High-throughput and automated diagnosis of antimicrobial resistance using a cost-effective cellphone-based micro-plate reader	*Nature*	www.nature.com/ scientificreports/ on December 16, 2016	3,494	Biological Engineering
20	Genetically manipulated phages with improved pH resistance for oral administration in veterinary medicine	*Nature*	www.nature.com/ scientificreports/ on December 16, 2016	5,497	Biological Engineering
21	Phospholipase D1 deficiency in mice causes nonalcoholic fatty liver disease via an autophagy defect	*Nature*	www.nature.com/ scientificreports/ on December 16, 2016	5,306	Molecular Medicine
22	Leisure-time physical activity and academic performance: cross-lagged associations from adolescence to young adulthood	*Nature*	www.nature.com/ scientificreports/ on December 16, 2016	5,505	Psychologic-al and Brain Sciences
23	Roles of human POLD1 and POLD3 in genome stability	*Nature*	www.nature.com/ scientificreports/ on December 16, 2016	5,333	Molecular Medicine

(to be continued)

No.	Article	Journal	Download Information	Word	Discipline
24	A window into the brain mechanisms associated with noise sensitivity	*Nature*	www.nature.com/ scientificreports/ on December 16, 2016	5,083	Medical Imaging
25	A critical, nonlinear threshold dictates bacterial invasion and initial kinetics during influenza	*Nature*	www.nature.com/ scientificreports/ on December 16, 2016	5,468	Medicine
26	Iron mineralogy and uranium-binding environment in the rhizosphere of a wetland soil	*Science of the Total Environment*	www.elsevier.com/ locate/scitotenv/ on March 16, 2017	5,472	Environmental Science
27	Gunshot residue and brakepads: Compositional and morphological considerations for forensic casework	*Forensic Science International*	www.elsevier.com/ locate/forsciint / on March 16, 2017	3,142	Forensic Science
28	A bio-inspired novel optimization technique for reactive power flow	*Engineering Science and Technology, an International Journal*	www.elsevier.com/ locate/jestch/ on March 16, 2017	3,467	Electrical Engineering
29	An efficient approximate moment method for multi-dimensional population balance models: Application to virus replication in multi-cellular systems	*Chemical Engineering Science*	www.elsevier.com/ locate/ces / on March 16, 2017	6,400	Chemical Engineering
30	Evaluation for sheet metals under hot stamping conditions by a novel biaxial testing system and a new materials model	*International Journal of Mechanical Sciences*	www.elsevier.com/ locate/ijmecsci/ on March 17, 2017	5,368	Mechanical Engineering

(to be continued)

No.	Article	Journal	Download Information	Word	Discipline
31	Fast-match: fast affine template matching	*International Journal of Computer Vision*	http://link.springer.com/article/10.1007/s11263-016-0926-1 on March 16, 2017	6,964	Computer Science
32	Hollywood 3D: What are the best 3D features for action recognition?	*International Journal of Computer Vision*	http://link.springer.com/article/10.1007/ on March 16, 2017	8,116	Computer Science
33	Cadmium(II) inhibition of human uracil-DNA glycosylase by catalytic water supplantation	*Nature*	http://journals.sagepub.com/doi/pdf/10.1260/ on March 16, 2017	4,739	Biochemistry
34	Black hole kicks as new gravitational wave observables	*Physical Review Letters*	https://journals.aps.org/prl/abstract/10.1103/PhysRevLett/ on March 16, 2017	2,854	Theoretical Physics
35	I sleep, because we sleep: a synthesis on the role of culture in sleep behavior research	*Sleep Medicine*	http://dx.doi.org/10.1016/ on March 16, 2017	5,672	Medicine

Appendix II

Lexical Realizations of Quality-Thing Metaphors

No.	Fre.	Metaphorical form	Congruent form	No.	Fre.	Metaphorical form	Congruent form
1	62	presence	present	14	15	diversity	diverse
2	49	stability	stable	15	14	efficacy	efficacious
3	42	differences	different	16	14	safety	safe
4	40	difference	different	17	14	turbidity	turbid
5	32	accuracy	accurate	18	13	importance	important
6	32	activity	active	19	12	complexity	complex
7	27	intensity	intense	20	12	conductivity	conductive
8	22	sensitivity	sensitive	21	12	robustness	robust
9	21	heterogeneity	heterogeneous	22	10	availability	available
10	18	flexibility	flexible	23	10	instability	instable
11	18	variability	variable	24	10	strength	strong
12	17	efficiency	efficient	25	9	frequency	frequent
13	16	absence	absent	26	9	thickness	thick

(to be continued)

No.	Fre.	Metaphorical form	Congruent form	No.	Fre.	Metaphorical form	Congruent form
27	8	significance	significant	56	4	fitness	fit
28	8	similarity	similar	57	4	hypersensitivity	hypersensitive
29	8	viability	viability	58	4	lethality	lethal
30	7	contractility	contractible	59	4	linearity	linear
31	7	prevalence	prevalent	60	4	mobility	mobile
32	7	selectivity	selective	61	4	relevance	relevant
33	6	abundance	abundant	62	4	reproducibility	reproducible
34	6	ambiguity	ambiguous	63	4	resistivity	resistive
35	6	detectability	detectable	64	4	responsiveness	responsive
36	6	severity	severe	65	4	simplicity	simple
37	6	transparency	transparent	66	4	sustainability	sustainable
38	6	validity	valid	67	4	uniformity	uniform
39	5	difficulties	difficult	68	3	abnormalities	abnormal
40	5	difficulty	difficult	69	3	causality	causal
41	5	formability	formable	70	3	correctness	correct
42	5	homogeneity	homogenous	71	3	crystallinity	crystalline
43	5	invariance	invariant	72	3	discrepancies	discrepant
44	5	invariances	invariant	73	3	fluency	fluent
45	5	pathogenicity	pathogenic	74	3	infectivity	infective
46	5	productivity	productive	75	3	latencies	latent
47	5	reliability	reliable	76	3	noisiness	noisy
48	5	smoothness	smooth	77	3	priority	prior
49	5	specificity	specific	78	3	scarcity	scarce
50	4	clarity	clear	79	3	seniority	senior
51	4	compatibility	compatible	80	3	versatility	versatile
52	4	connectivity	connective	81	2	biostability	biostable
53	4	deficiency	deficient	82	2	continuity	continuous
54	4	density	dense	83	2	deficiencies	deficient
55	4	effectiveness	effective	84	2	discrepancy	discrepant

(to be continued)

No.	Fre.	Metaphorical form	Congruent form
85	2	disparities	disparate
86	2	equity	equal
87	2	friendliness	friendly
88	2	hardness	hard
89	2	inertness	inert
90	2	inhomogeneity	inhomoge-neous
91	2	instabilities	instability
92	2	integrity	integrate
93	2	malignancy	malignant
94	2	nonlinearity	nonlinear
95	2	nonuniformity	nonuniform
96	2	repeatability	repeatable
97	2	resilience	resilient
98	2	responsibilities	responsible
99	2	responsibility	responsible
100	2	seasonality	seasonal
101	2	sensitivities	sensitive
102	2	stiffness	stiff
103	2	suitability	suitable
104	2	susceptibility	susceptible
105	2	toxicity	toxic
106	2	variety	various
107	2	virulence	virulent
108	2	wakefulness	wakeful
109	2	wettability	wettable
110	1	breadth	broad
111	1	abruptness	abrupt
112	1	accessibility	accessible

No.	Fre.	Metaphorical form	Congruent form
113	1	acuity	acute
114	1	ambiguities	ambiguous
115	1	applicability	applicable
116	1	aromaticity	aromatic
117	1	asymmetry	asymmetric
118	1	benignity	benign
119	1	biodiversity	biodiverse
120	1	brevity	brief
121	1	brightness	bright
122	1	comfort	comfortable
123	1	commonalities	common
124	1	completeness	complete
125	1	comprehensi-veness	comprehensive
126	1	conductivities	conductive
127	1	consistency	consistent
128	1	controllability	controllable
129	1	deformability	deformable
130	1	descriptiveness	descriptive
131	1	directivity	directive
132	1	dryness	dry
133	1	durability	durable
134	1	ease	easy
135	1	efficiencies	efficient
136	1	elasticity	elastic
137	1	entirety	entire
138	1	equivalence	equivalent
139	1	fatality	fatal
140	1	fidelity	fiddly

(to be continued)

No.	Fre.	Metaphorical form	Congruent form
141	1	fluorescence	fluorescent
142	1	freedom	free
143	1	functionality	functional
144	1	generality	general
145	1	generalizability	generalizable
146	1	genotoxicity	genotoxic
147	1	heterozygosity	heterozygous
148	1	humidity	humid
149	1	hydrophilicity	hydrophilic
150	1	hygroscopicity	hygroscopic
151	1	hyperpermeability	hyperpermeable
152	1	immunoreactivity	immunoreactive
153	1	inadequacy	inadequate
154	1	inconsistencies	inconsistent
155	1	inconsistency	inconsistent
156	1	indistinctness	indistinct
157	1	insecurity	insecure
158	1	insufficiencies	insufficient
159	1	intelligence	intelligent
160	1	intensities	intense
161	1	lability	labile
162	1	latency	latent
163	1	loudness	loud
164	1	maturity	mature
165	1	missingness	missing
166	1	musicality	musical
167	1	nonpolarizability	nonpolarizable

No.	Fre.	Metaphorical form	Congruent form
168	1	novelties	novel
169	1	observability	observable
170	1	phototoxicity	phototoxic
171	1	popularity	popular
172	1	porosity	porous
173	1	potency	potent
174	1	predominance	predominant
175	1	reactivity	reactive
176	1	realism	real
177	1	reversibility	reversible
178	1	richness	rich
179	1	saliency	salient
180	1	security	secure
181	1	shortage	short
182	1	silence	silent
183	1	similarities	similar
184	1	solubility	soluble
185	1	sparsity	sparse
186	1	stabilities	stability
187	1	superiority	superior
188	1	supremacy	supreme
189	1	tenability	tenable
190	1	terracentricity	terracentric
191	1	thicknesses	thick
192	1	toxicities	toxic
193	1	tractability	tractable
194	1	tunability	tunable
195	1	unpleasantness	unpleasant
196	1	unsuitability	unsuitable

(to be continued)

240

No.	Fre.	Metaphorical form	Congruent form
197	1	variance	variant
198	1	veracity	veracious
199	1	vigilance	vigilant
200	1	viscidity	viscid

No.	Fre.	Metaphorical form	Congruent form
201	1	viscoplasticity	viscoplastic
202	1	warmth	warm

后　记

本书是在我的博士论文基础上修订完成的。本书的出版得到了很多人的帮助。首先，我要衷心地感谢我的导师张德禄教授。张老师把我领进了系统功能语言学的大门，并指引我走上学术研究之路。我从对系统功能语言学的懵懂无知，到博士课题的完成，一路走来，老师的悉心指导、谆谆教诲、鼓励支持给了我前进的动力。张老师为人谦逊的涵养影响着我，深邃渊博的学识吸引着我，严谨治学的态度激励着我。跟随老师学习的几年间，每每遇到难题困惑向老师请教，老师总是在第一时间回复，循循善诱，耐心解答，为我打开一扇扇智慧之窗，让我享受语言学研究的乐趣。老师不仅是我学术道路上的领路人，也是我人生道路上的一盏明灯，老师高尚的师德和低调的处世态度一直潜移默化地影响着我。"做学问不可急功近利，研究的过程就是锻炼观察能力和耐力的过程。"老师的谆谆教诲我将铭记在心。同时，我要感谢师母王志兰老师对我的诸多帮助和鼓励。

我还要衷心感谢主持我博士论文答辩和担任教育部人文社科项目结题评审的诸位专家。他们是复旦大学的朱永生教授和杨雪燕教授，华东师范大学的杨延宁教授，上海交通大学的杨炳钧教授和王振华教授，上海大学的邓志勇教授，同济大学的戴劲教授、梁洁教授和李梅教授。感谢各位老师的答疑解惑、悉心指点及为本书提出的宝贵修改意见。

此外，我要感谢诸多同学和朋友的一路相伴与支持。感谢青岛大学的布占廷师兄在软件使用方面给予的热心指导，感谢我在同济大学的同学瞿桃博士、郭恩华博士、胡瑞云博士、郝兴刚博士、喻志刚博士、韩艳方博士在语料分析、论文答辩、书稿修改等方面给予的无私帮助，感谢上海理工大学的董榆萍副教授和郭影平副教授在本书撰写期间给予的大力支持和精神鼓励。

最后,我要特别感谢我的家人,尤其是父母全心全意的付出和支持。在我求学期间,父母放弃舒适安逸的退休生活在沪帮忙照看孩子,使我能安心完成学业。父母恩重如山,无以为报。

本书的出版得到了教育部人文社科青年基金(项目编号:14YJC740017)和上海理工大学外语学院博士启动基金的资助,特此致谢。同时,感谢中国海洋大学出版社领导和编辑的辛勤付出。

限于研究水平,本书定有不当之处,敬请学界前辈和同仁以及广大读者批评指正。

董娟

2020 年 8 月 8 日

于上海理工大学